Empathy and Deliberation

Value Inquiry Book Series

VOLUME 421

Studies in Existentialism, Hermeneutics, and Phenomenology

The titles published in this series are listed at *brill.com/vibs* and *brill.com/se*

Empathy and Deliberation

The Case for a Phenomenological Approach

By

Eugenia Stefanello

BRILL

ISSN 0929-8436
ISBN 978-90-04-74535-3
ISBN 978-90-04-74536-0 (PDF)
DOI https://doi.org/10.1163/9789004745360

Library of Congress Control Number: 2026904949

Brill and Koninklijke Brill BV are part of De Gruyter Brill.
www.degruyterbrill.com

Questions about General Product Safety Regulation: productsafety@degruyterbrill.com

Cover illustration: *Drawing of a blue bird and a red bird*, Fons Heijnsbroek. Photo by Fons Heijnsbroek on Unsplash.

Contents

PART 2
A Critique of the Standard Definition of Empathy and Its Role in Deliberation

PART 3
A Different Road: Phenomenological Empathy as a Better Ally for Deliberation

Acknowledgments

This book emerged from countless conversations and encounters that have shaped both its arguments and my thinking during my Ph.D. and postdoctoral period at the University of Padua. I have many people to thank for its existence.

First and foremost, I am deeply grateful to Professor Antonio Da Re, who supervised my dissertation and guided me through the preparation of this book with continuous support and invaluable advice. I also owe an enormous debt to my colleagues in the Ethics Research Group at the FISPPA Department – Professor Francesca Marin, Professor Simone Grigoletto, and Professor Federico Zilio – who have generously shared their expertise and wisdom throughout this journey, patiently answering my many questions and encouraging me at every step.

This book would not have been possible without Professor Elisa Magrì, who not only welcomed me to Boston College – an experience that profoundly shaped both my career and, perhaps more importantly, my character – but also taught me much of what I know about Edith Stein and the phenomenological method. Any errors are, of course, entirely my own. I am equally grateful to the philosophical community at Boston College, particularly Professor Dermot Moran, Professor Andrew Barnett, Professor Gregory Fried, and Professor Giovanni Pietro Basile, who provided invaluable feedback on my work, especially regarding the phenomenological approach to intersubjectivity.

I am also indebted to Professor Andrea Staiti, Professor Andrea Altobrando, Professor Anna Donise, and Professor Søren Overgaard, who generously dedicated their time to commenting on and improving this work at different stages of its development. My thanks extend to the anonymous reviewers who challenged me to clarify and refine the arguments presented here, as well as to all the researchers and scholars who posed questions and shared their insights at the numerous conferences and workshops where I have presented this work.

I am deeply grateful to my parents, Vinicio and Stefania, who have always given me the space and freedom to become who I wanted to be, while celebrating every small achievement along the way, and to my grandmothers, Franca and Ines, each of whom taught me, in her own way, never to be afraid to speak my mind – a lesson I carry with me every day. Finally, my most profound gratitude goes to Edoardo, whose unwavering faith in me has sustained me through every challenge and who believes in me even when I doubt myself.

To them, my family, I dedicate this book.

Introduction

The ever-growing popularity of empathy in public discourse and academic debate is hardly controversial. Empathy seems to have the power to solve just about everything. It is often seen as a powerful tool for bridging the various divides in our contemporary societies, because by putting oneself in the other's shoes, it seems to be able – or so it is hoped – to, at least, reduce, if not close, the emotional and cognitive distance between different subjects, and thus mitigate or avoid misunderstandings and conflicts (Rifkin, 2009; Waal, 2009). This hopeful view of empathy and its supposed ability to build a shared experience based on mutual understanding and emotional sharing has been enthusiastically embraced by those of us concerned about our increasingly fragmented, unequal, and conflict-ridden world as a clear and programmatic antidote to these challenges.

In addition to this general appeal, empathy has often been considered by scholars as essential to our epistemic and moral lives. Understanding and sharing the inner state of the other, both cognitively and affectively, is said to be relevant to us as knowers and as moral agents. In particular, empathy is thought to be a valuable ally for our moral and epistemic deliberative processes, since it is supposed to help us decide what belief to adopt about the other person's state after we have accessed the contents of her mind, and what action to take after we have felt what she is feeling. For example, understanding through empathy that my friend believes it is better to lie to someone to prevent them from suffering may lead me to believe that she is either a good or a bad person, depending on my own beliefs about the situation. Similarly, sharing my little cousin's distress over her lost toy may move me to help her look for it.

While I believe that the involvement of empathy in our deliberative processes is undeniable, I think that both concepts, especially empathy, how they relate to each other, and the implications of this relationship should be better explored. Despite the rather overwhelming amount of literature on empathy, there are two theoretical gaps that I believe are worth attempting to fill. On the one hand, there is no systematic account of how the role of empathy in deliberation changes depending on the definition of empathy that is adopted. On the other hand, due to the widespread belief that empathy is inherently positive, there is a lack of discussion regarding the potential negative effects that empathy can have when involved in deliberation. In this book, I will attempt to address these gaps. In addition, I will suggest that by rethinking empathy and its role in deliberation in a different theoretical light,

 | HTTPS://DOI.ORG/10.1163/9789004745360-002

namely a phenomenological light, these negative effects can be reduced or eliminated.

The book has three main goals. First, to define how empathy and deliberation are conventionally understood in contemporary literature, and to identify how empathy is thought to affect the deliberative process accordingly; second, to argue that this way of framing empathy and its role in deliberation can be particularly problematic from both an epistemic and a moral perspective; third, to propose an alternative approach to defining empathy and its role in deliberation. Specifically, I will argue that a phenomenological account of empathy, as opposed to the standard way in which empathy is characterized in the contemporary debate, is a better way to understand the specific nature of the phenomenon and a better ally in our deliberations because it avoids some of the problems of the standard definition of empathy.

I intend to approach these problems primarily from a conceptual point of view and, due to the nature of empathy, the discussion will range from epistemology to folk psychology, metaethics, and normative ethics. I will also discuss empirical evidence, especially from neuroethics and applied psychology, but always in a non-reductionist way. Finally, I hope that this work can contribute to strengthening what I consider a fruitful methodological approach, namely bringing two theoretical perspectives and traditions into dialogue. As Dan Zahavi – among others – has argued effectively for some time (Zahavi, 2014b), the phenomenological tradition, especially the early phenomenological tradition, has much to say about contemporary discussions of empathy in both social cognition and moral theory. Following his suggestion, I will try to show how useful and fruitful this interaction can be for understanding the empathic phenomenon and how it functions in deliberation.

The book is divided into three parts, each consisting of three chapters. In Part 1, I will define the concepts of empathy and deliberation, and the relationship between the two. In Chapter 1, I will propose a definition of empathy that I will call the standard definition (SD), which seems to be able to condense the multiple definitions found in the literature. According to the SD, empathy consists of three phenomena, namely cognitive empathy understood as perspective taking, affective empathy understood as emotional sharing, and sympathy understood as concern for the welfare of others. I will also discuss how these three components of the SD are characterized within the contemporary debate, specifically within the epistemological debate on other minds and simulation theory, the moral debate on sentimentalism, and the moral-psychological debate on altruism.

In Chapter 2, I will propose a standard definition (SD) of deliberation, according to which the deliberative process is characterized as a mental activity aimed at deciding, by weighing different kinds of reasons, what to think (theoretical deliberation) and what to do (practical deliberation). I will focus on what I call "other-directed deliberation," that is, those deliberative processes that involve or have as their object one or more people. Specifically, the purpose of other-directed theoretical deliberation is to decide, by weighing different kinds of reasons, what beliefs to adopt about another person, while the purpose of other-directed practical deliberation is to decide how to act toward that person. When moral considerations are also involved, the deliberative process is called moral.

As I will make clear from the outset, I have two very different positions with regard to the SD of empathy and the SD of deliberation. While I think – and will try to show – that the former fails to capture the nature of the empathic phenomenon and is also problematic when it comes to its involvment in other-directed deliberation, I find the latter to be a compelling way of framing what our deliberative processes consist of.

In Chapter 3, I will identify and discuss three ways in which empathy, as defined in the SD, appears to contribute to other-directed deliberation. First, cognitive empathy as perspective-taking is thought to play an epistemic role in other-directed theoretical and practical deliberation because it provides the subject with information about the other's internal states that can be used as a basis for deliberating about the intelligibility of the reasons for the other's actions and how the empathizer should respond to them. Second, affective empathy seems capable of normatively grounding our moral judgments, which are special cases of deliberation. Third, empathy is assigned a motivational role in that it constitutes the source of the agent's motivating and normative reasons for other-directed practical deliberative processes, especially when the situation requires altruistic and moral action.

In Part 2, I will show that empathy as defined by the SD is not the best candidate to play the three roles identified above, but on the contrary, its involvement in other-directed deliberation can have problematic consequences. In Chapter 4, I will challenge the idea that cognitive empathy as perspective-taking is the best option for fulfilling the epistemic role in other-directed deliberative processes. First, cognitive empathy in its most basic forms does not seem to guarantee the recognition of like-mindedness as it is supposed to do. Second, cognitive empathy seems to be dangerously inaccurate due to its many cognitive biases which can negatively affect the deliberative process. Third, cognitive empathy, especially when characterized as a simulation-plus-projection routine, poses a threat to the target's agency that compromises the epistemic accuracy and morality of our other-directed deliberative processes.

In Chapter 5, I will question the assumption that empathy, especially affective empathy, is the best source of moral motivation and moral judgments. Empathy – both cognitive and affective – seems to engage in some sort of selection process regarding whom to help and whose actions to approve or disapprove of. In this regard, I will discuss the empirical evidence for the affective biases of empathy when it comes to recognizing, understanding, and sharing the emotions of others. This will highlight how the selective and partial nature caused by these inherent biases directly affects the motivating reasons provided by empathy, potentially leading to immoral actions. Second, I will challenge the claim that affective empathy is the best available basis for approval and disapproval, and ultimately for moral judgments, because it risks producing highly flawed, if not immoral, outcomes.

In Chapter 6, I will discuss the problematic consequences of characterizing empathy – as the SD does – as independent of the broader sociocultural, historical, political, and economic context in which it occurs. On the one hand, I will argue that both the overall character of the subjects involved in the empathic relationship and the broader context in which this relationship is embedded have a profound impact on the empathic relationship, its epistemic and moral outcomes, and, consequently, on the other-directed deliberative processes in which empathy is engaged. On the other hand, as anthropological studies have shown, the broader context not only can directly influence whether empathy will lead to problematic epistemic and moral outcomes but also appears to be responsible for revealing those outcomes. In particular, because empathy between privileged and nonprivileged individuals can foster instances of epistemic injustice, considering the broader context of these relationships can help reveal these epistemically unjust behaviors and their morally troubling consequences.

In Part 3, I will propose a phenomenologically inspired account of empathy in light of the problems of the SD. In Chapter 7, I will argue that a phenomenological account of empathy, particularly one inspired by Edith Stein's proposal, might be able to better describe what the empathic phenomenon is and avoid or mitigate some of the problems of the SD of empathy. First, I will analyze Lipps' account of empathy, not only because it was the first to characterize empathy as a tool for understanding the interiority of others, but also because it became a target of criticism for the early phenomenological movement. Then, I will discuss Husserl's account of empathy and the conceptual tools he developed to analyze and describe our intersubjective experience. This will shed light on the continuity between Husserl's ideas and Stein's innovative analysis, while also highlighting how Stein built upon and advanced the work of her mentor. I will then outline the main aspects of Stein's innovative theoretical approach to empathy as developed in her book *On the Problem of Empathy* (1917). As a result of this analysis, I will tentatively define what phenomenological empathy is, drawing primarily on Stein's account and, to a lesser extent, on other early and contemporary phenomenologists.

In Chapter 8, I will highlight the differences between a phenomenological account of empathy and the SD of empathy, and how these differences allow the former to mitigate or avoid the problems that the latter encounters when involved in other-directed deliberation. I will first show that phenomenological empathy is fundamentally different from cognitive empathy in that it does not involve any form of mirroring, simulation-plus-projection, or first-person perspective-taking. Rather it is a quasi-perceptual and quasi-imaginative grasp of the other's inner states as expressed in their living body, which also allows the empathizer to grasp the other as a person, that is, as a bearer of motives and values. Because of this crucial difference, phenomenological empathy seems able to guarantee the recognition of the embodied mind of the other, mitigate the dangers of inaccurate empathic understanding, and respect the agency of the other. Phenomenological empathy also seems able to avoid all the problems that affective empathy encounters when it is involved in moral other-directed deliberation because, on the one hand, it does not involve affective sharing and thus does not have to worry about its shortcomings; on the other hand, in the phenomenological approach, empathy is distinct from sympathy and does not play a foundational role in morality. Finally, phenomenological empathy seems better equipped to deal with the influence of the broader context in which both the empathic relationship and the deliberative process take place, not only because it is more aware of its influence, but also because empathy alone would never be able to understand this context satisfactorily. For this reason, the phenomenological approach invites us to expand the resources we use to understand others and navigate our moral lives, which can help those who empathize to be aware of power dynamics and potentially mitigate instances of epistemic injustice.

This will allow me, in Chapter 9, to rethink the role that empathy can play in the deliberative process, that is, an eminently epistemic role. However, this epistemic role is greatly diminished compared to that ascribed to empathy by the SD. As I understand it through a phenomenological lens, empathy cannot normatively ground our deliberative processes and thus never guarantees the accuracy or morality of the reasons it provides. Rather, empathy allows us to grasp what the other person is thinking or feeling, but always in a partial, sometimes superficial, and never definitive way. Specifically, it allows the empathizer to grasp the other's inner states and motivational context, but without claiming to understand them in their entirety and complexity. Moreover, a specific epistemic achievement of a phenomenological account of empathy is its ability to grasp the hierarchically organized values of the other person as revealed in her emotions. As a result, the empathizer recognizes the other as a person with motives and values. Although this achievement is not moral in itself, but rather epistemic, it is capable of providing the space within which our moral discourse and action can take place.

PART 1

Empathy and Deliberation: Definitions and How They Relate to Each Other

CHAPTER 1

The Standard Definition of Empathy

Given its popularity and relevance in both our everyday discourse and academic debate, one might expect a clear definition of what empathy is (Boella, 2018). Instead, when empathy scholars are asked to provide a definition of the empathic phenomenon, things get immensely complicated. The problem is not a lack of definitions. On the contrary, it could be argued that there are too many. The point is finding a *common* definition of empathy among the plethora of possibilities (Batson, 2009; Coplan, 2011a; Cuff et al., 2016).[1] It is not uncommon for each author writing on the topic to propose his or her own definition(s).[2] This would be less of a problem if the number of researchers studying empathy were not so large, which has led to a dramatic increase in the number of publications on empathy over the past 25 years.[3] Moreover, the empathic phenomenon can be studied by a variety of disciplines: from medicine, psychology, social sciences, and philosophy to neuroscience and even engineering.[4] This adds another layer of confusion, as each field has its own specific terminology and methodology (Songhorian, 2015).

However, these two factors are not the only, or even the main, reasons for the lack of a common definition of empathy. The most problematic aspect is the nature of empathy itself. As I will try to show in this work, empathy is an

1 For instance, Batson identified eight phenomena that have been labeled "empathy": knowing another person's internal state, including his or her thoughts and feelings; adopting the posture or matching the neural responses of an observed other; coming to feel as another person feels; intuiting or projecting into another's situation; imagining how another is thinking and feeling; imagining how one would think and feel in the other's place; feeling distress at witnessing another person's suffering; feeling for another person who is suffering (Batson, 2009). Cuff and colleagues found 43 discrete definitions of empathy in the literature and "eight themes relating to the nature of empathy emerged: 'Distinguishing Empathy from Other Concepts'; 'Cognitive or Affective?'; 'Congruent or Incongruent?'; 'Subject to Other Stimuli?'; 'Self-other Distinction or Merging?'; 'Trait or State Influences?'; 'Has a Behavioural Outcome?'; and 'Automatic or Controlled?'" (Cuff et al., 2016, p. 144).

2 Famously, de Vignemont and Singer stated: "there are probably nearly as many definitions as people working on the topic" (de Vignemont & Singer, 2006, p. 435).

3 *Scopus* trend for the term "empathy" (year: number of citations): 2000: 620; 2010: 1,688; 2020: 4,745; 2024: 6,372.

4 *Scopus* trend for documents about empathy by subject area (subject area: number of documents) from 2000 to 2024: Medicine: 24,181; Social Sciences: 19,460; Psychology: 16,147; Arts and Humanities: 9,485; Nursing: 7,593; Computer Science: 4,843; Neuroscience: 4,482; Business, Management and Accounting: 3,559; Engineering: 2,886.

 | HTTPS://DOI.ORG/10.1163/9789004745360-003

incredibly complex, nuanced, and multifaceted phenomenon. As such, the label "empathy" has inevitably come to refer to a large number of phenomena that can differ, even drastically, from one another. As we will see in this chapter, empathy can range from basic affective phenomena, such as emotional contagion (Hume, 1739; Slote, 2009), to more complicated and strictly cognitive mechanisms, such as perspective-taking (Goldman, 2006; Smith, 1759), to being synonymous with the precursor of sympathy (Simmons, 2013) or even the basis of morality itself (Slote, 2016). It is this inherent complexity that makes it so much more difficult, yet crucial, to agree on a common definition.

To say that it is crucial to find a common definition of a concept in order to understand it may seem like an outrageously banal statement. And yet, when it comes to empathy, crafting and choosing a definition is of the utmost importance, not only to "tidy up" the definitional chaos I mentioned above, but also, and most importantly, to clarify its role in the affective, cognitive, and moral life of the subject.

With this purpose in mind, in Chapter 1, I will explore what I call the standard definition (SD) of empathy, which I believe is a valid candidate for a common definition of the empathic phenomenon based on the current state of the literature. According to the SD, empathy consists of three phenomena: cognitive empathy, affective empathy, and sympathy. Broadly speaking, *cognitive empathy* refers to the process by which we are able both to recognize others as like-minded creatures and, through imaginative perspective-taking, to access the contents of their minds in order to understand or predict their actions and decisions (Spaulding, 2016). *Affective empathy* requires the empathizer to share the other's emotional state, and it can include different phenomena with varying requirements regarding the similarity and isomorphism between the emotional states of the two subjects (Maibom, 2017). Finally, *sympathy* consists of an active concern for the welfare and general well-being of the other person (Darwall, 1998).

Note that SD is a success definition, meaning that we can legitimately define as cognitive empathy, affective empathy, and sympathy only those processes that successfully achieve their respective goals. In other words, only when access to the epistemic content of the other's mind is gained through perspective-taking do we have cognitive empathy, and only when the other's emotional state is actually shared do we have affective empathy, or when there is concern for the other's welfare do we have sympathy. According to SD, merely attempting these processes without successfully carrying them out is not sufficient to define them as empathy.

Two preliminary caveats are in order. First, the distinction between the three phenomena is justified on conceptual grounds, since cognitively accessing the content of others' minds is a conceptually distinct operation from experiencing the emotional states of others or feeling concerned about their condition and alleviating their suffering. Relevantly, these operations are also different from the subject's experiential point of view: they feel qualitatively different. Moreover, they have different goals and roles: interpersonal understanding, motivating pro-social actions, and caring for others (see Chapter 3). This tripartite distinction also seems to be supported by the results of several empirical studies, especially neuroscientific ones (Guo, 2017), which attest to the involvement of different neural pathways when it comes to cognitive and affective empathy-related phenomena (Decety & Cowell, 2014). As a result, there is a fairly broad consensus in the literature on the distinction between the affective and cognitive aspects of empathy:

> Empathy requires both the ability to share the emotional experience of the other person (affective component) and an understanding of the other person's experience (cognitive component). Some scholars favor in their definition one aspect or the other.
>
> DECETY AND JACKSON, 2004, pp. 73–74.

Second, the claim that empathy consists of three distinct phenomena does not mean that they cannot or do not overlap in our everyday experience: cognitive empathy and affective empathy can occur simultaneously as a result of the same interaction with the other person. However, they can also be in asynchronous relationships: cognitive empathy can cause affective sharing or vice versa. Moreover, according to some scholars (Batson, 2011; Denham, 2017), empathy, especially affective empathy, can cause, motivate, or lead to sympathetic actions, which can be characterized in terms of altruistic and/or moral actions (see Section 1.3). For others (Battaly, 2011; Prinz, 2011b), cognitive and affective empathy have nothing to do with sympathy or morality. Thus, the effort to define empathy not only concerns each of its three components but also requires an exploration of their relationship to each other (see Chapters 3, 5, and 8).

For these reasons, Chapter 1 is devoted to analyzing each of the components of the SD of empathy, which will allow me to provide an overview of the current literature on the topic and set the stage for discussing the role of empathy in deliberation. However, my ultimate intention is to reject the SD of empathy: I will use it as a negative archetypal model against which to propose my definition of the empathic phenomenon, inspired by the phenomenological tradition (especially Edith Stein's account) and its role in our moral and theoretical deliberative processes. While the SD has the merit of providing a common ground and a useful starting point, as I will show in Part 2 (see Chapters 4, 5, and 6), I believe it poses more problems than it solves, especially when it comes to the deliberative process, and does not accurately capture what we do when we empathize with others (see Chapter 8). But let us not get ahead of ourselves. Let us begin with the essential task of trying to understand how empathy has been defined according to the SD.

1 Cognitive Empathy as Perspective-Taking

Cognitive empathy, very broadly, is defined as "the capacity to understand another person's state of mind from her perspective" (Spaulding, 2017, p. 13). Specifically, in order to achieve the goal of understanding the other's perspective, we can follow two different strategies, which are not mutually exclusive:[5] one based on the Theory Theory (TT) account and one based on the Simulation Theory (ST) account. For both accounts, the ultimate goal is to gain access to, i.e., to understand, the other person's mental state, be it desires, beliefs, or emotions, and to predict or retrodict the other person's future or past actions.

Relevantly, both approaches exclude the possibility of a direct perception of the inner state of the other: it must be mediated either by a folk-psychological theory in TT or by a simulation process in ST. The (not so) implicit assumption is that the minds of others are inaccessible in a direct way because they are opaque to all but their owners (for a critique of this position, see Zahavi, 2011; see Chapter 8). It follows that, to overcome this, it is necessary to employ mediating strategies involving either theoretical inferences or inner simulation processes.

Beyond this common requirement of mediated access, TT and ST differ dramatically. Generally speaking, TT can be equated with "an *information-rich* inference to the best explanation" (Spaulding, 2017, p. 14). The basic idea is that we understand other people's behavior based on a folk-psychological theory or, better, theoretical models that allow us to infer their mental states with some degree of certainty. When we try to understand other people's mental states, we combine what we can infer from their behavior with what we already know about human behavior and mental states in general from other sources

5 As argued by Spaulding, "Most contemporary theory theorists and simulation theorists recognize the inadequacy of *pure* TT and *pure* ST. Most theorists in this debate endorse an hybrid account that involves both theoretical and simulational elements. The consensus is that sometimes we theorize to understand another person's perspective, while other times we mentally simulate. The current debate concerns under what conditions we use each of these strategies" (Spaulding, 2017, p. 16).

of knowledge, such as interpretative processes, intuitions, assumptions, heuristics, and cognitive and domain-specific models (Maibom, 2009; Nichols & Stich, 2003). Relevantly, cognitive empathy is rarely mentioned in the context of TT and usually does not play a specific role in this approach to mindreading.[6]

Conversely, empathy is a prominent feature of ST. For this reason, I will focus primarily on ST and its relationship to empathy, using Alvin Goldman's account of ST because of its enormous influence on the debate.[7] Importantly, I consider ST in general, and Goldman's account in particular, to be the theoretical framework for understanding cognitive empathy as characterized by the SD.

1.1 *Reading Other Minds: Simulation Theory and Two Types of Empathy*

Very broadly, all proponents of ST believe that mindreading is essentially dependent on a simulation process, in which the subject imaginatively puts herself in the other person's mental condition and/or concrete situation and, using her own mind as a reference, understands the other's mental and emotional states and predicts or retrodicts her decisions. Unlike TT, the simulation process has been described as an "*information-poor* cognitive empathy process" (Spaulding, 2017, p. 15) because the main source of information is the target's internal state and no other theoretical folk psychological resources. Sometimes, especially in more complex cases, some prior knowledge of the target, not of general psychological processes, possessed by the subject is also employed.

It is precisely the characterization of cognitive empathy in terms of a simulation process that is central to my discussion. In ST, cognitive empathy is characterized not only as the general ability to understand the other's perspective, but, crucially, it also coincides with the specific process by which we are able to do so. In this sense, Goldman explicitly linked empathy to simulationist mindreading.[8] In particular, he distinguished between two distinct processes:

6 At best, we can be more or less "empathetic," i.e., have more or less familiarity with the folk psychological models (Spaulding, 2017, p. 15). However, this is a very peculiar and less common use of the term empathy within the Other Minds debate.

7 Other relevant figures in the ST debate are Robert M. Gordon and Jane Heal (Gordon, 1986; Heal, 1986).

8 Goldman on the relationship between empathy and simulation: "Other investigators are interested in empathy as a key to mindreading, and might even use the term 'empathy' to describe (what they take to be) the most common form of mindreading. In other words, they use the term 'empathize' as roughly equivalent to 'simulate' (in an intersubjective fashion). I myself am a partisan of this position (…)" (Goldman, 2011, p. 32). Even more strikingly, in *Simulating Minds* Goldman wrote: "the 'empathy theory' is another label for the simulation theory" (Goldman, 2006, p. 11).

low-level simulation and *high-level simulation*. These two processes can be characterized as "two routes to empathy" (Goldman, 2011, p. 31) that recruit different cognitive systems. Accordingly, Goldman argued for a dual-process theory of empathy: respectively, *mirroring empathy*, and *reconstructive empathy* (Goldman, 2006, p. 207).[9]

Low-level simulation processes are often automatic, primitive, and non-propositional in content. They are mostly unconscious because their goal is to recognize rather basic phenomena, typically very simple goal-directed actions and emotions, based on the other person's facial expressions and bodily gestures (Goldman, 2006, pp. 113–146). In the case of emotion, for example, I see the other person's frown; I recognize his expression as indicating displeasure or disapproval.

This ability to recognize others' goal-directed actions and their emotions appears to be partly based on mirroring and mimicry mechanisms, which, in turn, depend on mirror neurons (MNs), "since [according to empirical evidence] deficits in the experience of an emotion and selective deficits in the face-based recognition of the same emotion reliably co-occur" (Goldman, 2006, p. 119). Discovered in 1992 by Giacomo Rizzolatti and his team in a laboratory in Parma (Italy) (di Pellegrino et al., 1992), MNs represent a class of neurons that are activated both when the subject performs an action and when she observes the same (or similar) action being performed by another subject. This execution-observation matching system is not restricted to the F5 region of the vPm, which is responsible for goal-directed actions, but also appears to be involved in the somatosensory cortex and the insula or amygdala, and thus to be involved in emotional states (Carr et al., 2003).

According to ST proponents, especially Goldman and Vittorio Gallese – who was part of Rizzolatti's team and participated in the discovery of MNs – the existence of MNs is taken as (further) evidence in favor of the ST hypothesis, in particular at the low-level: "MNs activity seems to be nature's way of getting the observer into the same 'mental shoes' as the target – exactly what the conjectured simulations heuristics aims to do." While the link between low-level simulation and mirroring is explicitly established, Goldman also clarified that this mirroring provides a *potential* basis for low-level mindreading: "Although mirroring doesn't entail mindreading, as a matter of definition, it is entirely possible that mirroring is used as a basis of mindreading." Or, again, he reiterated to

9 As recognized by Goldman (Goldman, 2006, p. 207), this dual approach to empathy is inspired by Sara Hodges and Daniel Wegner's distinction between automatic and controlled empathy (Hodges & Wegner, 1997). Notably, Karsten Stueber also argued for a distinction between basic and reenactive empathy (Stueber, 2006). For a discussion of his account, see Section 3.1.

"not claim that whenever there is mirroring, there is also low-level mindreading. But wherever there is mirroring, the potential for simulation-based mindreading is there" (Goldman, 2006, pp. 134, 140).

The core idea is that low-level simulation based on mirroring is responsible for the recognition of the other's state (Ferrari & Coudé, 2018; Iacoboni, 2009; J. T. Kaplan & Iacoboni, 2006). This is particularly relevant in the context of emotion recognition: "To recognize someone's face as expressive of a certain emotion [via mirroring but not only] is to judge the person to be in that state and to categorize the emotion as being of the specified type" (Goldman, 2006, p. 114). Some have pushed the argument even further by claiming that "[W] hen people use the expression 'I feel your pain' [via mirroring] to indicate both comprehension and empathy, they may not realize just how literally true their statement could be" (Rizzolatti et al., 2006, p. 60, cited in Debes, 2017, p. 58, see Debes, 2017 for a critique of this position).

In Goldman's account, low-level simulation – of which emotional recognition based on MNs is one of the possible instances – is considered one of the routes to *mirroring empathy*. The main characteristic of this type of empathy is its automaticity, because the way in which mirroring empathy responds to a given stimulus is not spontaneous or open to infinite possibilities. On the contrary, mirroring responses are quite consistent for neurotypical individuals from infancy: seeing another person's disgusted facial expression reliably elicits an automatic mimetic response of disgust in neurotypical observers (Goldman, 2011, p. 36). In this sense, mirroring empathy is described as an "emotional and cognitive contagion and priming" phenomenon (Goldman, 2006, p. 207).[10] In addition, mirroring empathy usually occurs at a subconscious level, in the sense that "the receiver may not be aware, or not fully aware, of the mental state she is undergoing that happens to be congruent with an event in the sender" (Goldman, 2011, p. 34).

In contrast to low-level simulation, *high-level simulation processes* are characterized as voluntary, mostly conscious, and aimed at more complex states than low-level simulation, such as propositional attitudes (Goldman, 2006, pp. 147–191). Typically, the process involves imaginatively simulating the other person's situation, i.e., recreating the other person's emotions, beliefs, desires, and decision-making process in the simulator's mind, and then projecting, i.e., attributing them to the other person. High-level simulation can also be called a simulation-plus-projection process, which Goldman summarized in a three-step process (Goldman, 2005, pp. 80–81, cited in Gallagher, 2007, p. 355):

10 See Section 1.2 for a discussion of the difference between empathy and contagion.

> First, the attributor creates in herself pretend states intended to match those of the target. In other words, the attributor attempts to put herself in the target's "mental shoes." The second step is to feed these initial pretend states, e.g., beliefs, into some mechanism of the attributor's own psychology (…) and allow that mechanism to operate on the pretend states so as to generate one or more new states, e.g., decisions. Third, the attributor assigns the output state to the target (…) e.g., we infer or project the decision to the other's mind.

As Goldman pointed out, this process is run "*off-line*"[11] (Goldman, 2006, p. 20), meaning that the simulator does not act on the outputs of the simulation process, that is, on the other person's mental states (pretend beliefs, desires, or emotions) and decisions. In other words, the simulator's mental activities are disconnected from her motor system, so the pretend states do not translate into outward actions. The same applies to low-level simulation and mirroring empathy: mirroring is only "internal," never external. To recognize the other's frown as an expression of displeasure or disapproval, I do not have to frown myself: there are evidence that emotion recognition is possible even in the presence of paralyzed facial muscles (Goldman, 2006, p. 208).

Another element of high-level simulation is the need for the simulator to quarantine her mental and emotional states, beliefs, desires, and values that do not match those she believes the target of her simulation holds (Goldman, 2006, p. 29). Quarantining means excluding from the simulation routine those mental states that are not shared by the other person but are part of the simulator's perspective; failure to do so which is not a rare occurrence, as Goldman himself recognized, will result in inaccurate simulation routines. Similarly, the quantity and quality of prior information about the target and/or their situation will critically affect the accuracy of the process (Goldman, 2006, pp. 164–180; Goldman, 2011, pp. 43–44).[12]

High-level simulation constitutes the route to *reconstructive empathy*, which is the result of a – at least partially – conscious and effortful act: Unlike mirroring empathy, nothing about this process is automatic, because it involves demanding and often complex imaginative operations that cannot be achieved without some level of purposeful reconstruction of the other person's experi-

11 For arguments against the use of this term, see Jane Heal (Heal, 1996).

12 These failures can be extremely problematic for a deliberative process based on cognitive empathy understood as simulation-plus-projection (see Chapter 4).

ence and inner states (Goldman, 2011, p. 38).[13] Note that, according to Goldman, reconstructive empathy may sometimes differ from high-level simulation only in its final step, that is, when "one or more of the constructed mental states are categorized (commonly, in terms of both mental type and propositional content) and assigned to the target" (Goldman, 2011, p. 38). In other words, not all instances of reconstructive empathy necessarily involve the categorization element of the final step of high-level simulation.

Crucially, reconstructive empathy involves E-imagination, that is, a kind of imagination that does not simply presuppose a particular mental state but requires the literal enactment – or at least the attempt – of that state (Goldman, 2006, pp. 47–48). The goal of this type of imagination is to match the other's mental state "by recreating or pre-creating this state in oneself" (Goldman, 2011, p. 40). The products of E-imagination are precisely those pretend states that the simulator (re- or pre-)creates and then feeds into her cognitive system in order to (re)produce the other's state. The involvement of E-imagination in reconstructive empathy reiterates the difference in complexity of the two types of empathy, since mirroring empathy is "something much less complex than [constructing] an imagined scenario" and taking the other's perspective (Goldman, 2011, p. 37).

Another key difference between mirroring empathy and reconstructive empathy lies in their outcomes: while the former is more likely to guarantee that the subject will end up in the same type of emotional state as the target, the latter is more likely to provide some insight into the object of that state. It is worth noting that Goldman warns us about the reliability of the results of both simulative processes, with particular emphasis on the pitfalls of high-level simulation and reconstructive empathy: "(...) the reconstructive method is obviously capable of generating more and more detailed isomorphic states than mirroring. But is it more reliable? I am skeptical" (Goldman, 2011, p. 43). His skepticism stems from the two aforementioned failures that often plague reconstructive empathy, namely the lack of relevant information about the target and the failure to quarantine the subject's own mental states.

As has hopefully emerged from this discussion, Goldman's reconstructive empathy (and high-level simulation) is an instance of the broader phenome-

---

13 Goldman on reconstructive empathy and high-level simulation: "In what I call 'high-level' simulation, mindreading another person's mental state involves an attempt to replicate or re-experience the target's state via a constructive process. Exploiting prior information about the target, the mind reader uses 'enactment imagination' to reproduce in his own mind what might have transpired, or may be transpiring, in the target. This coincides with the reconstructive type of empathizing proposed here" (Goldman, 2011, p. 38).

non of imaginative perspective-taking and thus can provide a theoretical blueprint for cognitive empathy in the SD. Relevantly, this imaginative perspective-taking process can be achieved in two related but different ways: we can imagine what we would have done, felt, or thought if we were in the other person's situation, or we can imagine what we would have done, felt, or thought if we were the other person in his or her situation. These two approaches are called *self-oriented perspective-taking* and *other-oriented perspective-taking*, respectively (Coplan, 2011a). It is not a subtle distinction: one thing is to imagine or simulate *our own* reactions to the other's situation, and another is to try to replicate the other's thought process (emotional, mental, and decisional) *as if we were the other person.*[14]

While ST and cognitive empathy have received increasing attention and interest in contemporary debates about mindreading, folk psychology, and social cognition, the idea that we can imaginatively place ourselves in the mental shoes of others is by no means new. Its conceptual and historical roots can be traced back to the Scottish moral tradition of the eighteenth century, and in particular to Adam Smith. In his 1759 work *The Theory of Moral Sentiments* (TMS), the Scottish philosopher described sympathy – what we now call (cognitive) empathy – as "our fellow-feeling with any passion whatsoever" (TMS, I.i.1.5). While common usage of these terms often equates sympathy with pity and compassion, Smith points out that this is misleading. The fact that sympathy enables us to understand any passion felt by the other person clearly distinguishes sympathy from pity and compassion, which refer only to our empathy with the suffering of others (TMS, I.i.1.5). Interestingly, this distinction between sympathizing with the other's emotional states in general and feeling pity or compassion only for the other's suffering is reflected in the SD's separation of (affective and cognitive) empathy and sympathy.

According to Smith, our understanding of each other's passions is so pervasive and shared by all human beings – including transgressors of moral and societal laws – that there is almost no need to provide examples to prove its existence.[15] But how this fellow-feeling is achieved requires some clarification.

---

14 Note that for some scholars, such as Goldman himself or Amy Coplan (Coplan, 2011b), only other-oriented perspective-taking counts as empathy, while for others (Goldie, 2011), self-oriented perspective-taking is the only thing that we can actually pull off and thus counts as empathy. As we will see in Chapter 4, both have problematic implications that can severely impact an empathy-based deliberative process.

15 Smith on how obvious it is to understand each other's suffering: "That we often derive sorrow from the sorrow of others, is a matter of fact too obvious to require any instances to prove it; for this sentiment, like all the other original passions of human nature, is by

In this sense, Smith readily explained that imagination is the faculty that makes sympathy possible (TMS, I.i.1.2, my emphasis):

> (…) it is by the *imagination* only that we can form any conception of what are his sensations. Neither can that faculty help us to this any other way, than by representing to us what would be our own, if we were in his case. It is the impressions of our own sense only, not those of his, which our imagination copy. By the imagination we place *ourselves* in his *situation*, we conceive ourselves enduring all the same torments, we enter as it were into his body, and become in some measure the same person with him, and thence form some idea if his sensations, and even feel something which, though weaker in degree, is not altogether unlike them.

In order for the spectator to succeed in "changing places in fancy" (TMS, I.i.1.3) with the other person, first and foremost, the spectator must understand the other person's situation. Understanding the situation enables the spectator to grasp the *cause* of the other person's passion (Rick, 2007, p. 139). Thus, according to Smith, the sympathetic process has two steps: first, the spectator must understand the other's situation and have a general idea of his or her emotional state. Second, the observer must imaginatively recreate the other's situation, imaginatively putting herself in the other's place and imagining how she would react emotionally to that situation. The centrality of the other person's situation in Smithian sympathy is demonstrated by the fact that it is possible, and in fact quite common, to sympathize with someone simply because of their situation, even if they are not currently experiencing any particular emotional state (TMS, I.i.1.10). One of Smith's examples concerns second-hand embarrassment: "we blush for the imprudence and rudeness of another, though he himself appears to have no sense of the impropriety of his own behaviour" (TMS, I.i.1.10). Similarly, we can also sympathize with a dead person.

Interestingly, long before the contemporary debate, Smith was aware of the difference between the two different ways of taking the other's perspective. In fact, in Part I of TMS, Smith seemed to describe the sympathetic process in terms of self-oriented perspective-taking, while in Part VII of TMS, Smith referred to the possibility of actually becoming the other person (TMS, VII.

---

no means confined to the virtuous and humane, though they perhaps may feel it with the most exquisite sensibility. The greatest ruffian, the most hardened violator of the laws of society, is not altogether without it" (TMS, I.i.1.1).

iii.1.4) in order to sympathize with the other's grief, thus describing other-oriented perspective-taking. As Ben-Moshe points out, "this inconsistency has to do with the question of how much of the spectator's self is transported into the actor's situation when the spectator sympathizes with the actor" (Ben-Moshe, 2020, p. 739).

According to him, Smith's apparent inconsistency can be resolved if we take into account the metaethical goal of Smithian sympathy, i.e., a judgment of approval or disapproval of the other's action, and not merely an understanding of the other's mental states, which distinguishes it from the contemporary account of cognitive empathy. We need both types of perspective-taking to compare our imagined response with the other person's response. If these two reactions match, the other person's action is approved by the empathizer. More on the role of empathy in formulating our moral judgments will be discussed in Chapter 3. For now, suffice it to say that cognitive empathy, as understood in the SD, is an imaginative perspective-taking process that uses a simulation-plus-projection routine to gain access to the mental states of the other person.

2 Affective Empathy as Emotional Sharing

Understanding the inner states of others through perspective-taking is undoubtedly a complex and fascinating ability. However, as surprising as perspective-taking may be, perhaps even more interesting is the fact that we are able to feel what other people are feeling. Our susceptibility as human beings to be infected by the emotional states of others is something we have all experienced in our lives. This experience of affective sharing has been conceptualized in the SD as affective empathy. In what follows, I will first focus on the distinction between affective empathy and emotional contagion, which, despite some similarities, are two distinct phenomena. I will then explore how the contemporary debate on affective empathy in both psychology and philosophy understands it as a multifaceted and multilayered phenomenon closely related to both personal distress and sympathy.

2.1 *Being Infected by Others' Feelings: Affective Empathy and Emotional Contagion*

One of the most popular and cited definitions of affective empathy is provided by Martin Hoffman, whose primary interest has been in exploring the psychological mechanisms underlying affective empathy and the moral dimension of this phenomenon. Importantly, for his definition, Hoffman is a firm believer in the fundamental contribution of affective empathy to prosocial action and, more generally, to our moral life: "For me," he wrote, "empathy is the spark of human concern for others, the glue that makes social life possible. It may be fragile, but it has arguably endured throughout evolutionary times and may continue as long as humans exist" (Hoffman, 2000, p. 3).

Hoffman defined affective empathy as those "psychological processes that make a person have feelings that are more *congruent* with another's situation than with his own situation" (Hoffman, 2000, p. 30, my emphasis). More specifically, when Hoffman spoke of the prosocial "calling" of affective empathy, he had in mind a specific manifestation of it, namely empathic distress, which is characterized as a feeling of discomfort or distress upon observing or experiencing the other's pain, fear, or negative feelings in general. This emotional response is intended to represent a powerful prosocial and moral motive that moves the subject from experiencing empathic distress to sympathy.[16]

There is a lot to unpack here. First, to say that in cases of affective empathy, my feelings are more congruent with the other person's situation implies that my feelings are caused by the other person's situation in general and the other person's feelings in particular. The causal relationship between my empathic feelings and those of the other person is even more evident if we consider a similar definition of affective empathy as a set of "emotional responses" to the other's condition (Maibom, 2017, p. 22).[17]

This is particularly important because the recognition that the feelings that empathizers experience have their origin in the other's situation is crucial to distinguishing between affective empathy proper and an adjacent but different phenomenon, that of emotional contagion.[18] The difference lies in the subject's awareness of the origin of the emotions: in affective empathy, the empathizer is always aware that she is experiencing an emotion, such as fear, as a result of the other person's fear, whereas in emotional contagion,

16 Hoffman's account of empathy and its contribution to morality is far more complex than what I have just outlined. For example, Hoffman acknowledges the need for moral principles and empathy to interact with each other (Hoffman, 2000, pp. 221–272). I will begin to discuss the relationship between empathy, sympathy, and morality in the next section (1.3.2).

17 Maibom explicitly cited Hoffman's definition of affective empathy as the starting point of her account (Maibom, 2017, p. 23).

18 What happens in cases of emotional contagion can also be described as a lack of separation or fusion between the selves of the two (or more) subjects involved in the situation, which, as we will see, was already seen as problematic in the early phenomenological tradition. For a discussion of early phenomenologists' critique of emotional contagion (specifically Stein's), which they called "emotional infection," as a critical response to Lipps's account of Einfühlung, see Part 3 (Chapter 7).

the subject believes that the fear is hers and not someone else's, or, alternatively, she does not know where (and why) the emotions originated. Typical examples of emotional contagion are the phenomena of reactive crying in infants (Hoffman, 2000, pp. 64–67)[19] and the spread of panic in a crowd of people.

In the contemporary literature on empathy, this distinction is fairly uncontroversial and almost universally agreed upon (Coplan, 2011a; Decety & Jackson, 2004; Wispé, 1987).[20] This distinction does not mean, however, that these two phenomena cannot occur simultaneously or one before the other: "Emotional contagion may be related to this process [empathy] and may sometimes participate in it, but when we 'catch' the emotions of the other through emotional contagion, the emotions are not experienced imaginatively or in relation to another; we experience them as our own" (Coplan, 2011b, p. 9).

In this sense, emotional contagion is often seen as "the most simple expression of emotional sharing that does not need conscious awareness" (Decety & Jackson, 2004, p. 77), which in turn is seen as a stepping stone to affective empathy proper. Note that emotional contagion is unconscious in two senses: on the one hand, it is unconscious as to the origin of the emotion, as mentioned above; on the other hand, it is unconscious because it is based on mimicry and mirroring mechanisms of the other person's physical gestures, facial expressions, tone of voice, and so on. Another term for this specific phenomenon is "neural resonance," which occurs when "observed bodily states are automatically mapped onto an observer's own sensory, motor and affective representation" (Zaki & Ochsner, 2011, pp. 208–209).

Note that the underlying systems involved in emotional contagion are the same as those involved in Goldman's mirroring empathy. Moreover, both share the same phenomenology, i.e., the subjects involved in instances of mirroring empathy and emotional contagion end up experiencing the same emotional state (e.g., disgust, fear, joy, etc.). However, these two phenomena differ significantly in terms of their ultimate goal: while mirroring empathy aims to

---

19 Hoffman's definition of newborn reactive crying: "the newborn reactive cry is an innate, isomorphic response to the cry of another being of the same species, which survived natural selection and is adaptive" (Hoffman, 2000, p. 65).

20 It is worth noting that Maibom distinguished affective empathy from emotional contagion without using the criterion of awareness of the origin of the emotion. She defined affective empathy as "Person *S* empathizes with person *O*'s experience of emotion *E* in situation *C* if *S* feels *E* for *O* as a result of believing or perceiving that O feels *E*, or imagining being in *C*" and emotional contagion as "Person *S*'s feeling *E* is a case of emotional contagion if *S* feels *E* as a result of believing that person *O* feels *E*, perceiving that *O*'s expressing *E*, or imagining being in *O*'s situation" (Maibom, 2017, p. 22).

achieve emotional recognition of the target's emotional state, emotional contagion never produces this kind of output because the subjects experiencing emotional contagion are, by design, never aware of the source of that emotion. For this reason, I will discuss mirroring empathy in the context of cognitive empathy, rather than affective empathy, because I want to emphasize its epistemic dimension and its contribution to empathy-based social cognition, which in the debate is often seen as a stepping stone to more complex perspective-taking tasks, rather than simply a mechanism that makes us feel what the other is feeling (see Chapters 3 and 4).

The idea that emotions have a contagious quality, and that we as human beings are particularly susceptible to "catching" the emotions of others, is again not remotely a recent discovery. As with cognitive empathy and Smith, David Hume's account of sympathy has had an enormous influence on contemporary debates about emotional contagion in particular and affective empathy in general. In his 1739 *Treatise of Human Nature* (THN), especially in the Second Book about passions, Hume qualified sympathy as the most remarkable quality of human nature, since it enables us to "*receive* by communication their [others'] inclinations and sentiments, however different from, or even contrary to our own" (THN, p. 316, my emphasis). I find the use of the verb "receive" revealing of the passive nature of Humean sympathy, in that the sympathetic process begins independently of the sympathizer, whose associative faculties are automatically activated by the other person's passions.

This becomes clear when Hume describes how the sympathetic process works: first, the subject observes the "effects" (THN, p. 317) and the "external signs in the countenance and conversation" (THN, p. 317), that is, the behavioral evidence of passion in the other person (facial expressions, bodily gestures, verbal expressions, their tone, etc.). Second, these external effects produce an idea of passion in the subject. This idea is the result of an associative process in which the subject associates a certain external behavior (i.e., the effects of passion) with the fact that the other person has a certain passion. Third, "this idea is presently converted into an *impression*, and acquires such a degree of force and vivacity, as to become the very passion itself, and produce an equal emotion, as any original affection" (THN, p. 317, my emphasis).[21]

21 Ideas and impressions are two central concepts in the THN and they are defined by Hume in the opening of the First Book: "All the perceptions of the human mind fall into two distinct kinds, which I shall call *impressions* and 'ideas'. These differ in the degrees of force and liveliness with which they strike upon the mind and make their way into our thought or consciousness. The perceptions that enter with most force and violence we may name 'impressions'; and under this name I bring all our sensations, passions, and emotions, as they make their first appearance in the soul. By *ideas* I mean

For this process to work, two premises are necessary. First, Hume postulated a strong similarity among human beings. We all share the same "fabric of the mind as with that of the body" (THN, p. 318). This allows a parallel to be drawn between our passions and those of others.[22] Obviously, the more other external factors outside our psychology are similar – for example, country, language, and so on – the easier the sympathetic relationship. This is problematic for a number of reasons, as Hume himself was well aware, which will be discussed later (see Chapter 5).

Second, the conversion from the idea to the impression and ultimately to the passion itself is also possible because of the permanent lively impression we have of ourselves (THN, p. 369). Crucially, because of the homogeneity among human beings, other people's passions cannot be foreign to us. We must have had at least one experience similar to theirs (THN, p. 369). Therefore, "I come to associate my idea of another person's emotion with my own experience of that emotion, and via my lively impression of myself, my idea of her [passion] is converted into the feeling of her [passion] in me" (Ilyes, 2017, p. 99).[23]

Note that Humean sympathy is not concerned with imagining the sympathizer's reaction if he were in the other's situation, as in Smith's account. On the contrary, it is about receiving and sharing the other's emotional state. This could not be clearer when Hume noted that all minds have a "mirroring quality." In what has become a *locus classicus*, he wrote precisely that "the minds of

---

the faint images of the others in thinking and reasoning: for example, all the perceptions aroused by your reading this book – apart from perceptions arising from sight and touch, and apart from the immediate pleasure or uneasiness your reading may cause in you" (THN, p. 1).

22 The conversion from observation of another's behavior to idea and finally to impression is possible because of the associative nature of our minds. Specifically, Hume identified three types of association: causality, resemblance, and continuity in time and place. These principles both inform how our minds naturally work (THN, pp. 13–15) and explain how the sympathetic process is possible. Observing the other person's behavior naturally leads me to think about its possible causes, in this context a passion. I can refer to my past experiences to realize that a certain behavior (smiling) is usually caused by a certain passion (happiness). This association produces in my mind the impression of the passion (happiness), which, according to Hume, has the ability to transfer "a share of its force and vivacity" (THN, p. 98) to the idea of the passion, transforming it into an experience of that passion.

23 In Hume's words: "We have a lively idea of everything related to us. All human creatures are related to us by resemblance. Their persons, therefore, theirs interests, their passions, their pains and pleasures must strike upon us in a lively manner, and produce an emotion similar to the original one; since a lively idea is easily converted into an impression" (THN, p. 369).

men are mirrors to one another" (THN, p. 365). It is no coincidence that Goldman included Hume among the precursors of ST, along with Smith and many others, citing this very passage as evidence (Goldman, 2006, p. 17).[24]

Hume also famously used the metaphor of contagion, whose influence on contemporary accounts of affective empathy cannot be overstated. According to him, "The passions are so contagious, that they pass with the greatest facility from one person to another, and produce correspondent movements in all human breasts" (THN, p. 605). The idea that emotions and feelings are virus-like entities that spread despite our conscious choice is entirely consistent with emotional contagion. In Humean sympathy, as well as in emotional contagion, the sympathizer has no say in whether to initiate the process. There is no conscious and deliberate effort involved in initiating the sympathetic process, just as it is impossible to decide whether or not to contract an infectious disease.[25] This is in stark contrast to Smith's account of sympathy, which requires active initiation and consists of a conscious act of perspective-taking.

More importantly, Smithian sympathy does not guarantee – or even require – that the sympathizer will end up in the same emotional state as the other person she is sympathizing with (recall the second-hand embarrassment scenario or sympathy for someone dead): the only thing the Smithian sympathizer needs to reproduce identically is the other person's situation. In contrast, for Hume, the whole point of sympathy is to mirror exactly the same passion as the other person, without any interest in the other person's situation and the cause of that passion. In other words, it is the passion itself that is responsible for directly causing sympathy in the spectator.

This marks another important difference between the two accounts: the different weight and role given to the imagination. Both Hume and Smith agreed on the private nature of feelings and their inaccessibility through the

24 As Fleischacker noted, Hume's account seems much more congruent with a TT account of mindreading than with ST. According to him, Hume is "closer (...) to what today we would call a 'theory theorist', for whom we work out what others are feeling from a causal inference from the way they behave" (Fleischacker, 2012, p. 276). However, he pointed out, there is a fundamental difference between Hume's account and TT: "The theory theorists says that we learn causal relationship between feelings and their expressions from a common stock of folk beliefs about such relationships, not form private observation of those relationships in our own case" (Fleischacker, 2012, note 20, p. 287). Moreover, the insistence on the contagion element of Hume's sympathy is far more relevant than this inferential aspect. Overall, then, Hume's perspective seems to differ from both ST and TT accounts of mindreading and empathy.

25 To be sure, in the case of infectious diseases, it is possible to reduce the risk of infection. However, as the Covid-19 pandemic taught us, it is impossible to completely control the spread of the virus, despite all the efforts and measures taken.

senses. But the agreement ends there. For Smith, the way we come to experience sympathy is distinctly imaginative: we imagine what we would feel if we were in the other person's situation. Conversely, Hume's approach relies much less on imagination: it allows us to experience for ourselves what the other person is feeling.[26] Interestingly, the different role of imagination in Smith's and Hume's accounts is worth keeping in mind, as it provides a useful conceptual tool to better clarify the distinction between cognitive and affective empathy in the SD, which also involves imagination very differently, much more in the case of the former and much less in the case of the latter.

2.2 *Sharing Others' Feelings: the Multifaceted Phenomenon of Affective Empathy*

The most important aspect of Hoffman's account is the concept of congruence: should we understand this concept as synonymous with emotional sharing? And if so, what does it mean to share another's emotions? There are conflicting positions in the literature. For some, the definition of empathizing with the other's emotion as having an emotional response that is more congruent with her emotional situation than that of the empathizer implies that the subjects involved in the empathic relationship must be in exactly the same emotional state. Thus, affective empathy requires emotional isomorphism between the emotional state of the empathizer and that of the other person.

The requirement for isomorphism can be interpreted in two slightly different ways. The strictest position argues for total sameness between the subjects, both in terms of the type of emotion and its intensity: if the other person is depressed, it is not enough for the empathizer to feel just a little down. It has to be a perfect match (Coplan, 2011a). Somewhat less demanding is to say that the emotions must be of the same type, but they can have different degrees of intensity: for example, there is empathy when the other person feels extremely

26 To explain this difference, Fleischacker used a clever metaphor: "We might call Hume's a microwave theory of the imagination's role in sympathy – the imagination heats up some ready-to-go ideas – while for Smith the imagination is a gourmet chef, preparing our sympathies from scratch" (Fleischacker, 2012, p. 292). The metaphor is meant to convey the different levels of activity of the imagination: for Smith, the imagination has a lot more work to do to ensure that sympathy arises, because it has to assemble all the different "flavors" of the other's situation and combine them to recreate the situation that allows the sympathizer to "taste" what feelings she would have. For Hume's imagination, the work is simpler: no fancy recipes or flavors. Instead, its job is to make sure that we experience firsthand what the other is feeling through association – or "reheating," if you will – between the vivid impression of ourselves and the idea of the other's feelings.

joyful and the empathizer feels moderately joyful in response. In any case, both positions require affective matching, that is, emotional isomorphism.

Alternatively, it can be argued that affective matching is too strong a requirement and that affective sharing is sufficient for affective empathy to occur. This means that the empathizer's emotional state must still be similar to the other person's state, but it can be of a different type. For example, affective empathy occurs when a mother is proud of her joyful daughter for graduating from college. Although pride and joy are not exactly the same emotion, so there is no affective match, they have the same valence, i.e., positive. Another classic example is the case of empathic anger: I empathize with the other person's pain caused by a third party, and in response I do not feel pain, but I do feel anger toward the perpetrator. It would be counterintuitive not to see this particular episode as an instance of affective empathy. But it would also be strange to say that the mother empathizes with her daughter when the former is sad and the latter is happy. For this reason, affective empathy requires that the empathizer and the target share an affect that has at least the same valence. Thus, congruence with the other's emotion is understood here in terms of sharing the valence of his or her emotion (de Vignemont & Jacob, 2012).[27]

According to an alternative perspective, affective matching and sharing are not essential for affective empathy. This is because there are instances where one can grasp what another person is experiencing without being in the same emotional state or in any emotional state at all. For example, one can empathize with someone's anger while feeling peaceful, or one can grasp another person's emotion without feeling it (Zahavi & Overgaard, 2011). As will be discussed (see Chapter 8), this understanding of empathy differs significantly from the definition of affective empathy as emotional matching and/or emotional sharing.[28] For now, suffice it to say that there are two competing and opposing accounts of (affective) empathy: one that requires emotional sharing and one that does not. According to the SD and most contemporary accounts

27 De Vignemont and Jacob argued for a set of conditions that must be met for empathy to occur: "i) *Affectivity condition*: X is in some affective state or other s^*; ii) *Interpersonal similarity condition*: X's affective state s^* stands in some similarity relation to Y's affective state s; iii) *Causal path condition*: X's being in state s^* is caused by Y's being in state s; iv) *Ascription condition*: X is aware of Y's being in s" (de Vignemont & Jacob, 2012, p. 306). The similarity of the empathizer's emotional state to that of the target is what distinguishes affective empathy from sympathy, understood as feeling sorry for whatever negative emotional state the other's is experiencing.

28 I agree with Zahavi's rejection of the isomorphism/matching condition, which he borrows from the early phenomenological tradition, including Stein (see Chapters 7 and 8).

of affective empathy, affective sharing (or, in some cases, even affective matching) is necessary for affective empathy to occur: if the other's affective situation is of a positive valence, the empathizer's response must be congruent with it, that is, it must share the valence of the other's emotional state. In this sense, affective empathy is "the vicarious sharing of an affect" (Stueber, 2019).

Another way to look at the problem is to consider the object of the emotional states involved in the empathic relationship. Every emotion has an object, that is, "it is about something" (Maibom, 2017, p. 24). The aboutness of our emotions is quite intuitive: I'm afraid *of* snakes, happy *about* my promotion, and sad *about* the end of the holidays. In the case of empathic emotions, their object can be either the other's emotional state or the object of the other's emotional state. I can be happy that you are happy, or I can be happy that you passed a class, which is the same object as your happiness.

Typically, accounts of affective empathy that require affective matching argue for the second type of aboutness: there must be congruence not only with the type and intensity of the emotions but also with the object of the empathic emotion and the emotion of the other person. In this sense, Stueber argues that it is not enough to be happy or unhappy because one's child is happy or unhappy (Stueber, 2019). This would simply be a case of an emotional response to a perception of the world (in which the other person, in our case the child, is feeling something) from our first-person perspective. According to this view, my emotional state must be a reaction to the other person's emotional state and therefore directed at the same object as that state.

However, as Maibom points out, "there is something odd about denying me empathic sadness in a case where my sadness has as its object just your sadness, but not the object of your sadness" (Maibom, 2017, p. 24). And I think most people would share that intuition, because that is how most of us commonly think affective empathy works. Maibom offered a solution to this apparent impasse: "Empathy comes in degrees" (Maibom, 2017, p. 24). Instead of disqualifying the case of feeling sadness simply because the other person is sad as non-empathy, it should be considered a less complete case of empathy than the case in which the object of the empathizer's emotions is the same as that of the other person. When this happens, we have "full empathy," that is, a perfect match between the empathizer's emotional state and that of the other person not only in terms of type and intensity but also of object.

In fairness, even in the case of full empathy, the object of the empathizer's emotion will not be *exclusively* the object of the other person's emotion – say, a promotion at work – because the other person's emotion – say, joy and satisfaction – will inevitably be somewhat involved in the object of the empathizer's emotional state. However, it is also possible to have affective empathy by meeting only the affective sharing requirement: different intensity, different type, but the same valence, and only with the other person's emotional state as the object. It will simply be a less complete instance of empathy. An interesting question would be whether there is a correlation between the degree of empathy and the motivational power or level of understanding of the empathizer. In other words, is a greater degree of empathy responsible for a stronger moral motivation (or a better epistemic understanding of the other person's emotional state)?

The final aspect of Hoffman's definition of affective empathy worth discussing concerns empathic distress and its relationship to prosocial behavior. According to Hoffman, there is a very important subcategory of affective empathy: empathic distress, which occurs when we share the other's discomfort or pain and become distressed as a result. Importantly, this phenomenon must meet two conditions: "[First], for a person to experience mature empathic distress, he must have a clear distinction between what happens to others and what happens to himself and [second] an understanding of how feelings are expressed and how they are shaped by events" (Hoffman, 2011, pp. 63–64). The ability to recognize self-other differentiation is a product of cognitive development that proceeds in stages and gradually achieves full awareness of self-other separation.

Following Hoffman's account, Maibom argues that the initial stage of affective empathy involves empathic distress, which is defined as the emotional matching between the empathizer and the other person's emotional state (Maibom, 2017, p. 26). Subsequently, the empathizer may experience *personal distress* and/or *sympathy*. Both personal distress and sympathy are emotional responses to the pain and suffering of another person. They have the same cause but differ in orientation. Personal distress is experienced as the empathizer's own pain, even though it initially arose from the other person's situation. Personal distress is considered *self-oriented* because the empathizer is the subject of the suffering, not the other person. Therefore, the response is not focused on the other person and alleviating their suffering, but on the empathizer herself. Empirical evidence has shown that personal distress often leads to egoistic actions rather than prosocial or altruistic ones (Batson, 2011).

Conversely, affective empathy is *other-oriented* since the empathizer is suffering not for her own condition but for the other person, which motivates them to act altruistically or pro-socially (Stueber, 2019). The empathizer experiences a combination of emotions, including pain, sympathy, and empathy. The resulting action, whether to help or not, depends on "how much of one versus the other [emotion] is felt, and how they relate to one another and the beliefs and attitudes of the person experiencing them" (Maibom, 2017, p. 26). This seems to partially answer the question of the correlation between the degree of empathy and its effect on the motivational (and epistemic) contribution of empathy: according to Maibom, it is not so much the degree of empathy, and thus the degree of affective sharing between subjects, that makes the difference when it comes to the prosocial and moral motivation of affective empathy. Instead, what matters is whether and how the empathic distress is transformed into either personal distress, which typically leads to withdrawal, or sympathy, which, as we will discuss next, is supposed to guarantee both prosocial and moral actions.[29]

A final clarification: the distinction between cognitive and affective empathy is valid, but it need not be exaggerated. To reiterate, despite solid evidence for different neural networks involved in these two phenomena (Decety & Jackson, 2004; Guo, 2017), it has also been shown that cognitive and affective empathy can occur simultaneously. This is because in real-life situations, as opposed to the experimental setting, the subject is presented with a variety of social cues, which in turn require her to engage both systems – the affective and the cognitive – simultaneously or, alternatively, one after the other (Zaki & Ochsner, 2011, p. 213). Moreover, there is evidence of interaction between the two systems, creating "a feedback loop that informs social information-processing as it unfolds" (Zaki & Ochsner, 2011, p. 214). Simply put, affective sharing processes appear to inform and influence cognitive processes, and vice versa.

3 Sympathy as Concern for the Other's Wellbeing

It now remains to provide a definition for the third and final component of the SD of empathy: sympathy. My aim is twofold: first, to define sympathy as active concern for the welfare of the other person, thus showing that empathy and sympathy are two distinct phenomena, and second, to begin to explore the nature of their relationship. As is already apparent, there is a high risk of contradiction: how can sympathy be anything other than empathy, if sympathy is considered a component of empathy? There are two possible answers: one possibility is to recognize the difference between the two phenomena, but at the same time to consider sympathy as a subcategory of empathy. This is the approach taken by the SD. Conversely, the other option – the one I favor and will defend in Part 3 (see Chapter 8) – is to separate the two phenomena. For

29 For a discussion of the motivational role of empathy and sympathy, see Chapter 3.

now, however, I will discuss how sympathy is characterized in the contemporary debate and begin to shed light on the interplay between empathy, sympathy, altruism, and morality.

3.1 *The Difference between Sympathy and Empathy*

Not without ambivalence, the SD of empathy distinguishes cognitive empathy and affective empathy from sympathy. At first glance, it seems clear that the former involves imagining the other's perspective (cognitive empathy) or sharing the other's emotional state (affective empathy), while the latter involves being concerned about the other's condition or even motivated to improve it. Recognition of the difference between these phenomena has gradually led most scholars to recognize the distinction between (cognitive and affective) empathy and sympathy (Darwall, 2010; de Vignemont & Singer, 2006; H. Maibom, 2014).

In this respect, Laura Wispé was one of the first to argue for a clear separation between these two concepts. According to her, they differ from each other on a historical-conceptual basis and, above all, on a psychological basis. Empathy and sympathy are two different processes with different goals: "Empathy is a way of 'knowing.' Sympathy is a way of 'relating'" (Wispé, 1986, p. 318). This characterization is already revealing: empathy has no reference to actively doing something for the other, while in sympathy the active and relational dimension is central. Accordingly, she defined sympathy as "the heightened awareness of the suffering of another person as something to be alleviated" and empathy as "the attempt by one self-aware self to comprehend unjudgmentally the positive and negative experiences of another self" (Wispé, 1986, p. 318). The key point is that the suffering of the other elicits a specific need in the empathizer, i.e., the need to alleviate that suffering. One thing is to understand that the other person is suffering (empathy), and another is to feel the urge to do something to stop that suffering (sympathy).[30]

Similarly, and even more influentially, Stephen Darwall offered a definition of sympathy that encapsulates all the crucial elements that distinguish it from empathy: "It is a feeling or emotion that (a) responds to some apparent threat or obstacle to an individual's *good* or *well-being*, (b) has that individual himself as object, and (c) involves *concern* for him, and thus for his well-being, for his sake" (Darwall, 1998, p. 261, my emphasis). Conversely, empathy

---

30 The intuition that empathy does not imply a prosocial or moral concern for the other's condition is by no means a recent discovery. As I will discuss in detail in Part 3, the early phenomenological tradition was well aware of the difference between empathy and sympathy (see Chapter 8). See, for example, Scheler's definition of both concepts (Scheler, 1913).

does not involve concern for the other person's welfare, since the empathizer is only interested in feeling what he or she believes or imagines the other person is feeling in his or her situation (Darwall, 1998, p. 261).

Thus, sympathy can be characterized as an active concern for the welfare of the other. Here I mean "active" only in the sense of eliciting some concerned response to the other's situation, which does not necessarily imply overt action to alleviate the other's suffering. A concerned attitude, composed of both affective and cognitive aspects, is sufficient for a sympathetic response. In this respect, I take compassion to be synonymous with sympathy: to be compassionate is not merely to be interested in or generally moved by the other's suffering, but must involve some form of actively expressed concern.

Despite the apparent consensus on the distinction between empathy and sympathy, there is much ambiguity in the literature. While it is usually recognized that empathy and sympathy are two separate phenomena, it is not uncommon to find expressions such as "sympathy is one of the empathic emotions," even though, it is the "most sophisticated" one (Maibom, 2014, p. 6). The idea behind this is that, regardless of the differences, sympathy is a special case of empathy or a subcategory of more general empathic attitudes. The SD of empathy that I discuss here reflects this ambiguity of recognizing these phenomena as distinct while also implying, more or less explicitly, some overlap. However, I find this way of framing the issue problematic. I think that a failure to recognize the inherently different nature of these two phenomena not only contradicts our everyday experience – knowing or feeling that the other person is in pain does not always translate into active concern for his or her well-being – but can also be misleading because it ascribes to empathy moral qualities that, as I will try to show in Part 2 (see Chapters 5–6), it simply does not have. Note that this is a highly controversial claim since empathy is believed by many to have a moral nature, and, consequently, to contribute prominently to morality, in general, and deliberation, in particular (see Chapter 3).

While the relationship between empathy and morality is nothing short of problematic, the same cannot be said for sympathy, which is almost unanimously seen as a positive force when it comes to morality (Hoffman, 2000). As Darwall pointed out, one reason for this is that it is a form of "concern for a person for *his own sake*" (Darwall, 1998, p. 274). In sympathy, when we are concerned about the other person's condition, we are concerned about her for her own sake, that is, because we care about her overall well-being, not merely because we don't want her to suffer. According to him, sympathy has a normative force precisely because it is directed toward the good of the other person for his or her own sake. It follows that sympathetic concern for the other's suffering acts as "a categorical reason for anyone to act on its behalf"

(Darwall, 1998, p. 276). Sympathy makes us desire the other's good for her or his own sake, which is not arbitrarily determined by the sympathizer: "Something is good for that person by virtue of being something it makes sense for anyone caring about her (perhaps she herself) to want for her sake" (Darwall, 1998, p. 277). In this sense, sympathy appeals to a definition of the good that aspires to universality.[31] More specifically, the primary locus of the concept of a person's well-being is not the individual's own desires, but rather the third-person perspective of someone who cares about that person.

Even if we do not subscribe to Darwall's (quasi)deontological and highly demanding account of sympathy, it is hard to deny that being actively concerned for the welfare of the other has something to do with morality. Note that I deliberately use an extremely vague phrase to characterize the moral nature of sympathy and its relation to morality, since all I need at this point is to establish that sympathy has some sort of moral aspect and, even more loosely, some involvement in the moral life of the subject. More details are needed, however, to clarify the persistent conceptual and terminological confusion about the relationship between empathy, sympathy, altruism, and morality: Is empathy the cause of sympathy, which in turn motivates altruistic and moral actions? Are altruism and morality the same thing? What follows attempts to provide some preliminary answers.

3.2 *Empathy as the Cause for Sympathy*

As mentioned above, the most common position on the relationship between empathy and sympathy is that the former can cause the latter (Hoffman, 2000; Maibom, 2017). The argument is fairly straightforward: cognitive empathy and affective empathy are responsible for inducing sympathetic attitudes because both imaginatively simulating the other's perspective or sharing the other's feelings are thought to lead to concern for the other's overall well-being. This is particularly evident in cases where the other person is in danger or suffering from various kinds of physical, emotional, or existential pain. In this context, the ability to understand and feel what the other person is going through should be what triggers the sympathetic response and thus the active concern for his or her welfare.

For example, I empathize with your grief by imagining what it would be like (for me or you) to lose a parent, and because of this act of cognitive empathy, I

31 Darwall's account of empathy and its contribution to morality is far more complex than these simple remarks. In particular, empathy, sympathy, and concern for the welfare of others are intrinsically linked to notions of recognition, respect, and the second-person standpoint (Darwall, 2009; Darwall, 1977).

now sympathize with you in the sense that I am actively concerned for your well-being. Similarly, I share your sadness about losing your job, and because of this instance of affective empathy, I now sympathize with you in the sense that I am actively concerned for your well-being. From these examples, it is easy to see why sympathy through empathy has been associated with morality in general and altruism in particular: sympathetic concern for the other person is supposed to motivate the subject to act altruistically, that is, with the other person's welfare in mind, rather than egoistically, that is, with only personal interest in mind.

To further complicate matters, it is not uncommon to discuss the relationship between empathy and altruism without explicitly mentioning sympathy. In particular, this relationship has been characterized in two ways: from a descriptive perspective or from a normative perspective (Schramme, 2017, pp. 205–206). On the one hand, the descriptive perspective examines why individuals are motivated to engage in altruistic actions and identifies empathy as a possible cause of these behaviors. This approach is very common in psychological research. The most famous theory that attempts to prove this causal relationship is the so-called "empathy-altruism hypothesis" proposed by Daniel C. Batson (Batson, 2011). According to him, based on decades of empirical evidence, "empathic concern produces altruistic motivation" (Batson, 2014).

Batson's proposal of the causal relationship between empathy and altruism has been a massive influence in literature. However, if we look closely at Batson's definition of empathic concern, it becomes clear that he is referring to neither cognitive nor affective empathy. Instead, he is referring to what I have called sympathy, following Wispé and Darwall. As if the use of the term "concern" were not enough to prove this, Batson explicitly defines "empathetic concern" as an "other-oriented emotion elicited by and congruent with the perceived welfare of a person in need" which, he claims, to include "a whole constellation [of emotions, such as] feelings of sympathy, compassion, softheartedness, tenderness, sorrow, sadness, upset, distress, concern, and grief" (Batson, 2014, p. 42).[32] Consistent with this interpretation of Batson's proposal, most evidence suggests that it is sympathy – not empathy – that leads

32 He then adds that "empathic concern is other-oriented in the sense that it involves feeling *for* the other – feeling sympathy for, compassion for, sorry for, distressed for, concerned for, and so on." And, finally, he explicitly states that "Knowing another's thoughts and feelings, adopting the posture or matching the neural response of another, coming to feel as another feels, feeling distress at witnessing another's suffering, imagining how one would think and feel in another's place, imagining how another thinks and feels, a general disposition (trait) to feel for others [are] distinct from other-oriented empathic concern. The empathy-altruism hypothesis makes no claim that any of these

to altruistic actions (Maibom, 2012). Thus, it seems reasonable to say that the "empathy-altruism hypothesis" has been responsible for trying to prove the causal link between sympathy and altruism.[33]

On the other hand, the normative perspective focuses on the reasons that motivate and justify moral actions in general and altruistic actions in particular (Schramme, 2017, pp. 211–212). According to this approach, empathy is the cause of altruism in the sense that empathy is seen as the reason for acting altruistically. Specifically, when empathy is understood as the affective sharing of feelings the normative framework is a sentimentalist one, whereas when empathy is understood as perspective-taking the normative theory is a rationalist one. In the former case, empathized emotional states are responsible for providing the subjects with reasons to act both altruistically and morally (Slote, 2009, 2015). In the latter case, it is the ability to take the other's perspective that elicits altruism (Nagel, 1978) (see Chapter 3).

Two other aspects are worth discussing. First, it is crucial to clarify this supposed "causal chain" between empathy, sympathy, and altruistic and/or moral action. Arguing for the existence of a causal link between empathy and sympathy is different from arguing for the existence of a causal link between sympathy and altruism. In other words, there are two possible claims: First, empathy causes sympathy, and second, sympathy causes altruistic behavior. It seems to me that we need two different sets of evidence and arguments to justify the two versions of the causal chain. To prove the first version, we need to show that empathic perspective-taking, or sharing of the other's emotional states, is causally linked to experiencing active concern for his or her walfare.

Conversely, to prove the second claim, we need to show that feelings or mental states of concern for the other person's well-being are causally related to altruistic and/or moral motivations, which in turn can lead to altruistic and/ or moral actions. In this sense, I believe that Batson's experiments and the "empathy-altruism hypothesis" can at least partially prove the second version of the causal chain, i.e., that sympathy causes altruism, but they say nothing about the first version. More work seems to be needed to prove the validity of the first claim.

---

other phenomena produces altruistic motivation, except if and when that phenomenon evokes empathic concern" (Batson, 2014, p. 42).

33 For a different interpretation of Batson's thesis, see Schramme (2017), who believes that what Batson has in mind when he speaks of empathic concern is affective empathy or, more generally, the emotional aspect of empathy (Schramme, 2017, p. 210). I disagree with his claim because the definition of empathic concern never mentions the emotional state of the other, only the welfare of the other.

Second, the use of "and/or" when discussing altruistic and moral actions is not accidental: an altruistic action does not always coincide with a moral action. Consequently, it is also important to discuss whether empathy and sympathy lead only to altruistic actions or also to moral ones. In this sense, Batson himself has made it clear that altruistic actions are not necessarily moral. On the contrary, altruistic actions can be a-moral or even immoral. Just because an action is altruistic, that is, the consequence of "a motivational state with the ultimate goal of increasing another's welfare" (Batson, 2014, p. 46) does not mean that the same action is also moral. This is because a moral action has a different goal than an altruistic action, namely "to promote some moral standard, principle or ideal" (Batson, 2014, p. 46).

This becomes clear in the following scenario: If I choose my sister over other more qualified candidates in a job interview in order to increase her welfare, I am unquestionably doing something altruistic for her. Getting a job will increase her welfare, and it will not increase my welfare (i.e., it is not selfish). It could be argued that this action might even harm my welfare if my boss were informed of my biased choice. And yet I am not acting morally. Quite the contrary: I am acting immorally because I am being unfair to the other candidates, and I am not promoting the principle of impartiality and fairness that a moral action, specifically a fair action, would do.

Batson's distinction directly affects the ultimate goal of the "empathy-altruism hypothesis": it was never intended to prove a causal link between empathy or sympathy and morality itself. As he explicitly states, "(…) there are reasons to doubt the assumption that empathy-induced altruism is moral" (Batson, 2014, p. 45). Hence, the correct way to characterize this type of altruism is as "amoral" (Batson, 2014, p. 47): an altruistic action can be a moral action, but it is not necessary, as it can happen the opposite, that is, an altruistic action can also be immoral.

Batson's proposal is an example of the more modest claim that empathy can sometimes lead to sympathy – especially if we adopt a minimal definition of empathy as simply recognizing the other's condition (DeSteno, 2015) – which is only responsible for altruistic behavior. This argument acknowledges that there are instances in which altruistic and moral actions do indeed coincide, but according to it, empathy does not necessarily entail moral outcomes: it is perfectly possible to just empathize with someone and do absolutely nothing about it, not even feeling any form of interest, much less concern for the other person's situation. Needless to say, in this version of the argument, empathy and sympathy have no intrinsic moral quality, and their connection to morality is not constitutive (Decety & Cowell, 2014; Song, 2015; Songhorian, 2019; Ugazio et al., 2014).

In contrast, there is a stronger version of the causal argument, according to which empathy is capable of causing sympathy, which in turn motivates moral action. In this approach, there is no distinction between altruistic and moral action, as it implies a direct link between empathy and morality through the mediation of sympathy. The causal link between empathy and sympathy is usually assumed to be necessary and sufficient: every time I empathize with someone, I aim to sympathize with them. Another implicit but fundamental assumption of this version is that empathy and sympathy are inherently moral, or at least related to morality (Eisenberg, 1992; Hoffman, 2000; Simmons, 2013; Slote, 2016) (see Chapters 3 and 5).

Crucially, there is also a third way of characterizing the relationship between empathy, sympathy, altruism, and morality: there is no relationship. According to some, not only do empathy and sympathy have nothing to do with morality or altruism, but it can be detrimental to them, that is, empathy can lead to selfish and/or immoral outcomes (Bloom, 2016; Prinz, 2011a). I will discuss this perspective in Part 2. Before doing so, however, I need to address another definitional task: the definition of deliberation. This is essential to achieving the ultimate goal of my work, which is to better understand the impact of empathy on the deliberative process.

CHAPTER 2

The Standard Definition of Deliberation

So far, my efforts have been directed toward exploring the empathic phenomenon as defined by the SD, i.e., as composed of cognitive empathy, understood as perspective-taking; affective empathy, understood as affective sharing; and sympathy, understood as active concern for the welfare of the other. However, empathy is only half of my concern. Since my main goal is to investigate how empathy affects the deliberative process, I need to define what deliberation is. Admittedly, compared to empathy, it seems to be easier, or at least less controversial, to find a common definition of what deliberation *is*, but the same is not true for how deliberation actually *works*.

Fortunately, I only need a basic definition of deliberation and an even looser idea of how it works to discuss what role empathy is supposed to play. Starting from common distinctions in the literature, I will provide and adopt a hopefully non-contentious definition of deliberation, which I will call the standard definition (SD) of deliberation. I will then focus on a particular type of deliberative process, characterized as other-directed, because it seems to be particularly prone to the influence of empathy. Finally, I will consider the relationship between affective states and deliberation.

But first, a terminological clarification is needed. I have chosen to use the term deliberation rather than decision-making because the former has a philosophical specificity that seems better suited to the present discussion, which aspires to be philosophical in nature and scope, while the latter is mostly used in psychology, neuroscience, and economics (Bartels et al., 2015). This does not necessarily mean that deliberation and decision-making have two radically different meanings. They both refer to the process by which we arrive at a decision.

Finally, a warning: I will try to cover a lot of ground in this chapter. And yet, it is not intended to be exhaustive. For my argument, I do not need to provide a comprehensive review of the literature, settle every controversy about how people make decisions, or adopt a particular theory of decision-making. Instead, the aim of this chapter is more modest but no less important: although empathy is my primary focus, it is crucial to clarify what deliberation is in order to understand both the ways in which empathy is involved in deliberation (see Chapter 3) and the ways in which this involvement can cause problems (see Chapters 4, 5, and 6).

HTTPS://DOI.ORG/10.1163/9789004745360-004

1 Theoretical and Practical Deliberation

I will begin with two preliminary distinctions borrowed from Gilbert Harman. First, I will examine what kind of activity deliberation is, that is, I will examine it "as something that people do" rather than from the perspective of formal logical arguments (Harman 2011, p. 263). The focus will be on showing how we normally make decisions in everyday life. In keeping with this approach, my goal will be to explore how empathy affects, especially negatively, the way people *actually* deliberate in general and toward others in particular.

The second distinction is between deliberation "*with other people*" and deliberation "*by and for oneself*" (Harman 2011, p. 263). Deliberation can be either collective or individual: the difference is not so much that only in collective deliberation subjects can discuss and confront each other, as it is quite common that even in individual deliberation the subject openly discusses her deliberative process with others (e.g., to ask for advice). The point is that in the case of individual deliberation, the final decision ultimately rests with the subject alone, whereas in the case of collective deliberation – to be truly collective – the final decision must be the result of a shared deliberative process.

Moreover, precisely because collective deliberation is a shared process, it is also a public process. Conversely, individual deliberation is private in the sense that the final decision must be made only by the subject. This point is not as trivial as it might seem, since the public nature of collective deliberation makes it an excellent candidate for solving problems related to decision-making in organizations and institutions of democratic societies. In this sense, one can speak of deliberative democracy, which "refers to the idea that legitimate lawmaking issues from the public deliberation of citizens. (…) In short, it presents an ideal of political autonomy based on the practical reasoning of citizens" (Bohman and Rehg 1997, p. ix).

In the context of deliberative democracy, the term "public" is used in a loosely Kantian sense: collective deliberation is public when it requires and involves "the public use of one's reason" (Kant 1784, as cited in Bohman and Rehg 1997, p. x). Through the exercise of public deliberation, citizens or elected representatives should be able to reach an agreement around a shared concept of the common good despite their competing interests and goals. Importantly, according to proponents of deliberative democracy, the deliberative process is strongly understood in an epistemic sense: it is cognitive in nature, and its outcome can be either correct or incorrect based on an independent standard (Bohman and Rehg 1997, p. xvi). For example, Joshua Cohen broadly defines deliberation as the activity of "weighing the reasons relevant to a decision with a view to making a decision on the basis of that weighing" (Cohen 2007, p. 219) and summarizes the essence of deliberative democracy as follows (Cohen 2007, p. 220):[1]

> It is about making collective decisions and exercising power in ways that trace to the reasoning of the equals who are subject to the decisions: not only their preferences, interests, and choices, but to their reasoning. Essentially, the point of deliberative democracy is to subject the exercise of power to reason's discipline, to what Habermas famously described as "the force of the better argument", not the advantage of the better situated.

Relevant to and consistent with the epistemic characterization of the process, Cohen clarified that decision-making can be considered deliberative only if reasonableness, and not merely fairness, is the desired outcome of the process (Cohen 2007, p. 221).[2] Cohen's position is not an outlier in the debate: in most cases, deliberation means making a decision only if it is supported by good reasons, where reasons are understood in terms of rational arguments, and their goodness is judged by rational standards (Dryzek and Braithwaite 2000; Elster 1998, as cited in Cohen, 2007, pp. 221–222).

A clear example of how this approach can be applied in practice is provided by Amy Gutmann and Dennis Thompson in the context of bioethics. Echoing Cohen, they also define deliberative democracy as the exercise of "justify[ing] any demands for collective action by *giving reasons* that can be accepted by those who are bound by the action" (Gutmann and Thompson 1997, p. 38, my emphasis). The need for deliberation is particularly urgent in the bioethical debate because disagreements and value conflicts are pervasive, and deliberation seems particularly suited to dealing with them because it encourages participants to be more open to others' perspectives, forcing them to better justify their positions.[3]

The collective and public deliberative process is usually considered to be the specific domain of empathy. As we will see below (Chapter 3), the reason for this is quite clear: since empathy is able to "connect" us, either cognitively

1 The quote from Habermas is from *Between Facts and Norms* (Habermas, 1998).

2 According to Cohen, if participants only care about advancing their own interests and that this process is fair, we have only "aggregative democracy" (Cohen 2007, p. 221).

3 For another concrete application of public deliberation in the context of deliberative democracy, see the Deliberative Polling method proposed by Fishkin and colleagues at the Deliberative Democracy Lab at Stanford University (Fishkin, 2021).

or emotionally, it should at least play a role in – if not enable – collective deliberative processes. This is why some advocates of deliberative democracy give empathy a prominent role in their accounts (Goodin, 2003; Krause, 2008; Morrell, 2015). Nevertheless, my main focus will be on discussing what happens when empathy is involved in *individual* and *private* deliberation, as I am particularly interested in understanding how we as individuals deliberate in our everyday lives. This does not mean, however, that I will not consider the larger sociocultural, political, historical, and economic contexts in which the empathic relationship and the deliberative process take place (see Chapter 6).

In defining deliberation, the most important distinction of all is that between theoretical deliberation and practical deliberation. In the contemporary debate, there have been attempts to define deliberation in both practical and theoretical terms. In particular, Nomy Arpaly and Timothy Schroeder propose an account of deliberation that includes both a practical and a theoretical characterization. In their view, "theoretical deliberation is primarily concerned with what to believe, while practical deliberation is primarily concerned with what to do" (Arpaly and Schroeder 2014, p. 22). They consider both types of deliberation to be "kinds of action" (Arpaly and Schroeder 2014, p. 22). Therefore, like other actions, deliberation is voluntary, and its feasibility depends on the circumstances. As they argue, we choose to deliberate as we choose to drink a glass of wine, and there are cases where deliberation, like running a marathon, is simply not possible due to external or involuntary factors, such as severe illness.

Moreover, deliberation is subject to the same failures as other actions: sometimes we may be alienated from our own deliberations, or their end may be opaque even to ourselves, or we may deliberate absent-mindedly. Finally, deliberation is something that may or may not be expected of us by others, depending on the circumstances (Arpaly and Schroeder 2014, pp. 22–23).[4] Because deliberation has the same characteristics as other actions, the authors concluded that deliberation is indeed an action.

---

4 Arpaly and Schroeder's examples for each of the similarities between deliberation and actions: alienation ("I could hardly believe I was contemplating covering up my misbehavior"); opacity ("I found myself thinking about the facts of the case, uncertain as to why my mind was drawn to them but unwilling to stop myself"); absentmindedness ("I suddenly realize that, in my mental wanderings, I had started going over all the reasons I had given myself for ending my past romances"); demanding to deliberate ("figure out whether the company has a genuine obligation to continue supporting breast cancer research, and then write up a memo on it"); censuring for not deliberating ("I told you to have something figured out") or for deliberating ("I told you to stop wasting time thinking about our so-called moral obligations; just figure out the legal angle") (Arpaly and Schroeder 2014, p. 23).

An important clarification is needed: the term "theoretical deliberation" may rightly raise some eyebrows. After all, the deliberative process is inherently practical. This is undoubtedly true, and neither the authors nor I wish to deny it. In fact, the practical character of deliberation is preserved even in its theoretical characterization, since this kind of deliberation is first and foremost an *activity*, albeit mental, whose goal is to decide which course of *action*, albeit mental, to follow. The adjective "theoretical" does not mean that the process itself and the results it produces are not practical. On the contrary, it only indicates that this type of deliberation is related to the cognitive domain. In this sense, "the product of theoretical deliberation is perhaps a new belief (or entrenchment of an existing belief), or a new credence in a possible state of affairs, or a sincere thought about the truth of a proposition, or something similar" (Arpaly and Schroeder 2014, p. 22). All "products" of theoretical deliberation can be considered cognitive *activities* and, in this sense, practical. In line with this, cognition is broadly defined as "the mental *action* or process of acquiring knowledge and understanding through thought, experience, and the senses" ("Cognition" 2023, my emphasis).

To be fair, "cognitive deliberation" or "theoretical evaluation" might have been better alternatives to "theoretical deliberation." However, to remain faithful to the authors' original definition, I will use the term "theoretical deliberation" with the caveat just discussed: theoretical deliberation is itself, and the result it produces, practical. This fact does not deny the difference between theoretical and practical deliberation, since the latter is a mental activity whose results are directly aimed at producing concrete action or intention to act: "The product of practical deliberation is perhaps a new intention (or entrenchment of an existing intention), or an action, or something similar, in which case it is purely practical" (Arpaly and Schroeder 2014, p. 22).

I find this definition quite effective because it has the merit of being extremely clear without being reductive. Moreover, as the authors have openly stated, this definition has been formulated to be as uncontroversial as possible. I sympathize with the authors' attempt, and for this reason, I will consider their definition of deliberation as the basis for what I will call the standard definition (SD). According to this definition, deliberation is a (mental) activity that "aimed at determining what to think [theoretical deliberation] or do [practical deliberation]" (Arpaly and Schroeder 2014, p. 22).[5] There is also a special kind of

5 Deliberation is a mental activity in the sense that it is a reflective activity performed by the subject. As Arpaly and Schroeder note, during deliberation, the subject may use "nonmental aids (notepaper, calculators, interlocutors, the sound of one's own voice speaking out loud ...)" (Arpaly and Schroeder 2014, p. 22). This does not change the fact that deliberation is primarily a mental activity. Note that this also confirms my claim about the possibility of

deliberation, namely moral deliberation. Specifically, theoretical deliberation and practical deliberation are characterized as *moral* when the deliberative process "is influenced by moral considerations" (Harman 2011, p. 264).

For these reasons, I will not challenge this definition of deliberation. In fact, unlike in the case of the SD of empathy, I believe that this particular one does a good job of providing a common definition of the phenomenon, which is all I need here. This is not to say that the SD of deliberation is unproblematic, especially in its implications. It definitely is. However, if the conceptual core of this definition is at least acceptable, then it is solid enough to begin my discussion of the role of empathy in our deliberative processes.

An important implication of this way of defining the deliberative process is that theoretical deliberation and practical deliberation can be concerned with both a factual question and a normative question (Wallace, 2020).[6] Theoretical deliberation can be responsible for figuring out what we believe (factual question) and what we ought to believe (normative question). Practical deliberation allows us to decide what to do or not to do (factual question) and what we should or should not do (normative question). The same is true for both moral theoretical and moral practical deliberation.

It follows that, on the one hand, theoretical deliberation involves some kind of reference to the truth of the facts and beliefs held by the subject and the reasons for their acceptance or rejection (Wallace, 2020). For example, deliberating whether to believe that the Covid-19 vaccine is safe or not is a case of theoretical deliberation. Deliberating whether to believe that the Covid-19 vaccine mandate is fair or unfair is a case of moral theoretical deliberation because it involves moral considerations. On the other hand, practical deliberation aims to determine which actions are more desirable or valuable and why (Wallace, 2020). For example, deliberating about whether it is more convenient to bike to work or drive is a case of practical deliberation. Deliberating about whether it is more ethical to bike to work than to drive is a case of practical moral deliberation because moral considerations are involved.

Importantly, the distinction between the two types of deliberative processes should not be exaggerated, since they are both considered activities or "attitudes," with the difference that the former "leads to modifications of

individual deliberation being carried out with interlocutors, but still remaining "by and for oneself."

6 In particular, some have argued that only practical deliberation poses a factual and a normative question, while theoretical deliberation is concerned only with a factual question (Wallace, 2020). However, I find that theoretical deliberation does imply a normative dimension since we can and do ask ourselves what beliefs we should hold about a given situation or issue.

our beliefs" and the latter "leads to modifications of our intentions" (Wallace, 2020). Notably, "modifications" are not the only thing that can happen: beliefs or intentions do not *have to* change. After deliberation, the subject may also confirm his or her beliefs and intentions, thereby strengthening his or her conviction. For this reason, Arpaly and Schroeder added that a possible outcome of deliberation is also the entrenchment of what the subject already believes or intends to do. Finally, they can also overlap, such as when theoretical deliberation results in a belief about which action to perform. For example, deliberating whether to believe that taking the Covid-19 vaccine is the best thing to do is a case of overlap, or more precisely, practical deliberation is a "subtype" of theoretical deliberation (Arpaly and Schroeder 2014, p. 22).

Moreover, according to the SD, deliberation is always done for a reason, which is a fairly common way of characterizing our deliberative processes. As Arpaly and Schroeder noted, Anscombe, Davidson, and Korsgaard all claimed that actions are always done for some reason, and since is an action, deliberation is always done for some reason (Anscombe, 2000; Davidson, 2001; Korsgaard, 1996). Thus, involuntary actions, such as breathing, or involuntary thought processes, such as those involved in some psychopathologies (e.g., obsessive-compulsive disorder), are not instances of deliberation because they lack the essential voluntary element. It would be puzzling to argue that we deliberate about breathing or whether to let our heart beat. Similarly, obsessive thoughts are so intrusive and disruptive precisely because they are not the result of the will of the subject, who consequently struggles as she is unable to make them stop. Conversely, as we decide whether and when to act, we also decide whether and when to deliberate.

It is important to note that the reason for deliberating does not have to be a good reason. As Arpaly and Schroeder note, absurd, false, and stupid reasons also count as reasons. It follows that the SD of deliberation is not a success definition: we can still have deliberation even if it fails, that is, even if it is motivated by the wrong, e.g., irrational, reasons. As Arpaly and Schroeder remind us "the word 'rational' in the expression 'rational deliberation' is thus not a redundant one: irrational deliberation is possible" (Arpaly and Schroeder 2014, p. 27). However, irrational deliberation is still an instance of deliberation because the subject is still deciding what to think or do. For example, it is irrational to deliberate whether or not to put the ice cream back in the freezer when the ice cream has been out for hours and is hopelessly melted and spoiled. Nevertheless, the actual act of deliberating about what to do with the ice cream counts as an act of (practical) deliberation.

Let me now turn to how we deliberate, that is, how we determine what to think and what to do. From a purely conceptual perspective, a very basic claim is that deliberation deals with reasons. Usually, deliberation is considered to be a reason-assessing or reason-giving activity: when deliberating, the subject chooses between different possible reasons for thinking or acting in a certain way (reason-assessing). In light of this, the subject can also explicitly give reasons for adopting certain beliefs or behaviors, if necessary (reason-giving).

For example, I may deliberate whether to believe that the Covid-19 vaccine is effective and safe or ineffective and potentially harmful. The deliberative process amounts to considering all the different reasons for each belief and finally choosing the preferred one, because the subject has evaluated some reasons for adopting (or not adopting) a belief as more true, appropriate, or generally preferable than others. Similarly, in deliberating whether to take the car or the bike to work, the subject considers all the reasons for the two different courses of action, based on the ones she thinks are most valuable, consistent with her other beliefs and actions, or generally preferable, and she makes her decision.

There are several ways to characterize this reasoning process. One way is to compare it to a weighting operation in which reasons have different factual, normative, and/or motivational weights for the deliberator (Raz, 2010; Wedgwood, 2009, 2013). Of course, the core question of this perspective is how the scale is calibrated, i.e., what the criteria are according to which some reasons are weightier than others, and who established them. This is particularly problematic when moral considerations are involved, and we need to compare moral and non-moral reasons, or different moral reasons. In this context, different moral theories will provide different criteria for weighting these reasons, leading to potentially conflicting deliberative processes and outcomes.

One possible solution to this problem, in favor of a weighing model of deliberation, might be to adopt a pluralistic framework that seems able to overcome the need to choose a particular moral theory as the sole normative source for deliberation (Gaut, 1993; Ross, 1930; Sen, 1980).[7] In particular, axiological pluralism and methodological pluralism seem to be better able to account for the complex and multifaceted nature of our moral experience as deliberators than a monistic approach (Grigoletto, 2019). According to the former, there is a pluralism of values that have different weights each time the subject deliberates. According to the latter, the subject does not have to follow the same ethical theory in every single case of moral deliberation. This means that on some occasions a deontological approach might be preferable to a consequentialist one, and, on other occasions, virtue ethics might be more

7 Other authors who argued, in different ways, for moral pluralism are Bernard Williams (Williams, 1973), John Kekes (Kekes, 1996), and Martha Nussbaum (Nussbaum, 2001a).

appropriate to help the subject weigh her reasons in the deliberative process. Importantly, even those who disagree with moral pluralism – about which much more could be said than is possible here – can subscribe to the SD definition of deliberation as moral pluralism is not necessarily implied by it.

Two issues need to be clarified. First, what constitutes a reason? Second, what exactly is the role of reasons in deliberation? Let's start with the first question. In keeping with the SD of deliberation, I will take the broadest possible definition of what constitutes a reason in the deliberative process. In general, not only "things outside of human heads," such as facts and events, but also internal states, both cognitive and affective, constitute reasons in (moral) theoretical and practical deliberation (Arpaly and Schroeder 2014, p. 53). In this respect, it is possible to distinguish between "objective reasons" and "rationalizing reasons" (Arpaly and Schroeder 2014, p. 54, my emphasis):

> *Objective epistemic reasons* are determined by the facts of the world, whether or not they are believed in. *Rationalizing epistemic reasons* for a person are determined by what a person believes to be the facts of the world, rather than the actual facts. Similarly, *objective practical reasons* are determined by something that prioritizes possible states of affairs (something that might be independent of desires, or largely independent, or identical to desires) plus the facts of the world, whether or not they are believed in. And *rationalizing practical reasons* are determined by whatever prioritizes possible states of affairs plus what a person believes to be the facts of the world, rather than the actual facts.

For example, the fact that it is raining outside is a reason (an objective epistemic reason) for my decision to drive to work instead of riding a bicycle. My belief that the Covid-19 vaccine is a tool used by the government to control people is why (a rationalizing epistemic reason) I decided not to take it. In parallel, my dislike of sweating plus the fact that it is raining outside is a reason (an objective practical reason) for my decision to drive to work. Finally, my dislike of sweating plus my belief that wearing a turtleneck to work is necessary to look professional constitutes a reason (a rationalizing practical reason) for my decision to wear a turtleneck and drive to work instead of riding a bicycle. Rationalizing reasons are most relevant here because the reasons provided by empathy as understood in the SD can be characterized as both rationalizing epistemic and practical reasons for our deliberative processes (see Chapter 3).

The second question allows me to touch briefly on two extremely complicated facets of this debate: motivation and normativity. In the deliberative process, the role of reasons can be twofold: motivational and normative (Davidson, 2001).[8] On the one hand, reasons are thought to have the function of motivating the deliberated beliefs or courses of action. When this is the case, reasons are referred to as motivational (or explanatory) reasons (Finlay & Schroeder, 2017). When we use expressions such as "the reason why I did what I did" or "the reason why I think that is the case," we are saying nothing different from "what motivated me to act in this way is this reason" or "what led me to think that is the case is this reason."

It is hardly controversial that the reasons we encounter in our deliberative process, and which we then adopt, can be understood as sources of our motivation. For example, the fact that my doctor told me that the Covid-19 vaccine is safe motivates me to believe that it is safe. A dislike of sweating is what motivates me not to ride my bike and to drive my car instead. Valuing fairness is what motivates a hiring manager not to favor her sister in a job interview. Note that in the second example, an emotional state (dislike) is a motivating reason for practical deliberation.

On the other hand, reasons can have a normative role (Finlay & Schroeder, 2017). In the case of normative reasons, the focus is not on the subject's motive but on the justification for the belief or action. For example, the fact that my doctor told me that the Covid-19 vaccine is safe counts as a reason in favor of my belief that it is safe. Similarly, hating to sweat counts as a reason against taking the bike to work. Believing fairness to be morally right is a reason against favoritism. Note that the normative standpoint is not the default. To reiterate, it is possible to simply ask a factual question (What do I think or do about the Covid-19 vaccine?), which is different from asking a normative question (What should I think or do about the Covid-19 vaccine? Or what is it the reason in favor or against my belief or action in regard to the Covid-19 vaccine).

The distinction between motivating reasons and normative reasons is fairly well established. Much more problematic is the discussion of the relationship between normative reasons and motivation, especially in the context of practical deliberation. The claim that normative reasons are related to motivation is typically seen as the core claim of an internalist approach to reasons (Korsgaard, 1986; Schroeder, 2007; Williams, 1981). According to this view, since my dislike of sweating justifies my choice to drive to work, i.e., it counts in favor of this action, it also motivates me to drive instead of bike. In this sense, internalism "denies that someone can judge, and possibly know, that it is right for him

8 For a more detailed taxonomy of reasons for action and a discussion of Davidson's account, see Hieronymi (Hieronymi, 2011).

to perform a certain action in the given circumstances whilst being entirely unmotivated to perform that action" (Döring 2007, p. 363).

An externalist approach, on the other hand, denies this relation and argues for the possibility that there are normative reasons unrelated to motivation, and thus that it is possible to believe that something is wrong or right and not be motivated either to not do it or to do it. In the externalist approach, motivation depends on other external reasons and factors that are not part of the subject's internal motivational set. Indeed, externalism claims that "human motives are to be developed in such a way that normative reasons are always accompanied by appropriate external motives" which seems to make this relationship contingent (Döring 2007, p. 366).

Admittedly, this is a very rough summary of these problems. Still, my only goal here was to sketch out a very broad definition of deliberation and a conception of what constitutes a reason. In particular, I am interested in understanding what happens when the deliberator uses empathy as a source of motivating and normative reasons for thinking or acting in a certain way. This is because, on the one hand, the idea that empathy is an exceptionally powerful motivational force in the deliberative process, especially in moral deliberation, is perhaps the most widely held claim in the literature, and, on the other hand, empathy is often thought to be capable of constituting a normative reason for (moral) deliberation and for judging the goodness or badness of an action (or belief).

Finally, I do not want to give the impression of overintellectualizing how we make decisions in our everyday lives. In particular, practical rationality and moral reasoning are not solely the product of conscious deliberation. On the contrary, as Irene McMullin has rightly pointed out, there is a much more pregnant sense of what it means to think, act, and ultimately be in the world (McMullin 2019, p. 35):

> (…) our characteristic way of being is best understood as a kind of pre-theoretical normative attunement to the world – an implicit understanding of one's possibilities in terms of conditions of success and failure, good and bad responses to the reasons that claim us. It is a background sense of oneself as being called to do only what one has reason to do. Though it is possible to engage in explicit deliberation, this only sometimes occurs in an average human life – it cannot be taken as the norm in our understanding of human agency.[9]

9 According to McMullin, the subject can flourish, that is, live a good life, only when it is able to (precariously) balance three normative perspectives that claim the subject: the first-

In a similar vein, Arpaly and Schroeder warn us that "deliberation is a valuable but imperfect tool for improving our more valuable but even more imperfect abilities to think and act for reasons without it" (Arpaly and Schroeder 2014, p. 51). That is, there are other processes (e.g., desiderative ones) that are not deliberative, in the sense of an explicitly cognitive process, that enables us to think and act for reasons. Leaving aside these specific accounts, I welcome the warning not to overintellectualize the way we think, act, and live.

2 Other-Directed Deliberation and (Empathic) Affective States

I am specifically interested in a particular kind of deliberation: *other-directed deliberation.* I call other-directed those deliberative processes that have another person as their object, that is, the object of the deliberative process is the other person. In particular, according to the SD of deliberation I am discussing here, the purpose of *other-directed theoretical deliberation* is to decide what beliefs to adopt about another subject, whereas the purpose of *other-directed practical deliberation* is to decide how to act toward the other. It is in this type of deliberation that the contribution of empathy seems most relevant, hence its centrality to this work.

One thing is to deliberate whether I believe that I will be happier in my new job, and another is to deliberate whether I believe that Edoardo will be happier in his new job. In the first case of theoretical deliberation the subject and the object of the process (myself) overlap, whereas in the second case of theoretical deliberation the subject (myself) and the object (Edoardo) of the process are different. Only the latter is an instance of other-directed theoretical deliberation. Similarly, it is one thing to deliberate whether to accept a job offer abroad, while it is another to deliberate that I will book a piano teacher for my daughter, since I have decided that she must have piano lessons every week. Again, there is a clear distinction between subject and object in the second case, which makes it an instance of other-directed practical deliberation.

To be clear, I do not want to give the impression that the criterion for identifying instances of other-directed practical deliberation is a purely consequentialist one, in the sense that practical deliberation is other-directed if the consequences of the deliberated action affect someone other than the

person normative perspective, which is about the self; the second-person normative perspective, which has its source in the other person; the third-person normative perspective, which depends on the shared world in which the self and other subjects live (McMullin, 2019).

subject of the deliberative process. Instead, my idea is more basic and less theory-laden: practical deliberation can be characterized as other-directed if the subject of the deliberative process is not the only one involved in the deliberated action. Similarly, theoretical deliberation can be characterized as other-directed if the subject of the deliberative process is not the only one involved in the deliberated belief.

The other-directedness of deliberation becomes particularly relevant when moral considerations enter the picture. For example, deliberating whether to believe that Ludovica was disrespectful to Eleonora is an instance of moral other-directed theoretical deliberation. Similarly, deliberating about which of five homeless people should get the only public housing unit available is an instance of moral other-directed theoretical deliberation. Moral other-directed theoretical and practical deliberation, and the morally relevant implications of other-directed theoretical and practical deliberation, are particularly relevant to my work.

Specifically, I am interested in investigating what happens when empathy, as defined in the SD, is the source of deliberation, that is, when the reasons, or at least some of the reasons, for the deliberative process are constituted by empathy. In short, empathy can be thought of as an epistemic source of information about the other person that potentially provides the deliberator with reasons, i.e., beliefs of the subject or even facts of the world. Moreover, empathy can be characterized as an affective phenomenon that can inform us about the state of the other person and potentially provide reasons, i.e., emotional states that prioritize some state of affairs, for the deliberative process. In the next chapter, I will elaborate precisely on the role that empathy, as both an epistemic and an affective phenomenon, is thought to play in other-directed deliberation (see Chapter 3).

However, it has not always been obvious to recognize the influence of affective states[10] – and thus of affective empathy as a specific source of affective states[11] – on the deliberative process. On the contrary, for a long time, in both theoretical and practical deliberation, affective states have been thought to cause the subject to make irrational and immoral decisions. Thus, deliberation has typically been understood as a fundamentally emotionless endeavor and an impartial and exclusively rational process. This characterization of deliberation also implies an anthropological consideration: deliberation should be a

10 Following Lerner and colleagues, I define affective states (or affects) as "unspecified feelings; the superordinate umbrella of constructs involving emotion, moods and emotion-related traits" (Lerner et al. 2015, p. 801).

11 As noted in Chapter 1, empathy, especially affective empathy, is not an emotion per se "but a *way* of feeling emotions" (Maibom 2014, p. 9).

rational process carried out by a rational subject who is – at least in theory – always capable of choosing the right course of action. Standard examples of this approach are decision theory and game theory (Fudenberg & Tirole, 1991), where the general idea is that deliberation should be based on probabilistic calculation and utility theory (Harsanyi, 1977; Mill, 1861; Sidgwick, 1962).

In this context, little or no attention was paid to affective states and their role in decision-making: "Decision makers were assumed to evaluate the potential consequences of their decisions dispassionately and to choose actions that maximized the 'utility' of those consequences. Once chosen, it was assumed that the utility-maximizing course of action would be implemented automatically" (Loewenstein and Lerner 2003, p. 619). This is consistent with the traditional approach to collective deliberation in the deliberative democracy debate, where although utilitarian considerations are not necessarily the only criterion for choice, deliberation must be reasonable in the sense that it must be impartial, rational, and exclude the influence of affective states (Cohen, 1989; Elster, 1998b; Habermas, 1998).

In recent years, especially after the so-called "affective turn" in the humanities began in the mid-1990s, the assumption of rationality has been challenged both theoretically and empirically across disciplines, including economics, psychology, neuroscience, and philosophy.[12] It has become increasingly clear that "emotions powerfully, predictably, and pervasively influence decision making" (Lerner et al. 2015, p. 802). There is no doubt that both integral emotions (Haidt, 2001; Solomon, 1993) and incidental emotions (Andrade & Ariely, 2009; Yang et al., 2020) have both positive and negative effects on deliberation.[13]

---

12 To be clear, emotions were given a crucial role in deliberation long before the affective turn. Consider Aristotle and Hume, to name only the most important. At the beginning of Book VI of the *Nicomachean Ethics*, Aristotle asserts that "thought by itself moves nothing"; only thought that is practical, that is, moved by desire, is capable of motivating the agent (1139a35–36). Desire, however, must be of a certain kind, since it must be directed toward the good (1113a22–27), that is, it must be the right desire. Thus, we as human beings are a mixture of reason and desire. Moreover, when we choose, which is a distinctively human activity, we need both the rational and the desiderative. In this sense, our choices are also a mixture of reason and desire. And right decisions are a mixture of good ends and deliberative desires. Similarly, Hume's formulation of the supremacy of the passions is as popular as it is memorable: "reason is, and ought only to be the slave of the passions, and can never pretend to any office than to serve and obey them" (THN, p. 415). For an in-depth discussion on moral sentimentalism, empathy, and deliberation see Chapter 3.

13 I follow Lerner and colleagues' distinction and definition: *integral emotions* are those emotions that arise directly from the deliberative process, whereas *incidental emotions* are those emotions that arise in a particular situation and are carried over to the next

More relevant here, emotions are thought to play different roles in deliberation, and several philosophical accounts aim to clarify what these roles are (Nussbaum, 2001b; Prinz, 2009; Solomon, 1993; Tappolet, 2009). One of these is defended by Patricia Greenspan who offers a systematic account of the role of emotions in deliberation, especially practical deliberation. Greenspan argues for a hybrid characterization of emotions as they seem to have a dual content: an evaluative element and an affective element. For example, "emotional discomfort both evaluates something negatively – has a negative evaluative content – and feels bad" (Greenspan 2020, p. 253).

Therefore, every emotion feels either good or bad (affective element) and implies a positive or negative evaluation of something (evaluative element). The feeling of disgust feels bad and implies the thought that something is actually disgusting, which means that it is the affective element of emotions that "does the evaluating" (Greenspan 2019, p. 77). This should also prevent us from thinking of the two elements as distinct from each other and, more importantly, as one causing the other: the distinction is merely logical, since in practice these two elements are so closely related that they are essentially the same thing (Greenspan 2019).[14] Note also that Greenspan allows for the possibility that complex emotions can simultaneously have positive and negative valence, and positive and negative appraisal.[15]

It follows from this definition of emotions that their role in practical reasoning is precisely to provide reasons. Specifically, emotions "can provide a reason – both a motive and a normative reason – to act to falsify the evaluation, in the sense of making it applicable by changing the situation" (Greenspan 2020, p. 253). First, emotions can motivate action because of their evaluative content. When something feels bad, (when we fear a snake), it implies a negative evaluation of both the subject's bodily sensations (the bodily sensations the subject is experiencing amount to a negative feeling) and the object of the emotion (the snake in front of the subject is evaluated as scary and therefore negative).[16]

---

situation and influence the related deliberative process, even if those emotions have no normative relevance in that context (Lerner et al. 2015, pp. 802–803).

14 Greenspan uses the term "bonded elements" (Greenspan 2019).

15 Greenspan on complex emotions: "Love and anger, for instance, may both include negative evaluations of an unfulfilled desire, for closeness or for retribution, though the primary evaluative content of love – evaluating the object of love, the person or thing loved – is of course positive" (Greenspan 2020, p. 252).

16 The motivational contribution of emotions seems plausible, since a solid body of empirical evidence correlates neurosomatic alterations or deficits in experiencing and recognizing emotions with suboptimal decision-making ability (Bechara, 2004; Damasio, 1994; Gupta et al., 2011).

It is the negative emotion that directly evaluates its object as negative. The emotional discomfort, as Greenspan called it, "embodies an evaluation," specifically a negative one, about the object of the emotion (Greenspan 2019, p. 83). Negative emotions and the discomfort they cause play a critical role in practical reasoning and deliberation because they motivate the subject to change the situation in order to change the evaluation and the phenomenal feeling from bad to good. In short, "given that one naturally wants to avoid or escape discomfort, the negative evaluation of one's own feelings explains how emotions add motivational force to a 'cool' judgment – of danger, distance, a failure to retaliate, or what have you" (Greenspan 2019, p. 84).

At the same time, emotions can also play a normative role in practical reasoning. Emotional discomfort provides "a higher-order normative reason against discounting reasons" for taking a particular course of action that is already considered the right one (Greenspan 2020, p. 259). In addition to avoiding the discounting of deliberate reasons and postponing action, emotions can provide the subject with reasons for action. In this sense, emotions act like a magnifying glass, as they can "direct attention" to the subject's reasons for action and provide reasons against discounting them (Greenspan 2020, p. 260). By virtue of their evaluative and affective elements, they make these reasons "bigger," i.e., heavier and more difficult to ignore. In sum, Greenspan's account assigns emotions both a motivational and a normative role in (practical) deliberation, openly rejecting the idea that emotions are an alternative to practical reasoning. On the contrary, they have not only a legitimate but also a necessary place in practical deliberation. In short, emotions are not an obstacle to deliberation; they are an essential part of it.

In this chapter, I have defined other-directed deliberation as a process that involves one or more people other than the one who is deliberating. I believe that this particular type of deliberative process is more susceptible to the influences of empathy. In this respect, there was no need to justify the possibility of the epistemic influence of empathy on deliberation. If empathy is understood as a purely cognitive operation whose goal is to provide facts or beliefs about another person as another object in the world, then the fact that empathy can contribute to deliberation is easy to concede. This is not to say that the epistemic contribution of empathy does not raise problems, because, as we will see in Part 2, it certainly does.

In contrast, the affective influence of affective states and, thus, of affective empathy as defined in the SD, on deliberation required more justification given the long-held belief that deliberation is an eminently rational process. For this reason, I discussed Greenspan's account, according to which affective states – of which empathically shared affective states are a subcategory – can be part of the deliberative process and constitute motivating and normative reasons within it. This is particularly useful here because, as I will discuss in the next chapter, affective empathy is seen as capable of providing both motivating and normative reasons in deliberation (see Chapter 3). But enough foreshadowing: it is now time to discuss exactly how empathy is thought to contribute to deliberation from both an epistemic and an affective perspective.

CHAPTER 3

Empathy and Its Many Roles in Deliberation

Note that we have introduced the standard definition (SD) of empathy and the SD of deliberation, let us analyze how they interact. In particular, I want to examine how their relationship has been characterized in the literature and provide a taxonomy of the roles that empathy is thought to play in the deliberative process. Let me reiterate that in Part 2, I will offer what I hope will be a compelling critique of the positions discussed in this chapter.

I will identify and discuss three ways in which empathy is thought to contribute to deliberation. First, cognitive empathy as perspective-taking is thought to play an *epistemic role* in other-directed theoretical and practical deliberations by providing the subject with information about the other's inner states that can be used as a basis for deliberation about what to believe and what to do with respect to the other. Second, following the sentimentalist approach, affective empathy seems capable of *grounding* our *moral judgments*, i.e., it constitutes the source of normative reasons for our moral judgments, which are special cases of deliberation. Third, empathy is assigned a *motivational role*, that is, it constitutes the source of the agent's motivating reasons for other-directed practical deliberative processes, especially when the situation requires altruistic and moral actions.

1 The Epistemic Role of Empathy

According to proponents of simulation theory (ST), empathy, understood as a simulation-plus-projection routine, is an incredible source of information about other people because it allows us to explain and predict their actions and behaviors (see Section 1.1.2). If this claim is accepted, it is easy to see how empathy can contribute to other-directed deliberation. For example, understanding through cognitive empathy that the other person is yelling at the television because she is cheering for her favorite soccer team and not because she is scared or angry is a reason to believe that she is happy (other-directed theoretical deliberation) and a reason to give her a high five of approval because I am also a supporter of the same soccer team (other-directed practical deliberation).

The above example is an extremely simple case of (mirroring) empathy and other-directed deliberation. It could also be argued that I could have reached

HTTPS://DOI.ORG/10.1163/9789004745360-005

the same conclusion without the help of empathy: other sources can provide the deliberator with the same information about the other person's condition. In this case, it may be sufficient to use very basic perceptual resources: to see that the other person is wearing the scarf of her favorite soccer team around her neck and to infer that she is indeed cheering for her favorite soccer team, without having to mirror her facial expressions, let alone take her point of view and simulate the reaction given her situation.

While cognitive empathy may not seem particularly useful in a case as simple as that of the soccer fan, the same does not seem to be true for more complicated scenarios. Consider this case. Pam and Jim have been friends for a long time. Jim is having a very difficult time in his marriage, and divorce is imminent. Pam knows that Jim's partner cheated on him after they decided to take a break from their relationship. Jim has no idea about the cheating, but he knows that his marriage is over and agrees with his partner that the relationship is over. However, Jim is understandably very upset and needs his dear friend Pam.

Now, Pam is faced with a dilemma: whether or not to tell Jim about the cheating. After some consideration, she decides not to tell him. After all, she thinks, there is no point in adding to Jim's suffering, since the decision to end their marriage had already been made by both of them, and the cheating did not affect it. Pam sees her decision as a white lie: she believes that telling the truth would be both irrelevant and cause suffering, hence the decision to omit this information for the sake of her friend. Then there is Michael: he sees this situation unfolding and wants to understand Pam's behavior and inner states. Can empathy help him do that? For proponents of an empathy-based approach to social cognition, especially proponents of ST, Michael will find empathy to be a valuable ally, indeed the most valuable ally.

For example, according to Karsten Stueber, "empathy should be seen as the epistemically central, even if at times limited, default method of gaining knowledge of the minds of other individual agents" (Stueber 2006, p. 19). In particular, Stueber argued that empathy has a special function: it enables us to understand the other person's beliefs and desires as her reasons for acting (Stueber 2009, p. 537).

This claim has two implications. First, empathy allows the empathizer to distinguish between actions taken for reasons and actions taken merely as a consequence of a change in circumstances. For example, Pam's decision is the consequence of her beliefs and desires regarding Jim's specific situation and more general considerations. Conversely, a sneeze or a yawn are actions that cannot be understood in terms of reasons, but are simply the consequences of physiological changes that constitute the internal causes of these actions

(Stueber 2009, p. 539). Second, although folk psychology is also a causal explanation of actions, it differs fundamentally from the physical sciences in that it is "adopted from an engaged perspective," that is, a perspective that requires the subject to be empathically engaged with the other person's in order to understand her internal states as reasons for her actions (Stueber 2009, p. 537).

Specifically, consistent with ST's definition of empathy, Stueber argued for two distinct types of empathy: basic empathy and reenactive empathy. Basic empathy is characterized as a "quasi-perceptual ability to recognize other creatures directly as minded creatures" (Stueber 2006, p. 20). We have this elementary ability to inwardly imitate the other person's expressions or gestures, which, as mentioned, seemed to be confirmed by the discovery of MNs. However, the most important acquisition that basic empathy provides us with is an awareness of how fundamentally similar we are, which is ultimately the condition for the possibility of mutual understanding. Basic empathy confirms the engaged character of folk psychology, since the recognition of the other person as a like-minded creature depends directly on the first-person involvement, i.e., the employment of the empathizer's mirroring resources.

However, as Stueber notes, this basic form of empathy will not get us very far in more complex situations such as the white lie case. It is reenactive empathy that allows us to understand the complexity of such cases:

> Only through *reenactive empathy* – that is, only by using our cognitive and deliberative capacities in order to *reenact* or *imitate* in our own mind the thought processes of the other person – are we able to conceive of another person's more complex social behavior as the behavior of a rational agent who acts for a reason.[1]
>
> STUEBER 2006, p. 21, my emphasis

Note that basic empathy and reenactive empathy are almost entirely consistent with what the SD of empathy called cognitive empathy, and in particular with Goldman's notions of mirroring empathy based on low-level simulation and reconstructing empathy based on high-level simulation (see Section 1.1.1).

A relevant difference between reenactive empathy and reconstructive empathy, however, is that the former is more interested in the other person's overall perspective on the world than the latter, which is more focused on the

1 The idea that empathy consists of a process of reenactment is another way of framing the central thesis of ST. One of the first authors to think of empathy in these terms was Ravenscroft in his classic paper *What Is It Like To Be Someone Else? Simulation and Empathy* (Ravenscroft, 1998).

other person's particular mental act. In fact, reenactive empathy allows the empathizer not only to grasp the other person's beliefs and desires and to understand them as reasons for her actions, and thus to recognize the other person as a responsible rational agent who can be praised or blamed for her actions. But it also allows the empathizer to reproduce the other person's more general deliberative process, which "requires figuring out which of [her] many other thoughts are relevant for consideration in a specific situation in order for a specific belief–desire pair to be a reason for acting" (Stueber 2009, p. 541).

This way of framing cognitive empathy assigns it a crucial task, that is, the ability to solve the so-called frame problem. In cognitive science, the frame problem consists of the difficulty of identifying which thoughts are relevant to the other person's deliberative process. According to Stueber, reenactive empathy is capable of overcoming this difficulty "by imaginatively putting ourselves in a particular situation, by engaging those thoughts in our own mind and by using them as a basis for our own deliberative encounter with the world" (Stueber 2009, p. 541). It is possible to imaginatively reproduce the other person's deliberative process, and the result of this reproduction or reenactment will provide the empathizer with epistemically relevant information about the reasons for the other person's actions. However, the reasons captured by reenactive empathy are not only limited to the immediate belief – desire pair that directly affects the action, but also include the background beliefs and desires that, although indirectly, also count as reasons for the other person's action.

In other words, reenactive empathy seems capable of grounding the empathizer's own other-directed deliberative process: the understanding or lack thereof of the other's reasons for acting via reenactment constitutes the empathizer's reasons for deliberating about those actions and the other's deliberative process as a whole. Interestingly, the lack of understanding is epistemically unsettling for the empathizer because it implies a diminished or null explanatory power of the information gained via reenactive empathy. This usually occurs when an action is so bizarre that the agent's reasons for it are completely opaque or when the social and cultural contexts of the empathizer and the target are vastly different. To mitigate these instances, additional tools are needed to understand what is going on, usually contextual information that comes from an epistemic source other than reenactive empathy. Even in this case, however, reenactive empathy is crucial because it allows us to recognize that additional sources are needed (Stueber, 2006, especially Chapter 6).

Let us see how Stueber's account might work in the white lie case discussed above: Pam did not tell Jim that his partner was cheating on him. Now Michael wants to understand why she made that choice. First and foremost, through basic empathy, Michael recognizes Pam as a fellow human being with a mind that functions like his own: she, too, is a rational agent who acts for reasons. But that is not enough: Michael wants to know the reasons for her particular decision. To do this, he needs reenactive empathy. He imaginatively puts himself in Pam's mental shoes and reproduces or reenacts her deliberative process, quarantining those beliefs, desires, and values that he believes Pam does not share. The result of this imaginative perspective-taking is that Pam's omission is the consequence of her belief that Jim would be better off not knowing about the cheating as well as her desire for his well-being. This is the direct belief–desire pair, and thus the direct reasons for Pam's action.

Through reenactive empathy, Michael is also able to pick up other indirect contextual information as he has the chance to briefly discuss the issue with Pam: Pam believes that Jim's happiness trumps his right to know the truth because when the same thing happened to her years ago and her sister decided to tell her about her partner's cheating, she felt ten times worse than before. In addition, Pam liked Jim's former partner and, perhaps implicitly, is trying to protect that person. All of this information also counts as reasons, albeit indirect, for Pam's action.

Taken together, these direct and indirect reasons provide the epistemic basis for Michael's other-directed deliberative process since, through reenactive empathy, Michael is able to reproduce, and thus understand, Pam's action. He also realizes that these reasons could have been his own reasons for acting as Pam did, and as a result he believes Pam to be a loyal friend and decides not to tell Jim about his partner's cheating.[2]

Although the primary goal of folk psychology and cognitive empathy is epistemic in general and explanatory in particular, there is also a moral implication. Stueber recognizes that reenacting the other person's reasons for acting can produce "an 'inner' conversation with this person" that can deepen the understanding of both the other person and the empathizer in the form of "self-reflection" (Stueber 2009, p. 544).[3] As noted above, this leads the empathizer to accept or reject the other person's reasons after her own deliberative process, that is, to critically evaluate the other person's reasons for acting.

2 These are instances of moral other-directed theoretical and practical deliberations, respectively.

3 On this point, Stueber partially disagrees with simulation theorists: "Yet in focusing only on simulation's contributions in reaching the cognitive goals of explanation and prediction, contemporary simulation theorists fail to sufficiently reflect on the vital role that the cognitive stance embodied in our folk psychological practice plays not merely for understanding other agents but also for the formation of ourselves as social and moral agents" (Stueber, 2009, pp. 543–544).

According to Stueber, Far from being a flaw and a potential source of bias, as some ST proponents fear, the inclusion of the empathizer's critical faculties and the potential internal dialogue between the two subjects is what makes mutual understanding normatively possible: "[the other person's] reasons can be understood as reasons only if they are re-enactable by me and *a fortiori* my reasons are reasons that are re-enactable by him" (Stueber 2009, p. 545). In this sense, the evaluation of the other's action does not qualify as a judgment regarding the goodness or badness of that action, rather "it has to do with the fact that [the] consequences [of the other's action], if one considers them in one's deliberations, put into question the validity of one's original reasons for acting" (Stueber 2009, p. 542).

But what about emotions? While it is true that desires are considered part of the reasons for action, Stueber's account has not paid much attention specifically to emotional states. And yet, when we think of empathy, we think primarily of its ability to understand the emotional state of the other person. In line with this intuition, Olivia Bailey argued for a specific epistemic and moral contribution of empathy to our lives: empathy provides what she calls "humane understanding" (Bailey 2020, p. 2).

In her account, the epistemic relevance of empathy depends on a specific characterization of emotions as quasi-perceptual tools capable of registering the evaluative features of the world around us: if I am afraid, it means that I find some elements of my situations frightening, which in turn requires certain behaviors and responses on my part. Inspired by Smith's account of sympathy as an indicator of "the 'propriety' of others' emotions" (Bailey 2020, p. 5), Bailey defined emotions as proper when they reliably register the evaluative proprieties of the situation (the furious man pointing a gun at me is actually scary). Of course, as Bailey points out, it is possible that the evaluative content signaled by emotions is not correct, that is, that it does not accurately reflect the situation. I can be frightened by a field of daisies, even though fear does not properly capture the evaluative characteristics of that situation. In this sense, emotions "can *appear* to be proper without actually being proper" (Bailey 2020, p. 7).

Crucially, the propriety or appearance of propriety of emotions necessarily implies their intelligibility to the subject: we recognize our emotions as capable of accounting for some (apparent or not) evaluative properties of the world to which those emotions are directed. Even more relevantly, the intelligibility of emotions is possible only through the actual experience of those emotions. It cannot be derived from a purely emotionless cognitive process.

Given the ability of emotions to capture the evaluative properties of the situation and to make them intelligible to the subject experiencing them, it is quite clear how empathy, understood as affective perspective-taking, is supposed to provide the empathizer with the unique kind of other-understanding that Bailey calls "humane understanding". According to Bailey, "to humanely understand another's emotion is to have a first-hand appreciation of the emotion's intelligibility. Securing that appreciation means imaginatively taking up the other's first-personal perspective and seeing the world as calling for the emotional response that the other is experiencing" (Bailey 2020, pp. 8–9). Ultimately, empathy coincides with the ability (or inability) to see (i.e., understand) the other person's emotional responses as intelligible, that is, as appropriate responses to the other's situation.

Let us reframe the case of the white lie according to Bailey's account of humane understanding. First, we need to focus on the emotional aspects of the situation. When Pam is deciding whether to tell Jim about the cheating, she feels anxious and full of doubt. After she decides to withhold the information, she feels calm and satisfied. Michael empathizes with her emotional states: he imaginatively puts himself in Pam's place and first-personally experiences first the anxiety and then the serenity. In doing so, Michael finds both emotions to be intelligible, that is, appropriate responses to the situation, since having to choose between telling a devastating truth to a friend or lying for his sake is an anxiety-provoking situation. Similarly, making a decision that is believed to preserve the happiness of a close friend involves calmness and serenity. Michael's act of empathy toward Pam's emotional reactions allows him to humanly understand her. Bailey's account is particularly relevant because humane understanding can be the source of other-directed deliberation: its epistemic content, i.e., the humane understanding of the other person's condition gained through empathy, constitutes the reasons for Michael's decision that Pam is a loyal friend and that he will not reveal her omission to Jim.

This begs the question: Is it possible to find the other person's emotions unintelligible? It seems that there are several cases in which the other's emotions are not intelligible to us, at least not fully, usually because there are relevant differences in our emotional sensitivity. However, according to Bailey, even in these cases, the empathizer will still reach an epistemically relevant conclusion: that the other person's emotions are indeed not fully intelligible to her. In this sense, the case described above is the best-case scenario: Michael was able to take Pam's perspective perfectly, without making any mistakes or misunderstandings. This is not always possible, and Bailey recognizes how easy it is to make "some imaginative slippage" when empathizing (Bailey 2020, p. 9). For this reason, openness to correction and revision is always necessary.

Finally, humane understanding is not only epistemically good, but also ethically good. There is something intrinsically good about having one's emotions humanely understood by others. Humane understanding serves to alleviate the existentially painful and potentially pathological sense of alienation we feel when our emotions are perceived as completely unintelligible, that is, as making no sense to anyone else. Note that Bailey is not suggesting that we need our emotions to be approved or validated by others: I may think that your fear of spiders is excessive, but I can see that because spiders seem scary to you, your fear is an appropriate response to them, so it is intelligible. The point is less demanding and yet much more morally relevant: it is enough that others "recognize us as people whose emotions make sense" (Bailey 2020, p. 13).

2 The Role of Empathy in Moral Judgments

Empathy has been characterized not only as an epistemic source for deliberation, but also as capable of grounding moral judgments. I am interested in moral judgments because they are a special case of deliberation: judging an action, a belief, or an emotional reaction to be morally good or morally bad ultimately amounts to a deliberative process involving moral considerations (sometimes exclusively, sometimes a combination of moral and non-moral considerations). That some of these are other-directed is fairly obvious: "Pam's action of omitting the truth was morally wrong, so I think Pam is a bad person" or "Since Pam committed a morally wrong action, I will never speak to her again" are instances of moral judgments, i.e., other-directed moral deliberations, about other people's actions and/or character.

In particular, moral sentimentalism is the tradition that has given and continues to give empathy a foundational role in morality, making it the best candidate for analyzing its role in moral judgments. In a nutshell, sentimentalists hold that moral judgments depend not on concepts but on sentiments, especially moral approval and disapproval. In particular, empathy-based accounts of sentimentalism typically argue that "changes in empathic responses predict changes in moral judgments, other things being equal" (Kauppinen 2014, p. 106).

Famously, Hume was the first and most important proponent of the role of sympathy (now empathy) in the formation of moral approval and disapproval. According to him, we make moral judgments based on the pains and pleasures we experience in response to the character and actions of other people: "To have the sense of virtue, is nothing but to feel a satisfaction of a particular kind from the contemplation of a character. The very feeling constitutes our praise or admiration" (THN, p. 471). As discussed in his 1748 *An Enquiry Concerning Human Understanding* (Hume, 1748, EHU from now on), the goodness or badness of the character is felt, and therefore judged, according to whether it is beneficial, harmful, agreeable, or disagreeable to other people (EHU, p. 268). In other words, if a character trait or action produces pleasure based on one of these four criteria, the subject will judge it as virtuous. Conversely, if a trait or action produces pain based on the same criteria, the subject will judge it as vicious.

There is, however, an important limitation: in order for these feelings to effectively constitute moral judgments, they cannot contain any "reference to our particular interest," that is, they cannot depend exclusively on self-centered passions because of their extreme variability (THN, p. 472).[4] And here the role of sympathy is crucial: it is through sympathy, understood as emotional contagion (see Section 1.2.1), that we can directly feel the passions, pains, and pleasures of others, leaving aside our own interests (Rick 2007, p. 141).[5] At the same time, Hume readily recognized the inherently partial nature of sympathy, especially toward those who are spatially, temporally, and emotionally close to the sympathizer and those who resemble her. We simply sympathize better and more deeply with those who share these characteristics. However, our moral judgments do not vary according to fluctuations in sympathy (THN, p. 581).[6] On the contrary, they claim validity across cultures, space, time, and types of relationships: "Notwithstanding this variation of our sympathy, we give the same approbation to the same moral qualities in *China* as in *England*" (THN, p. 581).

Hume was well aware of the existing gap between the variability of moral approval, which depends on the pains and pleasures felt through sympathy, and the homogeneity of our moral judgments for the same character trait (Sayre-McCord, 2013). It is because of this observational truth that Hume argued that our moral considerations do not vary as sympathy does because our moral judgments are made from "the general point of view" whose aim is precisely to correct for the variations and partialities of sympathy (THN,

4 Hume's complete quote: "'Tis only when a character is considered in general, without reference to our particular interest, that it causes such a feeling or sentiment, as denominates it morally good or evil' (THN, p. 472). Hume also called this type of sentiments instances of "self-love" (EHU, p. 74).

5 As Rick noticed, in Hume's account, the function of sympathy seemed to be the assurance of "disinterestedness" in moral judgments (Rick 2007, p. 141).

6 Here is Hume's famous passage on the partialities of sympathy: "[we] sympathize more with persons contiguous to us, than with persons remote from us: with our acquaintance, than strangers: with our countrymen, than with foreigners" (THN, p. 581).

p. 881–882). Roughly speaking, in the general point of view, "while we judge her [the other person] for her character, our judgments turn (…) on a more general view of the effects of the kind of character she has" (Sayre-McCord 2013, p. 227). In short, according to Hume, it is sympathy coupled with the general point of view that makes moral approbation, and consequently moral judgment, possible.

The centrality of sympathy to moral judgments is also present in perhaps the most radical proponent of empathy in the contemporary debate: Michael Slote. Inspired by Hume, Slote argues that empathy – like causation for Hume – is "the cement of the moral life" (Slote 2009, p. 13). In this context, empathy is defined as the phenomenon of "having the feelings of another (involuntarily) aroused in ourselves, as when we see another person in pain," which, not surprisingly, is similar to how Hume defined sympathy, that is, as emotional contagion (Slote 2009, p. 15).

Slote claimed that empathy constitutes moral approval and disapproval, which in turn allows us to make (and understand) moral judgments. According to him, I approve of another's action or behavior when I empathize with their empathic concern for others, which produces a feeling of warmth in me, which in turn constitutes moral approval (Slote 2009, p. 27). Similarly, moral disapproval arises from the cold feeling that results from empathizing with the other person's lack of empathic concern.

Although Slote shares with Hume the basic sentimentalist intuition that moral approval and disapproval do not require concepts of right and wrong,[7] he rejects Hume's idea that moral approval and disapproval are the results of our sympathy with the pains or pleasures caused by the actions of others. Instead, he claims that it is necessary to shift the focus from the consequences of actions to the agent's motivation: as said, the basis of approval and disapproval depends on whether we feel warm or cold as a result of empathizing with the agent's empathic motives or lack thereof. Then, moral judgments about the rightness or wrongness of actions are based on this approval or disapproval, and since empathy was critical for the formation of moral approval and disapproval, it follows that empathy is also fundamental for making and understanding moral judgments (Slote 2009, p. 53).

What about the partial nature of empathy, i.e., the fact that we empathize more easily with those who are near and dear to us (see Chapters 4 and 5 for an in-depth discussion of empathy's biases)? It seems particularly problematic in this account, since there is a double empathic movement, that from the observer to the agent and that from the agent to the person who suffers, poten-

7 This is a major point of contention between sentimentalists and rationalists.

tially doubling the risk of bias. But not according to Slote, who believes that empathy's biases should be embraced, not fought: "[Empathy's biases] correspond to normative moral distinctions we intuitively and commonsensically want to make," so there is nothing to correct (Slote 2009, p. 6).[8] Thus, empathy seems to be the primary source of normative reasons for the agent's specific deliberative process of judgment formation.

This is a very bold (and problematic) claim that deserves to be explored in depth (see Chapter 5). What is relevant here is that the biases of empathy are not a problem; on the contrary, they have the dual role of grounding and making intelligible our moral judgments (something is wrong/right because we disapprove/approve of it, i.e., we are empathically chilled/warmed by the lack/presence of empathic concern). On the contrary, as I will discuss next, empathy, biases included, is supposed to motivate our moral actions (empathy enables us to disapprove/approve and judge an action as bad/good, and for that very reason, we are also motivated to avoid/pursue that action).

It is possible, however, to endorse a sentimentalist account of empathy's contribution to moral judgment without justifying, if not encouraging, empathy's biases. Antti Kauppinen, for example, argues for what he calls "*ideal-regulated* empathy," which consists of "a broadly affective response to another's perceived situation that is regulated by reference to an ideal perspective" (Kauppinen 2014, p. 105). In contrast to Slote's definition of empathy which coincides with emotional contagion,[9] Kauppinen thought of this kind of empathy as a combination between affective empathy and cognitive empathy as defined in the SD. More specifically, in this context, empathy coincides with the phenomenon of affective empathy caused by cognitive empathy.[10] Empathy understood this way is characterized as "reactive" because it is directed at the other person's reactive attitudes, that is, at the maxim of his or her action ("what she does and to what end") (Kauppinen 2014, p. 100).

Most importantly, consistent with the classical sentimentalist framework of both Hume and Smith, Kauppinen suggested that empathy can ground moral judgments if and only if the empathizer regulates her empathic responses "by reference to an *ideal*, which has the function of contrasting the empathic partialities" (Kauppinen 2014, p. 100). To do this, the empathizer must adopt the

8 See also Slote, *The Ethics of Care and Empathy* for a more detailed defense of this position (Slote, 2007).

9 Kauppinen defines Slote's empathy as "immediate empathy" or "hedonic empathy" (Kauppinen 2014, p. 100).

10 Kauppinen defines the empathic phenomenon he has in mind as "combined empathy," i.e., having "an emotion congruent with another's situation *as a result of* imaginatively placing ourselves in another's situation" (Kauppinen 2014, p. 100).

perspective of what Smith called "an impartial spectator" (TMS, III.i.1.2), which means modulating one's empathic response by either down-regulating it when in-group members – toward whom empathy is stronger – are involved, and up-regulating it when out-group members – toward whom empathy is weaker, if not absent – are involved. Only then can and should the moral judgments made through ideal-regulated empathy be shared by others who have also judged the situation by placing themselves in the position of the empathetic, impartial observer.[11]

Kauppinen is openly inspired by Smith's account of the impartial spectator, which he believes is better suited to achieving ideal-regulated empathy than Hume's "general point of view" account. Whereas Hume focused on the pains and pleasures caused to the spectator by the actions of others, and characterized the spectator's ideal perspective in terms of the "narrow circle," Smith's focus is on the *propriety* of the other's emotional reactions to the situation. This means that I approve of something someone has done if, after imaginatively taking the perspective of an impartial spectator, I find the person's passion to be appropriate, that is, if there is a congruence between what the spectator's passion would have been in the situation and the other person's passion (TMS I.iii.1.9). Thus, the spectator's approval or disapproval – and the resulting moral judgment – ultimately is "a 'fittingness assessment'" (Debes 2016, p. 196).[12] In short, approval and disapproval are only possible because of the impartial spectator, which is able to correct the distortions caused by self-love[13] and to introduce an impartial perspective from which to judge the situation in light of the competing interests of the people involved, especially those of the sympathizer (Ben-Moshe 2020, p. 748).[14]

---

11 For a discussion about the problematic relationship between empathy and group membership, see Chapter 4.

12 In Smith's words: "when the original passions of the person principally concerned are in perfect concord with the sympathetic emotions of the spectator, they necessarily appear to this last *just* and *proper*, and suitable to their objects; and, on the contrary, when, upon bringing the case home to himself, he finds that they do not coincide with what he feels, they necessarily appear to him *unjust* and *improper*, and unsuitable to the causes which excite them" (TMS, I.i.3.1, my emphasis). As said, Bailey's account of humane understanding is also based on the Smithian "fitting assessment" (see Section 3.1).

13 Smith on the impartial spectator and self-love: "It is from him [the impartial spectator] that we learn the real littleness of ourselves, (…) and the natural misrepresentations of self-love can be corrected only by the eye of this impartial spectator" (TMS III.3.4).

14 Kauppinen on this point: "It is the reactive attitudes of resentment and gratitude that lie at the foundation of moral blame and praise. They are the sentiments that motivate punishment and reward and are sensitive to the agent's motives as well as consequences. They appear justified when we take any reasonable would share them" (Kauppinen, 2014, p. 110).

Importantly, "Smith's idea is that many if not most of our moral judgments result from *reasoning* from principles rather than directly from empathetic sentiments. Nevertheless, our adherence to these *principles* is ultimately explained by disciplined sentiment" (Kauppinen 2014, p. 111).[15] More specifically, there seems to be a two-stage process to form our moral judgment: First, "moral sentiments that result from more or less successfully ideal-regulated empathy in small-scale paradigmatic instances initially explain beliefs about which act-types are wrong-making" (Kauppinen 2014, p. 111). Second, when it comes to judging particular cases, a combination of the general rules originally based on ideal-regulated empathy, particular facts, and beliefs about the specific situation at hand generates the judgment.

Consider the example of the white lie. If we subscribe to Slote's account, Michael is capable of judging, i.e., deliberating about the moral status of Pam's action, on the basis of his empathic response to the presence or absence of Pam's empathic concern for Jim. If Pam's omission was motivated by empathic concern for Jim's happiness, and if Michael, in judging her action, feels empathically warmed by Pam's motivation, he will judge Pam's decision to be morally right. If Pam's empathic concern is not present, then Michael, empathically chilled by it, will judge Pam's decision as morally wrong. Note that this empathy-based moral judgment can, in turn, lead to other-directed theoretical deliberations (e.g., "I do (or do not) believe that Pam is a loyal and good friend") and other-directed practical deliberations (e.g., "I will (or will not) reveal personal information to Pam in the future"). Most importantly, if Michael's degree of empathy with Pam is higher, i.e., if he is more likely to empathically recognize Pam's empathic concern because, say, Pam is his sister-in-law, then the judgment of the rightness of her action is not only acceptable, but also normatively justified and intelligible.

In contrast, according to Kauppinen this result would be unacceptable because it could not be shared by the majority of other people. Note that the problem lies in the kind of justification offered for the judgment (e.g., Pam's

15 Smith explicitly mentions the role of experience and induction in the formation of our moral maxims: "From reason, therefore, we are very properly said to derive all those general maxims and ideas. It is by these, however, that we regulate the greater part of our moral judgments, which would be extremely uncertain and precarious if they depended altogether upon what is liable to so many variations as immediate sentiment and feeling, which they different states of health and humor are capable of altering so essentially. As our most solid judgments, therefore, with regard to right and wrong, are regulated by maxims and ideas derived from induction of reason, virtue may very properly be said to consist in a conformity to reason, and so far this faculty may be considered as the source and principle of approbation and disapprobation" (TMS VII.iii.2).

action is morally right because Michael feels a greater deal of empathy for her because she is his sister-in-law) and, ultimately, in the kind of empathy involved, not in its involvement *tout court*. On Kauppinen's account, moral judgments must be based on empathy, but empathy must be ideally regulated: Michael judges Pam's action to be morally right not because of their relationship but because of his sentiment of approval of her emotional response and the resulting action based on it. This moral sentiment of approval is derived from a combination of judgment about the moral status of the action type instantiated by Pam's specific action and specific information and facts about Pam's particular situation.

Thus, on the basis of ideal-regulated empathy, the action type "saying a white lie to make a friend feel better" is judged to be morally right. The specific action, Pam's omission which is an instantiation of that action type, is judged to be morally right because of the general judgment about that type of action based on ideal-regulated empathy, and also because of particular beliefs and facts about the concrete situation, e.g., the fact that the cheating was not relevant to Jim's partner's decision to divorce. Incidentally, because of the possibility of cultural transmission of these widely held judgments about paradigmatic cases – which are so widely held precisely because they are the result of ideal-regulated empathy – it is not necessary to take the perspective of the impartial bystander for every moral judgment, "unless the various features of an action generate opposing responses" (Kauppinen, 2014, p. 111).

In sum, both Slote's and Kauppinen's accounts of moral judgments are sentimentalist and empathy-based. However, they differ significantly in what kind of empathy they think plays a role in moral judgments and how they deal with its partial nature.

3 The Motivational Role of Empathy

For many empathy, caused or not by sympathy (see Section 1.3), is capable of and responsible for motivating moral action. This assumption has important implications for moral other-directed deliberation: if we subscribe to this claim, empathy becomes the central motivating reason or one of the central motivating reasons in our other-directed deliberations. In particular, when deciding how to act toward others, the role of empathy is to provide the subject with motivating reasons, which I have already characterized as both cognitive and affective, to act in a morally good way.

A paradigmatic example of this position is offered by the psychologist Simon Baron-Cohen who has famously argued that we should abandon the term "evil" and replace it with "empathy erosion" (Baron-Cohen 2011, p. 6). In his view, the reason is simple: immoral actions are not caused by people being inexplicably evil, but by their lack of some or all of their capacity to empathize. Or, to be more precise, people commit evil acts because they lack empathy. It follows that the cause of good and moral action is the presence of empathy: the agent's ability to perform a morally good action depends on her ability to empathize. Drawing on Martin Buber, Baron-Cohen suggests that this is evident when we consider the ease with which people who lack empathy can objectify other fellow human beings (Baron-Cohen 2011, p. 6). This objectification reflects and results from an inability to perform the mental operation of considering the thoughts and feelings of others, not just one's own. In particular, according to Baron-Cohen, people who lack empathy are unable to engage in "double-minded attention," that is, they are unable to take into account the thoughts, feelings, and interests of others instead of focusing exclusively on their own internal states and needs (Baron-Cohen 2011, p. 16).

Based on a quantitative approach to the empathic phenomenon, the psychologist claims that the distribution of empathy in the population varies along a bell-shaped curve, where each individual can have high, low, or moderate levels of empathy. Of particular interest in this context are those subjects who are at the low end of the empathy spectrum, especially those who are in a state of "zero negative empathy," that is, they are completely and irreparably incapable of empathizing (Baron-Cohen 2011, p. 45). Whether the subject never had empathy in the first place or lost it along the way due to specific events or trauma, the result is that they "become capable of dehumanizing other people, of turning other people into objects, and this can have tragic consequences" (Baron-Cohen 2011, p. 20). While being in a state of zero negative empathy does not necessarily – though it sometimes does – result in acts of overt physical violence, such as murder, torture, or rape, it always results in some psychological, emotional, or non-fatal physical harm to the other person involved in the relationship with an individual in a state of zero negative empathy.

Subsequently, Baron-Cohen spends a great deal of time detailing who the people in this state are and describing their specific behaviors. In particular, based on a large body of empirical evidence, he argues that three specific psychopathological populations possess the state of zero negative empathy and may attribute their behaviors to this deficiency: individuals with borderline personality disorder, antisocial personality disorder, and narcissistic personality disorder (Baron-Cohen 2011, pp. 43–94).

Leaving aside the specific psychiatric implications of his argument, I am most interested in Baron-Cohen's definition of empathy as "our ability to identify what someone else is thinking or feeling and to respond to their thoughts and feelings with an appropriate emotion" (Baron-Cohen 2011, p. 16). This seems a very demanding way of framing empathy: not only must the empathizer recognize the internal affective and cognitive states of the other person, but she must also respond to this understanding in a way that is deemed "appropriate." Note that these two stages of empathy, recognition and response, are *both* necessary (and sufficient) conditions for empathy: responding in an appropriate way to the recognition of the other's state is not merely a consequence of an empathic act; but rather it is integral to successfully empathizing with the other person. In other words, recognition alone, without response, does not achieve empathy (Baron-Cohen 2011, p. 16).

Most importantly, this definition of empathy explicitly implies that the presence of empathy is capable of guaranteeing moral, or at least pro-social, behavior. The mere fact of recognizing how others feel or what they are going through seems to necessarily lead to these kinds of behavior. This supposed automaticity is evident in Baron-Cohen's words:

> When (…) you are able to both recognize and respond, you can not only ask someone how they are feeling, you can sensitively avoid hurting their feelings, think about how to make them feel good, and consider how everything you say or do impacts on them or others. (…) If they are suffering to any degree, you just know to offer comfort and sympathy.
>
> BARON-COHEN 2011, p. 17

Thus, knowing what the other is experiencing seems both necessary and sufficient to motivate sympathetic, pro-social, and/or moral responses in the empathizer. The overarching assumption seems to be that empathy can do it all, and when it is present, it never fails: not only "being able to empathize means being able to understand accurately the *other* person's position, to identify with 'where they are at,'" but also "empathy avoids any risk of misunderstandings or miscommunication, by figuring out what the other person might have intended. It allows you to avoid causing offense by anticipating how things will be experienced by another mind different from your own" (Baron-Cohen 2011, pp. 18–19). In this sense, empathy, thus defined, becomes the cornerstone of our interpersonal life and, consequently, of morality, and its absence the primary source of interpersonal conflict and immorality in general.

In his account, Slote takes Baron-Cohen's argument even further, arguing not only that empathy is always capable of motivating sympathy, but also that it should be the normative source of all moral action, since it is able to fix the reference for the terms morally wrong and morally right. Let's start with the motivation claim. In contrast to most account of empathy-based motivation, he argues that the connection between empathy, on one hand, and sympathy, benevolence, and altruism, on the other, is not merely empirical, but rather it is conceptual. This is because when we empathize with someone's distress, we necessarily experience a form of that distress ourselves. This shared emotional state, he contends, inherently constitutes a motivation to alleviate the other person's suffering:

> But then consider someone who empathizes with, who empathically takes in, the other person's distress at their pain. This means feeling distressed oneself about their pain, and, again *ex vi termini*, this constitutes motivation to alleviate that person's pain. Which is what we mean by altruistic or benevolent motivation. So on strictly conceptual grounds empathy involves sympathy with and motivation to help another person[16].
>
> SLOTE 2016, p. 15

To justify the conceptual connection, Slote draws an analogy with Elizabeth Anscombe's famous example of the unintelligibility of desiring a saucer of mud without any further reason. Just as we struggle to make sense of such a baseless desire, Slote argues that the concept of sympathy or altruism without an underlying empathic foundation is equally incoherent. Only by positing the existence of empathy as motivating sympathy, i.e., as the reason that motivates sympathy, we have the necessary intelligibility condition to understand our sympathetic and benevolent responses to the plight of others: "If desire has intelligibility conditions and cannot attach to some intentional object independently of those conditions, then sympathy and altruism, which involve specific (and positive) forms of intentionally directed desire, may have their own intelligibility conditions; and can one think of a better candidate for such a condition than empathy?" (Slote 2016, pp. 19–20).

The central – and rather bold – claim is that empathy accounts for "any non-egoistic motivation to help others" (Slote 2016, p. 23). According to Slote, this is true even of rationalist accounts, such as those proposed by McDowell and Scanlon, which attribute our motivation to help others either to our grasp of the relevant facts about the other's condition or to some reasons we all have for doing so. This becomes clear when we consider the case of psychopathy: while

16 Note that Slote distinguishes between two types of empathy: projective empathy, which involves imagining oneself in another's situation, and associative or emotional empathy, which involves being affected by another's feelings, i.e., sharing them. Consistent with his previous work, he focuses on the latter, arguing that this form of empathy is inextricably linked to sympathetic and altruistic motivations (Slote 2016, p. 14).

their cognitive ability to understand the other's condition through perspective taking is intact, psychopaths do not seem to be moved to help others, and similarly, while it seems plausible that neurotypical people have some reasons for helping others, these same reasons are not recognized by psychopaths. The only way to explain their behavior is to point to the fact that they lack affective empathy and thus any non-egoistic moral motivation to help others.

Another way in which Slote justifies the motivational claim is by arguing for the intrinsic motivational power of our moral judgments, which, as noted, are based on empathy: when we judge something to be morally right, we are motivated to perform that action, and when we judge something to be morally wrong, we are motivated not to perform that action. Specifically, he claims that "the empathy inherently involved in making genuine moral judgments is precisely the empathy that inclines us to do what we think of as right and avoid what we think of as wrong" (Slote, 2009, p. 53). There is an inclination to "act in accordance with" our moral judgments because those moral judgments depend directly on our ability to empathize with the agent's empathic concern (or lack thereof) (Slote, 2009, p. 54).

In other words, since we must be either empathically warmed or chilled by the other's motive in order to make a moral judgment, it is precisely this second-order empathy with the other's first-order empathic concern that leads us to either perform or not perform the act we have approved or disapproved of. This seems to be demonstrated once again in the case of psychopaths: they are not motivated to perform sympathetic/benevolent/altruistic/moral acts because they lack affective empathy, and thus the second-order empathy that enables neurotypical people to formulate moral judgments of rightness and thus to motivate the corresponding actions.

Finally, Slote defends the view that empathy is normatively directed toward what is morally right (Slote 2009, pp. 98–99). If the agent feels genuine empathy for the other person, she will necessarily and sufficiently be motivated to behave in a way that promotes the welfare and happiness of that person. Using his recurring example of a son caring for his elderly and ill mother, Slote argues that:

> normal, good, caring motivation toward a mother is more likely to eventually lead one to doing the right thing by her: even if a genuinely devoted son can get tired of helping and temporarily lose any (conscious) feeling of concern or empathy for his mother, his empathic concern is very likely to revive before he does something that threatens her future wellbeing in a serious way and thus before any serious wrong doing occurs.
>
> SLOTE 2009, p. 99

Note that the phrase "more than likely" does not refer to the possibility that empathic concern might not lead to the right actions, but rather to the possibility that external circumstances, such as the son's death, might prevent him from caring for his mother. Similarly, while Slote clarifies that "the motivation may not issue in action if stronger contrary motives are also in play in the given situation," i.e., if external circumstances, rather than the agent's internal opposing motives, arise, he ultimately seems to imply that empathy-based motivation always leads to actual sympathetic and caring action (Slote 2016, p. 3).

More generally, as Slote himself acknowledged, his account is probably the position that has given empathy the most prominent role not only in altruistic actions but in morality in general.[17] Because of its radicality, Slote's proposal has been the subject of several criticisms, which I will discuss in the next section (see Chapter 5). Nevertheless, the undeniable merit of his account is that it offers a comprehensive theory of what it would be like if empathy were indeed the center of our moral universe and everything revolved around it.

Consider now the "white lie" case. After empathizing with Pam's distress caused by Jim's situation, Michael takes in her distress and, motivated by it, deliberates that he will help Pam comfort Jim that night instead of watching his favorite TV show. Michael's altruistic and moral motivation depends on the fact that he empathized with Pam's distress and decided to help her alleviate that distress. Michael's motivation to help Pam is intelligible only because of his affective empathy, that is, Michael's empathic sharing of Pam's distress is the only way to explain his altruistic and morally good act.

Note that in this case, Michael's action is both altruistic (not motivated by self-interest) and moral, since it is morally right to help a friend in need. In this regard, it is because Michael has previously been empathically warmed by Pam's empathic concern when helping her friend in need, and therefore judges it to be morally right, that he is motivated to choose this course of action.

In Baron-Cohen's view, if Michael were a narcissist, hence in the zero empathy condition, he would never have been able to recognize Pam's distress, and consequently would not have been able to even consider an appropriate response, for example, the possibility of giving up his enjoyable evening as he would only be preoccupied with satisfying his own needs. Since he would be prone to objectifying Pam, he might also have been able to manipulate Pam

17 Slote on the radicality of his position: "All in all, then, I don't think we can have beneficent or helping moral motivation in the absence of empathy. This goes well beyond anything I or anyone else has previously said about the moral role of empathy, and it moves us toward the conclusion that empathy is probably the most significant factor in the moral life" (Slote 2016, p. 25).

into standing up Jim and spending the evening with him instead, thereby increasing her and Jim's distress and suffering.

So far, I have attempted to establish the conceptual framework of the issue at hand. First, I have provided a definition of the empathic phenomenon, the SD of empathy, which is consistent with the most widely accepted positions in contemporary academic debate. I have also proposed a definition of the deliberative process that is most influenced by empathy, namely other-directed theoretical and practical deliberations. I then analyzed how this influence can manifest itself by providing the epistemic, motivational, and normative reasons that underpin other-directed deliberation, especially moral other-directed deliberation. It is now time to show how problematic empathy, so defined, can be when involved in this kind of deliberative process.

PART 2

A Critique of the Standard Definition of Empathy and Its Role in Deliberation

CHAPTER 4

Issues with Cognitive Empathy and Its Epistemic Role in Deliberation

In this chapter, I want to put some pressure on the idea that cognitive empathy, understood as perspective-taking, is the best option for fulfilling the epistemic role assigned to it in other-directed deliberation. First, I will show why cognitive empathy is dangerously inaccurate due to its numerous cognitive biases and how this can negatively impact the deliberative process. Second, I will argue that cognitive empathy, especially when characterized as a simulation-plus-projection routine, can pose a threat to the target's agency that compromises the epistemic accuracy and morality of our other-directed deliberative processes.

To be sure, my point is not merely to show that empathy has flaws, but that these flaws make it a problematic candidate for the roles it is assigned in other-directed deliberation. If empathy is supposed to provide the reasons for other-directed deliberation, then it is not doing a good job. In this sense, I do not intend to argue that cognitive empathy is useless or plays no role in interpersonal understanding and other-directed deliberation. Instead, I want to question its trustworthiness from an epistemic point of view.

Importantly, in this section (Chapters 4–6), I will set aside any direct criticism of the standard definition (SD) of empathy. In fact, I will assume that the definitions of cognitive empathy, affective empathy, and sympathy provided in the SD are correct in order to show how problematic they are when involved in the deliberative process. Ultimately, however, I will argue in the final section that the source of these problems lies precisely in the way the SD conceptualizes empathy, and that one way to respond to these problems is to completely change the theoretical framework and definition of the empathic phenomenon.

Finally, in this section, especially in Chapters 4 and 5, I will review several empirical studies, especially neuroethical and psychological ones. Importantly, I want to avoid a reductionist approach: empathy cannot and should not be reduced to a cluster of neurons in our brains, especially if we want to explore its role in other-directed deliberation within a distinctive philosophical framework. At the same time, however, empirical evidence cannot be ignored because it provides crucial evidence of what we as humans are capable of

 HTTPS://DOI.ORG/10.1163/9789004745360-006

doing given our biological resources (Zilio 2021). The result of this methodological approach is, on one hand, to preserve the complexity of our epistemic and moral experience without reducing it to mere biological or neurological functions. On the other hand, this approach manages to take into account the rich contribution of neuroethics and applied psychology. In this sense, my critique of the role of empathy in the deliberative process will be primarily conceptual, and empirical evidence will serve either to confirm or to limit the feasibility of these claims.

1 Cognitive Biases and Inaccuracy in Cognitive Empathy

There is nothing particularly original about accusing empathy of being biased. It is almost old news, given that Hume and Smith were already aware of it in the eighteenth century (Hume, 1739; Smith, 1759) (see Chapter 3). But that does not make it any less relevant: the inherently biased nature of empathy cannot be overlooked, especially when it is considered a building block of interpersonal understanding and other-directed deliberation. For this reason, I will discuss cognitive biases in cognitive empathy and show how they can negatively affect our interpersonal understanding and ultimately our other-directed deliberative process, with problematic consequences at both the epistemic and the moral level.

A cognitive bias is broadly defined as a mental phenomenon associated with irrationality: "When confronted with evidence of type *X*, a judge will consistently choose alternative *B* instead of the expected alternative *A*" (Hilbert 2012, p. 211). The key here is the consistency of cognitive biases: because of the consistency of our biased choices, "rules that describe such biases have large predictive power" (Hilbert 2012, p. 211).[1] In addition, biases can be either implicit or explicit: when "prejudicial attitudes and stereotypical beliefs are activated spontaneously and effortlessly" (Hagiwara et al., 2020, p. 1457), we have an implicit bias (both affective and cognitive), while when these attitudes and beliefs are consciously and openly chosen, we have an explicit bias. In particular, a stereotype is "a semantic structure, and encodes descriptive proprieties of groups" (Westra 2019, p. 2824). Conversely, a prejudice is "an evaluative structure, and encodes valenced information" (Westra 2019, p. 2824).

The insistence on the impact of biases stems from the fact that they threaten the *accuracy* of the outcome of cognitive empathy. The psychological phenom-

1 See Baron (2008) and Ehrlinger et al. (2016) for a more in-depth discussion of cognitive bias and a detailed list of cognitive biases and heuristics.

enon of empathic accuracy is defined as "the ability to correctly infer the content of the discrete subjectively perceived mental events of another person as they occur over time" (Hodges, Lewis, and Ickes 2015, p. 319) and empathic inaccuracy is its opposite. Importantly, while cognitive biases do not necessarily lead to inaccurate understanding, they increase the risk of this happening because they favor efficiency and speed over accuracy (Ehrlinger et al., 2016). The risk of inaccuracy is a serious concern. After all, we engage in cognitive empathy because we want to accurately understand what the other person is thinking or feeling. Ideally, our goal is to understand the target's actual internal states, and indeed, we generally consider cognitive empathy to have failed if accuracy is not achieved.

Accuracy seems to satisfy two very basic human needs. On one hand, we want accuracy because we *need* accuracy: cognitive empathy provides a clear, albeit basic, evolutionary advantage by allowing us to predict and readily respond to the behavior of others (Smith, 2006). On the other hand, even when we engage in cognitive empathy with no apparent evolutionary benefit – for example, when we do so with fictional characters – we do so with the precise goal of gaining some accurate insight into their minds, otherwise we would not bother. This seems to signal that we seek accuracy beyond its evolutionary advantage. We seem to aim for accuracy because we *desire* accuracy when *we* are the target of cognitive empathy. When others are trying to understand our perspective, we want them to understand us as accurately as possible.

The desire for accuracy explains why "fake empathy" – when detected by the target – is experienced as a breach of trust (Morton 2017, p. 181). Fake empathy occurs when, in order to avoid the effortful operations required by cognitive empathy, the target uses a standardized set of expressions and gestures that attempt to mimic, almost mechanically, genuine empathic understanding. When fake empathy is recognized, it can lead to an erosion of trust between the subjects involved in the relationship. Interestingly, the reaction triggered by the recognition of this purely performative empathy can be seen as similar to the uncanny valley effect, which consists of an immediate disgust and aversion to those androids that resemble humans too closely (Gardner, 2015; Stefanello, 2021b). Faking something as human as empathic understanding produces the same negative and alienating effects as something that only pretends to be human. The point is that the intention behind cognitive empathy must be genuine, in the sense that the subject must want to pursue an accurate understanding of the other person's condition. This does not preclude the possibility of failure, which, as we shall see, is very likely.

So, given its importance, are we accurate perspective-takers and (cognitive) empathizers? According to empirical evidence, not really: "Strangers infer each other's thoughts and feelings with an average accuracy score of about 20%; close friends make these inferences with an average accuracy score of 30%; and married couples achieve average accuracy scores that usually range no higher than 35%" (Ta and Ickes 2017, p. 355).[2] The scores are well below 50%, which is discouraging if we are to use cognitive empathy as the default epistemic source for our other-directed deliberative processes.

This empirical data conflicts with our self-assessments and our common sense intuition that we are in fact quite capable of understanding others, especially people with whom we are close. In fact, one of the hallmarks of an intimate relationship is the belief that the more involved you are with the other person, the more you understand his or her mind. We usually say or think things like, "I know him, so I understand what he is thinking and feeling." We also get annoyed when someone claims to understand our friend's, partner's, or relative's mind better than we do. Even with strangers, we assume that we are better than empirical evidence suggests: our other-directed deliberations about people we do not know are based on assumptions of general epistemic correctness and general confidence in our empathic abilities. For example, when we deliberate about what the person sitting in front of us on the train is thinking about after listening to her work phone call, we assume (and hope for) a certain level of accuracy. Again, why else would we bother?

It seems that we overestimate our ability to understand other people accurately (Ames, 2004).[3] There could be a number of reasons for this: "A lack of interest in correcting our mindreading mistakes, a lack of feedback on errors, or an extreme instance of the Dunning-Kruger effect" (Spaulding 2016, p. 423). At its core, however, the source of inaccuracy is the fact that we are flawed knowers. Our knowledge is always partial, biased, and incomplete because we are inherently limited epistemic agents. Depending on the object of our knowl-

---

2 The definition of empathic accuracy in this context: "Empathic accuracy, as operationally defined, is a global measure of how accurately a perceiver is able to infer the specific content of all of the target person's thoughts and feelings. The accuracy of the perceiver's empathic inferences is based on trained raters' judgments of how similar each of the inferred thoughts and feelings were to the actual thoughts and feelings that the target person reported. The global (overall) measure of empathic accuracy is scaled as a percentage measure, with 0 indicating no accuracy and 100 indicating perfect accuracy. (More precisely, 0 indicates that the perceiver was awarded no "accuracy points" for any of his or her empathic inferences, whereas 100 indicates that the perceiver was awarded all of the available "accuracy points" by the trained raters.)" (Ta and Ickes 2017, p. 354). See also Ickes (Ickes, 1993).

3 For a position that argues that we should be agnostic about whether our mindreading ability are accurate or not, see Westra (2020).

edge, we are either better or worse at mitigating our biased tendencies, which are nonetheless inescapable.

In the case of cognitive empathy, the object is the other person's internal state, arguably one of the most complex and opaque subjects to master from an epistemic perspective. To get a sense of the complexity, consider that "neuroscientists calculate that a human brain could be in more possible brain states than there are elementary particles in the universe" (Eyal, Steffel, and Epley 2018, p. 547). To be clear, to say that other people's minds are complex is not to say that they are completely unintelligible. We would be hard-pressed to accept any kind of claim that postulates a fundamental and insurmountable lack of intelligibility between us. It is undeniably true that we are somehow able to understand each other, with all the limitations that entails. At the same time, however, it also seems true that other people will never be fully epistemically transparent to us: full access to their minds is not possible, despite our efforts to mitigate and correct our errors of perspective-taking.[4]

Given the importance of accuracy, it is necessary to analyze the main causes of inaccuracy, which, as mentioned, are the cognitive biases that influence the subject when performing cognitive empathy. In particular, I will focus on these biases and some broader related issues involved in the two different types of cognitive empathy as characterized in the SD of empathy (Goldman, 2006; Stueber, 2006).[5] On one hand, basic or mirroring empathy is responsible for guiding the subject in recognizing others, i.e., as worthy targets for cognitive empathy. On the other hand, reenactive or reconstructive empathy is one of the strategies through which the subject can gather information about her target and subsequently understand the target's internal states through simulation and projection.[6]

The function of basic empathy is to allow us to recognize other people as minded beings, just like ourselves. This is supposed to happen instantly and consistently because we are all endowed with mirror neurons (MNs), which makes this recognition spontaneous, direct, and automatic. For this to be true, two assumptions must be proven. First, MNs and related mechanisms must be uniquely responsible for this ability to recognize others as like-minded. Second, this first-order recognition must necessarily lead to a second-order rec-

4 See Chapter 9 for a discussion on this point.

5 See Sections 1.1.1 and 3.1 for a discussion on Goldman's and Stueber's accounts, respectively.

6 I will use Stueber's terminology from now on when discussing cognitive empathy as I am particularly interested in questioning the idea that cognitive empathy allows as to grasp the other's reasons for actions.

ognition: the recognition that other people qualify as potential targets for reconstructive or reenactive empathy.

The first assumption is based on the idea that recognizing that the other person's actions, like mine, are goal-directed and that the other person's facial expressions express emotions should lead to an understanding that we share a fundamental characteristic: we are both creatures with minds that function in the same way in important ways (Stueber 2009, p. 539). Gallese famously argued that "the *phenomenological level* [i.e., basic empathy] is the one responsible for the sense of similarity, of being individuals within a larger social community of persons like us" (Gallese 2001, p. 45). Similarly, Stueber, drawing on Meltzoff's "like me" analogy (Meltzoff & Brooks, 2001),[7] asserted that "imitation and its underlying mechanisms should be understood not only as allowing me to recognize others to be 'like me' but also as allowing me to recognize myself as being 'like you,'" distinguishing them from other inanimate objects that are incapable of human actions (Stueber 2006, p. 143). Note that this way of defining basic empathy and the role of MNs does not (yet) imply any kind of understanding-related claim: it does not imply that basic empathy is capable of providing the subject with any kind of rich understanding of the content of the other person's inner state (Goldman, 2006), which is a far more difficult claim to defend since it would imply an explicit embrace of behaviorism (Borg, 2007).[8]

However, it seems doubtful that the activation of MNs alone is sufficient for the attribution of like-mindedness. For this claim to be true, there must be a perfect causal relationship between the activation of MNs and the recognition of like-mindedness: every time my MNs are activated by someone else's actions, I must automatically and unambiguously recognize that the agent of

7 According to Meltzoff and Brooks, "infants' attention to and imitation of human acts has interesting developmental sequelae: The world of material objects is then divisible into those that perform human act (people) and those that do not (things). Because human acts are seen in others and performed by the self, the infant can represent the other as 'like me': I can act like the other and reciprocally the other acts like me. Persons are special entities, the only entities in the world with whom I can share behavioral states" (Meltzoff and Brooks 2001, p. 174).

8 There have also been claims of a closer relationship between MNs and empathic understanding. For instance, Kaplan and Iacoboni argued: "We believe that the data presented here suggest that the mirror neuron system supports a simulation-based form of the intentions of others while they perform everyday goal-oriented actions. Moreover, the functions of the mirror neuron system seem to map well onto important forms of social competence in adulthood, such as cognitive empathy" (Kaplan and Iacoboni 2006, p. 182). But also Gallese: "My proposal is that action understanding heavily relies on a neural mechanism that matches, in the same neuronal substrate, the observed behavior of the one executed" (Gallese 2001, p. 39).

that action *de facto* has a mind like mine. This does not seem to be the case. As Vincenzo Costa has rightly noted, there are cases in which our MNs are activated by some actions that do not imply the attribution of like-mindedness to the agent (Costa 2010, pp. 100–101).

In particular, empirical evidence shows that there are "no significant differences between MNs activity during the observation of robotic and human actions" (Gazzola et al., 2007, p. 1682), since our MNs fire even when we observe an industrial robot, rather than a human, performing goal-directed actions, such as grasping a cocktail glass or moving wooden blocks. Nevertheless, we certainly do not attribute a mind like ours to the robot, and thus we do not recognize it as a like-minded being. What seems more plausible is that MNs and thus basic empathy, defined as the activity of mirroring the actions and gestures of others, may be responsible for "codifying the structure of actions," i.e., identifying the actions as goal-directed (Costa 2010, p. 102). However, this does not necessarily imply that we ascribe a mind like ours to the agent of these goal-directed actions.

Now the second assumption: it must be true that for every instance of like-mindedness recognition, there is a second-order instance that recognizes the other person as a potential target of reconstructive or reenactive empathy. Because of our biased tendencies, we sometimes recognize others as like-minded, but not as potentially *worthy* of reconstructive or reenactive empathy (Gehlbach and Mu 2023, p. 8). Incidentally, no simulation theory proponent argues that basic empathy always leads to reconstructive or reenactive empathy, since this is clearly contradicted by our everyday experience: we often recognize others as having minds like ours and as potentially worthy of reconstructive or reenactive empathy, but we do not engage in any form of perspective-taking due to lack of time or resources. The problem is not that we do not always follow through with perspective-taking, but rather that the worthiness of this operation seems to be granted on the basis of biased considerations.

For instance, Gutsell and Inzlicht found that the neural mechanisms responsible for simulating the others' actions "are less responsive to outgroup members than to ingroup members" (Gutsell and Inzlicht 2010, p. 844). More importantly, they found that "prejudiced people fail to mentally simulate outgroup member's actions and this failure to simulate is particularly pronounced for disliked outgroups" (Gutsell and Inzlicht 2010, p. 844). Consistent with other empirical evidence (Likowski et al., 2008; Van Bavel et al., 2008), this study seems to confirm that the responsiveness to engage in mental simulation is strongly influenced by group membership. In this case, the mirroring networks of Caucasian subjects were significantly less active with African-Canadian, East Asian, and South Asian subjects than with other Caucasian subjects. Interestingly, there appears to be a vicious cycle between prejudice and motivation when it comes to basic empathy. The lower levels of basic empathy toward outgroup members that appear to be caused by prejudicial attitudes may lead to a decrease in the ability to engage in low-level simulation and thus to recognize them as worthy targets for high-level simulation, which in turn may lead to the reinforcement of prejudices and negative stereotypes.

Things are no easier when it comes to reconstructive or reenactive empathy, which has as many, if not more, problems with the accuracy of its results as basic empathy. First of all, reconstructive or reenactive empathy like the rest of "our social inferences [is] biased toward the most readily accessible information", namely "the most salient features of a person [which] tend to be their age, race, and gender" (Spaulding 2016, p. 427).[9] We do this because it is easier and more efficient than taking into account all of the information that the other person may be able to provide us, consciously or unconsciously. To avoid this costly and laborious process, we not only categorize people according to their salient features but also "spontaneously attribute personality traits such as trustworthiness, competence, aggressiveness, and dominance" or other personal characteristics as demonstrated by the implicit association task (Spaulding 2016, p. 427). In other words, "stereotypes are structured around *attributions of character traits*" based on extrinsic features of the subject (Westra 2019, p. 2824).

A typical example is when we attribute aggressiveness to black people, or when we associate women with weakness. This information is likely to be inaccurate because it does not take into account the specificity of the person and the situation at hand, but is instead based on stereotypes and implicit biases, that is, on characteristics that have nothing to do with the moral character or epistemic features of the person. It makes little difference whether the stereotype or bias is positive or negative. For example, being male is usually associated with being more competent, which is obviously a positive inference for men (but much less so for women).

But what matters from an epistemic point of view is the accuracy of the information, which these kinds of associations do not guarantee. Despite the fact that we all use these shortcuts and rapid inferences to understand other people, they do not seem to be able to achieve the epistemic goal desired by ST

9 Spaulding did not explicitly mention reenactive empathy or reconstructive empathy. She was referring to mindreading and ST in general. However, her critique is applicable to reenactive and reconstructive empathy because she understands mindreading as a simulation-plus-projection routine.

theorists, namely a detailed and accurate understanding of the other person's inner states and behavior. Understanding the other's action as a mere product of a stereotypical characteristic associated with their gender or race is not only ridiculously reductive, but also highly inaccurate, since that aspect may not even have any weight in that particular decision or behavior. Moreover, if they are lucky enough to contain some accurate information, their involvement in reenactive empathy can only result in a generalized and vague understanding of the other person's state and, thus, reasons for action (Lewis et al., 2012, p. 1041).

Interestingly, Ames and colleagues found that "higher levels of similarity were associated with greater projection and less stereotyping", meaning that when the subject perceives the target as less similar, they rely more on stereotypes and less on projecting their own internal states and deliberative processes onto the target (Ames, Weber, and Zou 2012, p. 108).[10] Thus, the use of stereotypes in reconstructive or reenactive empathy, especially when targets are perceived as less similar, seems to increase the risk of inaccurate understanding which, due to the vicious cycle mentioned above, is likely to reinforce biased attitudes toward outgroup members.

Note that the criterion of similarity involved in the study was characterized as "perceived similarity" rather than "actual similarity," with only the former correlating with modulation of projection and stereotyping (Ames, Weber, and Zou 2012, p. 98). Most importantly, as the authors made clear, "perceptions of general similarity seem fallible and malleable, susceptible to overgeneralization from limited evidence of similarities or differences and to focus and salience effects (e.g., focusing on similarities to a target tends to increase the subjective sense of general similarity)" (Ames, Weber, and Zou 2012, p. 98). Once again, the importance of group membership in modulating cognitive empathy seems inescapable, given that the parameters that draw the boundaries of the group of those perceived as similar to the empathizers are either entirely arbitrary or based on the typical salient characteristics by which we categorize each other (race, gender, and age).

Subject similarity is also relevant to empathic accuracy in another sense. It is generally assumed that if the subject perceives the other as similar or having

10 Note that the study refers to the domain of strategic interaction and does not directly address reenactive empathy. However, it does focus on mindreading and perspective-taking characterized in terms of "us[ing] the self, through projection or perspective-taking, as a template for intuiting others' desires, preferences, and intentions" which essentially coincides with the concept of cognitive empathy (specifically reenactive empathy) (Ames, Weber, and Zou 2012, p. 97).

the same life experiences as the target, perspective-taking will not only be less cognitively demanding since it would be mostly based on projection, but also more accurate. Empirical evidence suggests that this is not the case: having a similar experience is positively correlated with an increase in empathic concern (see Chapter 5), but does not affect empathic accuracy (Hodges, 2005). One of the studies conducted by Hodges et al. found that "people with [the same] experience may *feel* like they really do understand and care more (in line with our empathic concern results), but actual accuracy does not necessarily follow" (Hodges et al., 2010, p. 406). Having the same experience as the target only helped the "been there, done that" empathizer when the target's condition was substantially consistent with the relevant stereotypes for that condition.[11] This seems to confirm, on one hand, the gap between what the subject believes her level of empathic accuracy to be, based on shared experience with the target, and what it actually is, and, on the other hand, how strongly stereotypes are involved in cognitive empathy, even when the subjects share the same experience.

The second problematic aspect of reconstructive or reenactive empathy has been effectively labeled by Shaun Gallagher as the "diversity problem" (Gallagher 2012, p. 363). It refers to the concern about how to preserve the uniqueness and distinctiveness of the other person's point of view. This concern arises because the process of reconstruction and reenactment depends entirely on the empathizer's ability to simulate the content of the other's mind. In other words, the empathizer's mind is the basis for the simulative process. This problem becomes clear in the case of self-oriented perspective-taking, raising the following question: "When we project ourselves imaginatively into the perspective of the other, when we put ourselves in his or her shoes, do we really attain an understanding of the other or we are merely reiterating ourselves?" (Gallagher 2012, p. 363). Do we understand the other's reasons for acting or do we understand what our own reasons would have been for the other's action? The inevitable consequence of this way of understanding reconstructive or reenactive empathy is the introduction of "a consistent first-person bias in our understanding of others" (Gallagher 2012, p. 364).

The problem with projection is that it would lead to accurate understanding only when there is no significant difference between the subject and the

11 Specifically, "the benefits of experience on accuracy were limited: It did not help new-mother perceivers guess what a target was thinking at a specific point in time, it did not help new-mother perceivers do better than pregnant perceivers (who also had not yet had the experience), and it only helped new-mother perceivers do better than never-pregnant perceivers in guessing a target's attitudes toward motherhood to the extent that the target's attitudes resembled the average new mother" (Hodges et al. 2010, p. 406)

target. However, I have serious doubts that the absence of significant differences between the people involved in empathic understanding can happen very often, or perhaps at all. What usually happens is that we fail to notice important differences between ourselves and other people. In short, we seem epistemically incapable of seeing what makes us different. As Spaulding points out: "Errors arise when we *overestimate* the similarity between ourselves and the other person(s) and thus engage in more projection than is warranted" (Spaulding 2016, 431).[12]

Even assuming that the similarity between the subjects is appropriately assigned and the necessary adjustments are made, self-oriented perspective-taking does not guarantee accuracy, since it depends on the degree of accuracy of the introspective process that the subject has undertaken. In other words, if the subject is unable – for a variety of reasons – to answer correctly and accurately the question "What would I think or feel in the target's state?," then the information she will project onto the target will necessarily be inaccurate. More on this later (see Section 4.2).

The third and final concern with reconstructive or reenactive empathy challenges the assumption that cognitive empathy is the epistemically best tool at our disposal for interpersonal understanding and for gathering information about others' conditions that they would not otherwise have had access to (Eyal et al., 2018). Surprisingly, despite the popularity of this assumption, little attention has been paid to testing whether accuracy is indeed achieved through perspective-taking. In this regard, Eyal et al. found unexpected results:

> Across a wide variety of experimental tests, involving relationships that ranged from strangers to spouses, we found no evidence that perspective taking systematically increased one's ability to accurately understand the mind of another person compared with a control condition. If anything, we found that perspective-taking tended to decrease interpersonal accuracy.
>
> EYAL ET AL. 2018, p. 567

For example, the focus on perspective-taking may distract the subject from paying attention to other epistemically relevant cues and information about

12 Two instances of these errors are the false consensus effect and the curse of knowledge that, respectively, "occurs when we falsely assume that a group of people shares our perspective on some issue. [And when] we falsely assume that another individual knows what we know" (Spaulding 2016, 431).

the other person, or the empathizer may be unable to effectively quarantine his or her personal beliefs that he or she does not share with the target. In particular, this ability to correctly quarantine seems particularly demanding, since it implies a fairly deep understanding of both the empathizer's, i.e., a very accurate introspection, and the other's relevant beliefs and inner states for the given situation. Especially in complex situations, are we sure that either of these goals can be easily achieved? I will come back to this when I discuss Goldie's critique next.

The key point is that the empirical results seem to indicate that there is no strong correlation, let alone causation, between empathic perspective-taking and increases in accuracy, which is enough to cast at least some doubt on the epistemic role of cognitive empathy in interpersonal understanding and other-directed deliberation. In this sense, its supposedly crucial involvement in the deliberative process is probably one of the most important reasons for wanting our empathic understanding to be accurate, in addition to all the reasons mentioned above: if the empathizer does not accurately understand the other person's beliefs and desires, i.e., the reasons for his or her actions, the entire deliberative process may be compromised. Similarly, if cognitive empathy coincides with the ability to understand the other person's emotional reactions as intelligible, then the other person's emotions must be understood accurately in order for them to be considered appropriate and therefore intelligible (see Chapter 3).

Let's revisit the white lie case to see why accuracy is so important in empathic other-directed deliberation. Michael deliberates that Pam is a loyal friend (other-directed theoretical deliberation) and that he will not tell Jim about the cheating (other-directed practical deliberation). He is able to do this because he has empathically understood – via reconstructive or reenactive empathy – Pam's beliefs and desires as her reasons for acting, and the fact that he has understood them is the very reason for his decisions. In the best case scenario, Michael's empathic understanding is not influenced by any of the biases and stereotypes mentioned above.

This seems unlikely, however, given their pervasiveness. Perhaps the fact that Pam is a woman leads Michael to ascribe to her a greater desire to care for others, when in fact her reason for not telling Jim about the cheating depends on the fact that she also cheated on her partner and feels guilty about confronting a victim of that action. Or he may be overlooking an important difference between them: Pam does not share his perspective on the moral status of cheating. For her, there is no moral conflict; she simply does not believe that cheating is wrong, and therefore has no problem with not telling Jim. Without considering this salient difference, Michael has projected his perspective onto Pam, coming dangerously close to introspection rather than other-understanding.

Alternatively, Michael may perceive Pam as significantly different from him – perhaps because she is Japanese and he is Italian – and therefore be less inclined to engage in basic empathy and the simulation-plus-projection routine and instead use stereotypical tropes. He may believe that Pam's reason for lying about the cheating is because of her race and the fact that Japanese people have a stereotypical reputation for being reserved. In the specific case of emotions, due to various biases and/or simply the possibility of genuine error, Michael may imaginatively misrepresent her emotions, mistaking, for instance, Pam's disinterest for doubt. All of these cases share the same problematic outcome: inaccurate perspective-taking and empathic understanding leading to an epistemically inaccurate other-directed deliberative process (e.g., Pam is not a loyal friend and Micheal should tell Jim about the cheating).

Not to mention all the obstacles that basic empathy has to overcome in order to lead to the recognition that the other's perspective is worth simulating. It matters little that empathic understanding is inaccurate if the target's perspective is not first and foremost recognized as worthy of simulative engagement. If Michael does not recognize that Pam's perspective is worthy of imaginative reenactment, then inaccuracy is the least of our concerns. This is especially problematic because, as said, this recognition seems to be given or denied to the other person based on biased criteria as well, such as group membership.

Cognitive biases and inaccuracy also have morally problematic implications. The fact that lack of second-order recognition and inaccurate empathic understanding occur systematically when the target is perceived as an outgroup based on features of their identity (gender, race, age, etc.) may contribute to the reinforcement of prejudice and negative stereotypes, leading to potentially immoral and discriminatory actions (see Chapters 5 and 6). Finally, if we assume that mindreading is indeed an important part of moral judgments (see Chapter 5) and that cognitive empathy is the central tool for achieving it, then its accuracy is crucial to ensuring that the reasons that justify our moral judgments about the actions of others are accurate. For example, Michael might judge Pam's behavior to be morally wrong because, after engaging in cognitive empathy, he inaccurately believes that she did not tell Jim out of self-interest because she wanted to cut their meeting short to go to the movies that night. Despite his attempt at cognitive empathy, he misunderstands Pam's reasons for acting and wrongly concludes that she is selfish and that what she did is morally wrong.

2 The Problem of Agency in Cognitive Empathy

The tendency of cognitive empathy to be inaccurate also appears to have negative implications for the target's agency. This seems particularly true in the case of other-oriented perspective-taking, which requires the subject to imaginatively take the other person's perspective as if she were actually that person. In this sense, Peter Goldie famously argues that if we empathizers expect to assume the first-person stance of the target in the empathic act, then access to the other person's inner world is neither epistemically possible nor morally desirable (Goldie, 2011). According to Goldie, taking the other's perspective – what he calls "empathic perspective-shifting" – poses insurmountable epistemic challenges to the empathizer (Goldie 2011, p. 302).[13]

In his view, an external subject cannot take the same first-person position that the agent herself takes in her deliberative process: "Only the agent himself can take his stance towards her own thoughts, decisions, and intentions" (Goldie 2011, p. 303). It is possible to imagine being the other person only in what he calls "base cases," which involve a thin notion of agency, where the characteristics of the subject making a decision do not influence the decision itself. Thus, in a base case, all subjects who possess a minimum of rationality will formulate the same decision, because the deliberation process is independent of the relevant aspects of the subject's character. Who you are does not matter; therefore, deliberative subjects are interchangeable. On the contrary, in cases where a stronger notion of agency is involved, the attempt to take the first-person perspective from the point of view of another subject is bound to fail. In fact, in cases where a strong notion of agency is involved, the characteristics of the subject who decides, thinks, and experiences emotions are crucial to the deliberative process.

One thing is to imaginatively take the other person's first-person perspective when trying to simulate and understand the other person's decision to go to the nearest bookstore to buy the latest novel by his or her favorite author. Another is to imaginatively reproduce Pam's deliberative process and the consequent decision not to tell Jim about his partner's cheating from Pam's perspective, i.e., being Pam. In the first base case, the subject's agency is minimally involved, whereas in the second case, the entire deliberation and its

13 Goldie defined *empathetic perspective-shifting* as follows: "consciously and intentionally shifting your perspective in order to imagine *being* the other person, and thereby sharing in *his or her* thoughts, feelings, decisions, and other aspects of their psychology" (Goldie 2011, p. 302). Goldie also considered *empathetic perspective-shifting* as a synonym of Goldman's high-level mind-reading and Stueber's reenactive empathy (Goldie 2011, p. 304).

outcome depend on who Pam is as a person, which means that her agency is fully involved in the process. How the subject sees and experiences the world, her values and priorities, her imaginative projects for the future, her past experiences, and her emotional history are not only relevant but essential aspects of the deliberative process.

While it is true that we also use cognitive empathy, especially basic empathy, to understand the trivial behaviors and decisions of others, I would argue that most of the decisions we are interested in understanding through cognitive empathy involve a strong sense of agency. When we engage in more complex and cognitively demanding empathetic processes, such as in cases of other-oriented perspective-taking, our epistemic goals are highly ambitious. For example, we try to understand why our friend or partner is angry with us, or why our biological mother gave us up for adoption. Similarly, we try to understand the reasons behind even more complex situations, such as terrible and dilemmatic decisions: why someone took their own life, or why a parent decided to withdraw medically assisted nutrition and hydration from their terminally ill daughter.

Incidentally, it is worth pointing out that the assumed pervasiveness of reconstructive or reenactive empathy should also be questioned. Both Goldman and Stueber have argued that the simulative mechanism of cognitive empathy is the "default method" of mutual understanding (Goldman 2002, p. 7; Stueber 2006, p. 19), which implies that when we need or want to understand the other person's condition, we usually engage in an explicit and conscious empathic simulation, be it other-oriented or self-oriented. However, as Gallagher points out, there is a strong phenomenological objection to this supposed ubiquity: for the most part, we do not seem to have the phenomenological experience of explicitly simulating the other's situation in general, and following the steps described by ST proponents in particular. According to him, "there is no experiential evidence that I use such conscious (imaginative, introspective) simulation routines when I interact with or come to understand another person" (Gallagher 2007, p. 356). If we do so, it is because we are confronted with peculiar cases.

Beyond this important caveat, Goldie has convincingly argued that the epistemic route of other-oriented perspective-taking cannot be successfully pursued, especially in cases as complex as those mentioned above. The core reason is that four aspects of the deliberative process involved in non-basic cases cannot be faithfully reproduced by other-oriented perspective-taking. First, as already mentioned, the characterization of the subjects involved in the empathic process cannot be perfectly replicated because it involves character traits, intellectual characteristics, and emotional dispositions that are unique to each subject. Second, there are usually irrational influences that interfere with the subject's deliberative process, such as lack of sleep or irritability. Third, the subject's potential state of confusion about his own decision affects the deliberative process. Finally, conflict or doubt is also highly influential in the subject's deliberative process.

Importantly, all of these factors have two characteristics in common: first, they strongly influence the target's deliberative process that the empathizer is trying to understand, and second, they are incredibly difficult for the empathizer to reproduce. Thus, there is a *prima facie* difficulty with this kind of perspective-taking: it seems epistemically impossible for the empathizer to reproduce all these influences because of their sheer volume and complexity, which would require a cognitive effort on the part of the empathizer that seems impossible to perform.

One could argue that their difficulty and complexity do not in themselves prove the impossibility to imaginatively reproduce them: perhaps some of us are particularly skilled and able to reproduce the other person's deliberation in all its "epistemic glory." Goldie clarified, however, that even if the empathizer were somehow able to do this, it would still be impossible for her to reproduce all of the target's unconscious influences in the same unconscious manner. In other words, the main obstacle to their reproduction is the fact that all of these aspects are unconsciously influencing the target's deliberative process and thus are unlikely to be registered by the target as reasons for her decision.[14]

In contrast, in the empathizer's imaginative process, they would be reproduced as conscious reasons for the target's decisions, i.e., as additional information that the empathizer takes into account in the imaginative act: "B's [the target's] full-blooded agency, including his characterization, becomes merely another empirical fact for A [the empathizer] to take into account in her imaginative projects. And this produces a fundamentally distorted model of B's [the target's] thinking]" (Goldie 2011, p. 309). There would be a shift in the epistemic status of some elements of the target's deliberative process and the empathizer's simulated process, compromising the accuracy of empathic understanding. This shift and the resulting bias cannot be overcome by any empathizer, regardless of cognitive ability, and is therefore a strong theoretical reason to question the epistemic feasibility of other-oriented perspective-taking.

14 In Goldie's words: "The typical role of these dispositions is passive or in the background in the sense that our conscious thoughts and feelings that feature in our deliberations are shaped by, *but are not directed towards*, these dispositions" (Goldie 2011, p. 309).

Let us consider our white lie case and assume that Pam was sleep-deprived when she decided not to tell Jim about his partner's cheating, and that Michael is able to reproduce this state when he tries to simulate Pam's deliberative process as if he were Pam. To do so, he not only has to recreate Pam's worldview, values, and general character – which is challenging, to say the least – but he also has to account for the fact that Pam is working the night shift this month and is incredibly tired. The problem is that Pam did not take her sleep deprivation into account when she made her decision, and if we were to ask her about it, she would deny that it influenced her decision. Conversely, in Michael's empathic simulation, her lack of sleep would have the same epistemic status as all the other information about Pam and her situation (e.g., Jim's emotional state, the fact that Jim's partner's cheating was not part of the reason for the divorce, Pam's past experience with adultery, and so on). As the example showed, attempts at other-oriented perspective-taking in non-base cases seem to result in misrepresenting the other's deliberative process by mystifying or limiting his or her reasons for acting or behaving in a certain way, which Goldie characterizes in terms of "usurp[ing]" the target's agency (Goldie 2011, p. 316).

Note that restricting another person's agency is problematic not only from an epistemic standpoint, but also from a moral standpoint, because it compromises a crucial feature of being a rational agent, namely that one's decisions must be the result of one's agency in the stronger sense. More precisely, "one chooses to do what one believes one has reason to do, and the capacity for this kind of choice is what makes us agents in the first place" (Wallace 1999, p. 242). In this sense, the actions of rational agents are guided by and result from, their deliberations about the reasons they have for their actions. To deny this condition is to deny other people the status of rational agents.

Precisely for this reason, usurping or limiting the target's agency deprives her of the ability to claim that her decisions are directly dependent on her deliberations, i.e., her reasons for acting in a certain way. If the empathizer – as she inevitably will – only partially acknowledges these reasons, or assign them a different epistemic role, i.e., from unconscious to conscious, she risks restricting the target's agency and thus not fully recognizing her status as a rational agent. In this sense, restricting or taking away the other person's agency is morally troubling because it can be a first step in the process of dehumanization.

I find Goldie's argument compelling, particularly because, as he explicitly asserts, it operates at a conceptual level: "Empathetic perspective-shifting is *conceptually* unable to operate with the appropriately *full-blooded notion of first-personal agency* that is involved in deliberation" (Goldie 2011, p. 303, my emphasis). In this sense, empathic perspective-shifting, i.e., other-oriented perspective-taking, is conceptually the wrong tool for understanding another person's complex deliberative processes. Moreover, empathy's problem with agency highlights how intertwined the epistemic and ethical perspectives are: limiting the other person's agency not only leads to an inaccurate understanding of her reasons for acting, but also diminishes her status as a rational agent whose decisions and actions are the result of multiple reasons situated differently in the deliberative process.

However, I am not convinced by Goldie's conclusion. According to him, we should be content with "*in-his-shoes perspective-shifting*", i.e., *self-oriented perspective-taking* (Goldie 2011, p. 302)[15] While it is true that imagining what I would do, think, or feel in the other's situation seems to protect us from the risk of usurping the target's agency, since we are simply trying to figure out what our choices or actions would be in that situation and what reasons we would give to explain and justify them, this seems to be a valid alternative only if we do not then attribute the result of our imagination to the other person, as ST theorists tell us to do, otherwise, we would risk ending up with the same result, i.e., usurping the other's agency.

Nevertheless, even leaving aside the final projection/attribution step, self-oriented perspective taking still raises some doubts about its epistemic reliability. As the impressive amount of empirical evidence compiled by Maibom attests, our imagination has several structural limitations that prevent it from being trustworthy when it comes to offline simulation (Maibom, 2016). The entire simulation process hinges on the validity of a basic assumption: that we are able to predict with some degree of confidence and accuracy what we will do, think, or feel in a situation that, in the case of empathy, is the target's situation.

This does not seem to be the case for at least two reasons. First, as noted above in the discussion of introspection, our own reasons for acting in a certain way are opaque even to ourselves: the idea that we are aware of all the reasons for our actions when we act seems more like wishful thinking than a faithful representation of reality. Self-deception is a typical example of how unreliable our own reports are: we are unable or unwilling to recognize the influence of some environmental feature on our deliberative process, when in fact it was, in part or in whole, the reason for our decision (Hippel & Trivers,

15 Goldie defined *in-his-shoes perspective-shifting* as follows: "consciously and intentionally shifting your perspective in order to imagine what thoughts, feelings, decisions, and so on you would arrive at if you were in the other's circumstances" (Goldie 2011, p. 302).

2011; Nisbett & Wilson, 1977).[16] This is not to say that we are never aware of or capable of recognizing why we act in a certain way. Rather, the point is to challenge the assumption that the reasons behind our actual deliberative process are always fully transparent and accessible to us, which in turn casts even more doubt on our ability to access the reasons behind our *imagined* deliberative process.

Second, our imaginative simulation skills do not seem to be powerful enough: they are not able to "trick our psychological system into reacting the way that it would were we actually in the situation by merely imagining being in the situation" (Maibom 2016, p. 191). This inability is due to the fact that we lose certain aspects in the imagination that are extremely relevant when we are actually in the situation: "When we are in a situation, we have information available to us through sensory perception of an extraordinary richness that is simply not capture" when we simulate offline our potential reaction to the other person's situation (Maibom 2016, p. 202). Specifically, all of the implicit memories and gut feelings that are hugely influential in our deliberations are completely absent from the empathic simulation, not because we do not need or want to include them, but because our imaginative and empathic capacities are not equipped to reproduce them. As Maibom rightly points out, if our imaginations were capable of conjuring up the implicit memories and gut feelings that we would have in the real situation, we would probably just end up reacting in real time.

In short, we seem unable to provide an epistemically accurate template of our own cognitive and emotional reactions to the target's situation because of our inherently limited empathic imagination. At best, the result of self-oriented perspective-taking is our potential reaction if such a scenario were presented to us, or, alternatively, how a typical rational agent would react to the situation. This may still be epistemically relevant information, but it is far from the desired outcome. The main selling point of cognitive empathy, espe-

16 Nisbet and Wilson famously found that "Subjects are sometimes (a) unaware of the existence of a stimulus that importantly influenced a response, (b) unaware of the existence of the response, and (c) unaware that the stimulus has affected the response. It is proposed that when people attempt to report on their cognitive processes, that is, on the processes mediating the effects of a stimulus on a response, they do not do so on the basis of any true introspection. Instead, their reports are based on a priori, implicit causal theories, or judgments about the extent to which a particular stimulus is a plausible cause of a given response" (Nisbett and Wilson 1977, p. 231). In other words, as Hippel and Trivers summed up "People have limited conscious access to the contents of their own mind and to the motives that drive their behavior. In this manner the mind circumvents the seeming paradox of being both deceiver and deceived" (Hippel and Trivers 2011, p. 6).

cially in its more complex and sophisticated manifestations of self-oriented and other-oriented perspective-taking, is its purported ability to provide us with an understanding specifically tailored to that person's state, rather than some generalized knowledge of how an idealized version of us or a generic rational agent would act.

Note that there is a persistent tension between cognitive empathy's aspiration to understand the specific situation of a particular person and the empathizer's inherently limited resources, which in turn force her to resort to generalizations (such as stereotypes or prejudices, usually modulated by group membership) or imprecise and difficult attempts at introspection. To be clear, I am not suggesting that cognitive empathy has no epistemic contribution to make to our social cognitive endeavors and our interpersonal lives. My point is that it is not sufficiently accurate to be the default source of our reasons for our other-directed deliberations, especially if we want these deliberative processes to be epistemically faithful to the other person's state and respectful of the other person's agency.

CHAPTER 5

Issues with Affective Empathy and Its Role in Motivation and Moral Judgments

In this chapter, I want to challenge the assumption that empathy, especially affective empathy, is the best source of moral motivation and moral judgment. Simply put, the problem with affective empathy – as well as cognitive empathy (see Chapter 4) – is that it seems to engage in some sort of selection process about whom to help and whose actions to approve or disapprove of.

In particular, I will first enumerate empathy's affective biases in recognizing, understanding, and sharing others' emotions, and I will show that the selective and partial nature caused by these inherent biases has a direct impact on the motivational grounds that empathy provides for other-directed practical deliberation. As a result, empathy may be responsible for motivating immoral actions. Second, I will challenge the claim that affective empathy is the best available basis for approval and disapproval, and ultimately for moral judgments, because relying solely on empathy runs the risk of potentially misjudging the moral status of others' actions.

I intend to approach the discussion from three perspectives: the conceptual dimension, the empirical dimension, and finally the normative dimension. As mentioned in the previous chapter (see Chapter 4), my approach to empirical evidence will be non-reductionist. Finally, I will mostly deal with a sentimentalist framework, since empathy-based theories of moral motivation and moral judgment tend to belong to this tradition. This does not mean, however, that my critique is aimed at sentimentalism tout court: my sole focus is on the role of empathy in moral other-directed deliberation, not on the role of emotional states. Indeed, some of the most effective critiques of empathy's role in moral motivation and judgment have come from non-empathy-based sentimentalist accounts. Empathy, not emotions, seems to be the problem.

1 Affective Biases and Partiality in Affective Empathy and Moral Motivation

Accounts that assign both cognitive and affective empathy a role in moral motivation all share the same starting point: the agent must either *recognize* and *understand* (cognitive empathy) or *perceive* and *share* (affective empathy)

 | HTTPS://DOI.ORG/10.1163/9789004745360-007

the other person's emotional state. Some have argued that cognitive empathy is central to motivating the agent to act altruistically because it allows her to recognize that the other person is suffering or in distress. In this sense, Shaun Nichols argued that "altruistic motivation depends on the minimal mindreading capacity to attribute negative affective or hedonic states to others" (Nichols 2001, p. 436). According to him, this claim is able to explain two empirically proven phenomena related to our altruistic behavior: on one hand, people help others in need even when there is an easy way to escape the situation (Batson, 2011), and on the other hand, young children (1 and 2 years old) show comforting behavior after attributing pain and distress states to others (Wellman et al., 1995; Zahn-Waxler et al., 1992). In contrast, emotional contagion does not explain why people choose to help rather than leave and make their vicarious pain disappear when it is easy to do so. Similarly, more complex forms of mindreading, such as perspective-taking, are not yet developed in young children and therefore cannot explain their altruistic behavior.

Thus, basic empathy, the minimal form of mindreading that leads to the attribution of affective states to others, is responsible for triggering what Nichols calls the "Concern Mechanism": "The distress attribution might produce a kind of second-order empathic distress in the subject. For example, representing the sorrow of the target might lead one to feel sorrow" (Nichols 2001, p. 445–446). In Nichols's view, basic empathy produces affective empathy (emotional sharing), which in turn motivates the agent to act altruistically, even when it is easy to escape, because it produces "an enduring mental representation" that emotional contagion cannot provide, and it is also compatible with the cognitive and affective abilities of young children (Nichols 2001, p. 435).

In partial disagreement with Nichols, Batson argued on the basis of his experiments that more sophisticated forms of perspective-taking (such as reconstructive or reenactive empathy) are useful when it comes to altruistic and moral motivation: in asymmetric scenarios, that is, when the agent is in a position of clear advantage, imagining oneself in the other person's situation can motivate moral action (Batson et al., 2003, p. 1200). Importantly, the same type of imaginative perspective-taking seems to have the opposite effect in a symmetrical situation: "When each is in the same initial situation, imagining oneself in the other's place may lead one to focus on one's one interests, not the other's" (Batson et al., 2003, p. 1196).

Note that Batson's account seems much more conservative than Nichols's in that it does not attempt to prove that perspective-taking is the primary or most basic cause of all altruistic and/or moral actions. After all, as already discussed, Batson's famous empathy-altruism hypothesis establishes a causal link between empathic concern, what I called sympathy in the SD of empathy, and altruism (see Chapter 1). Accordingly, perspective-taking is only one of the possible ways to elicit empathic concern for the welfare of others, which is truly responsible for our altruistic motivation. More generally, for empathic concern to occur, the agent must perceive the other's affective and cognitive state, which, depending on its valence (positive or negative), will lead to an evaluation of the other's welfare.[1]

It is worth noting that in Batson's experiments, subjects are *instructed to* perform a perspective-taking task before deciding how to act toward the target, rather than simply witnessing the target's state and spontaneously engaging in perspective-taking. Instead, in real-life scenarios, we must voluntarily choose to take another's perspective and engage in reconstructive or reenactive empathy. For this reason, outside of the experimental context, the extent of the role of perspective-taking in our moral other-directed deliberations seems somewhat harder to demonstrate (see Chapter 6).

Consistent with Batson's approach, Baron-Cohen's account also requires the empathizer to recognize the other's cognitive and affective states in order to respond appropriately, which, in the case of the other's distress or pain, implies altruistic, pro-social, or moral actions (Baron-Cohen 2011; see Chapter 3). Again, it is the recognition – however, achieved – of the other's affective and/or cognitive states that drives the agent's motivations to act. Finally, according to Slote, only when the agent empathically shares the other's pain will she be motivated to alleviate that pain, because when someone is distressed, they are automatically motivated to make it go away because "that's just what distress *means*" (Slote 2016, p. 15). Thus, not only does affective sharing of another's emotional state occur automatically, but when this vicarious distress is experienced, the subject experiencing it should also be automatically motivated to alleviate it.

First, I am not sure that distress *necessarily* implies the need to alleviate it. On one hand, on a conceptual level, it seems possible to define distress independently of the desire to alleviate it: distress is a psychophysical state with specific characteristics and affective quality, while the need or desire to alleviate it is a distinct, though related, impulse to act in a certain way. On the other hand, this does not seem to be true from an experiential point of view either: there are instances in our everyday lives when we consciously choose to remain in a distressing state. For example, when something tragic happens

1 Specifically, participants in the perspective-taking conditions, were instructed to practice self-oriented perspective-taking: "In this exercise, we would like for you to *imagine yourself in the place of the other participant*") and other-oriented perspective-taking ("In this exercise, we would like for you to *imagine how the other participant likely feels*" (Batson et al., 2003, p. 1193).

to us, such as the loss of a loved one, it is psychologically common, if not healthy, to feel the pain of that event and not want to move on immediately. It therefore seems possible, both conceptually and on the basis of our everyday experience, to make a clear distinction between distress and the desire to alleviate it: the presence of the former does not automatically or necessarily imply the presence of the latter.

The same seems to be true for vicariously experienced distress: sharing another person's distress is conceptually distinct from wanting to alleviate it. I can imagine being emotionally infected by someone else's distress, but having no intention of alleviating it. For example, I can share the players' distress at losing the final game of the World Cup without having any impulse or intention to alleviate it. Thus, it is possible, from a conceptual point of view, to separate the two phenomena, i.e., shared distress and the need to alleviate it, without assuming a necessary causality between them.

This seems to be supported by empirical findings. For example, it is well established that the presence of other people in a dangerous situation reduces the likelihood that the individual will help (in this specific case, report the emergency). Importantly, in Farley and Latane's seminal experiment on the bystander effect, none of the bystanders who did not help the victim were "apathetic," but rather they "seemed more emotionally aroused than did the subjects who reported the emergency" (Darley and Latane 1968, p. 382). Thus, not only do they recognize the other's distress (basic empathy), but they also share that distress (affective empathy).

While the experiment suggests that the perceived level of danger increases arousal and thus willingness to help, it also shows that when other people are present, the agent's willingness to help is still lower than when she is alone, despite an increased level of arousal. This seems to prove that even in overtly dangerous situations, experiencing the victim's distress *alone* is not sufficient to motivate the subject to help her (Fischer et al., 2011). Moreover, the bystander effect seems to support the idea that experiencing the other's distress does not automatically guarantee that the empathizer will have the desire to alleviate it and that he or she will concretely help the victim, otherwise, the presence of other people will not modulate the helping response. In other words, while it is possible that on some or even many occasions vicariously experiencing another person's distress will lead to a desire to alleviate it, there is neither a necessary nor a sufficient correlation between the two.

If this is true, one might argue that empathy is only necessary to motivate supererogatory actions. In this regard, Maibom effectively argued that empathic understanding of what others are thinking and feeling has been shown to motivate helping behaviors that go beyond basic moral norms and to improve our interpersonal relationships by enhancing our social skills (Maibom, 2010).[2] In contrast, cognitive empathy does not seem to play a significant role in our motivation to follow basic moral norms such as not harming others, not lying, not stealing, and so on. People with autism seem to confirm this intuition, since some of them are characteristically unable (or find it very difficult) to take the perspective of others. However, their motivation to follow basic moral norms is unaffected by this lack of cognitive empathy (Kennett, 2002).

Relatedly, it seems too demanding, both cognitively and affectively, to claim that in order to act morally the agent must always enter into an empathic relationship, especially in terms of emotional sharing, with the targets of her actions, especially given the amount of pain and suffering we are exposed to in our globalized societies. Constant and unfiltered exposure to the plight of others can have the opposite effect: the suffering of others can be so overwhelming that the empathizer is motivated to alleviate her own distress by withdrawing from the situation and failing to help the victims. This happens not only by being physically present in these situations (e.g., first responders after a natural disaster) but also by viewing videos and photos of these events that are now available in ways never before possible (Kaplan, 2011).

When suffering is experienced on a daily basis, empathizers may experience burnout or compassion fatigue, one of the many problematic consequences of which is a reduction or suppression of motivation to engage with the source of pain. This is very common among health care workers who are consistently exposed to physical and psychological distress (Lamothe et al., 2014). Requiring them to be empathetic because empathy is the only or most effective moral or altruistic motive available to them, especially in terms of affective sharing, with every patient seems unsustainable and potentially dangerous. Even with cognitive regulation, "it is important to note that a modicum of negative arousal is necessary to help physicians attune to and empathically understand patients 'emotions'" (Gleichgerrcht and Decety 2013, p. 11). Thus, it seems that a certain amount of emotional fatigue is inevitable for the person, in this case the physician, who wants or needs to be empathic in the sense of sharing the other's emotional state as a precursor to sympathy.

So far, I have raised some doubts about the claim that affective and cognitive empathy are necessary and/or sufficient to motivate our altruistic and/or moral response, especially when the other person is suffering. Further doubts about empathy's ability to motivate altruistic and/or moral action

2 Maibom defines supererogatory norms as those "norms the living up to which is more praiseworthy than obligatory" (Maibom 2010, p. 35).

are raised by our own common experience as moral agents: we do not empathize with everyone in the same way, or in some cases at all. When something happens to someone, we see as similar to ourselves, we feel their emotions more, we want to and do understand them better, we worry more, we care more, and ultimately we are more likely to help them. This seems to be confirmed by the impressive body of empirical evidence attesting to the biases of cognitive and affective empathy in recognizing, understanding, and sharing emotions.[3] These biases and their implications for our empathic responses, I will argue, should make us wary of claims that identify empathy as the sole or most effective source of motivating reasons in other-directed deliberation.

In a nutshell, empathy seems to have the same problems, if not more, with emotional states as it does with mental states: it is very much influenced by group membership. This seems particularly true when it comes to *emotion recognition*, which is one of the desired outcomes of basic empathy: "Perceivers are faster and more accurate at recognizing [faces of] members of an in-group as compared to members of out-groups," meaning that in-group emotional expressions are more recognizable than out-group expressions (Echols and Correll 2011, p. 57). This, in turn, directly affects the level of motivation perceivers have to engage in basic and reenactive empathy.

Sadly, but not surprisingly, race appears to be the more powerful factor in modulating emotion recognition. In this regard, Michel et al. showed that "SR [same race] faces are perceived more holistically than OR [other race] faces" (Michel et al., 2006, p. 612). Holistic perception is more accurate than processing only parts of the face, which happens to be the default method for faces of members of other races. In addition to and consistent with the evidence discussed in the previous chapter (see Chapter 4), Chiao and colleagues found that "cultural group membership of both the expressor and perceiver of the fear signal modulates the magnitude of the response within the limbic region" (Chiao et al., 2008, p. 2171). Specifically, perceivers showed greater activation in the amygdala when viewing in-group (same race) expressions of fear than when viewing out-group expressions of fear, resulting in faster and more accurate recognition of their emotional state.

This result is particularly relevant because fear is one of the mental states, along with distress, grief, and sorrow, whose recognition and representation Nichols believes is capable of producing altruistic motivation (Nichols 2001, p. 436). It is easy to see where the problem lies: if the empathic agent does not

3 I follow Echols and Correll's categorization of emotion recognition, affective arousal, and emotion understanding (Echols & Correll, 2011).

recognize that an out-group member (e.g., a person of a different race) is experiencing fear, then no lasting representation of that fear will arise, and thus no altruistic motivation. Again, the problem is the desire to identify only one possible source of altruistic motivation, in this case basic empathy, which inevitably makes it impossible to ignore its limitations, since it must be able to operate in any situation in which altruism is required.

More complex forms of *emotional understanding*, such as those obtained through reconstructive or reenactive empathy, do not appear to be less prone to bias. For example, subjects tend to attribute secondary emotions, i.e., more complex emotional states that only humans experience, such as grief, anguish, and remorse, only to in-group members and not to out-groups, to whom they attribute only primary emotions. Notably, most of the mental states that Nichols enumerated as causes of altruism when empathically recognized can be classified as secondary emotions, which seem to be difficult to capture even with more complex empathic tools when it comes to out-group individuals.

According to one study, in the context of Hurricane Katrina, Caucasians subjects attributed fewer secondary emotions to African American victims than to Caucasians victims (Cuddy et al., 2007). This is because, as said (see Chapter 4) when we ascribe emotional states to in-groups, we typically use projection since we view them as similar and thus capable of both primary and secondary emotions. Conversely, when attributing emotional states to out-group members, we use stereotypical inferences, reflecting the underlying assumption that people who are different from us are not as complex as we are and, ultimately, not as human as we are. Identifying others as out-groups and consequently denying them full human status is a phenomenon known as "infrahumanization," which involves attributing fuller mental and emotional capacities only to those recognized as members of the in-group (Leyens et al., 2003; 2000). More alarmingly, the dehumanizing attitudes fostered by this lack of attribution of secondary emotions were directly related to a decrease in helping behavior toward out-group members (Cuddy et al., 2007).

Another group of empirical studies of particular interest is related to the study of how we respond to the pain of others. Studying our cognitive and affective responses to another person's pain yields incredibly revealing results for at least two reasons. First, from a methodological standpoint, the neural mechanisms underlying first-person experience of pain are well understood, and these same mechanisms have been shown to be activated when we witness or imagine someone else in pain (Decety & Jackson 2004; Price 2000). Moreover, measuring subjects' responses to perceived and imagined pain allows researchers to test for the influence of various interpersonal factors, such as how the characteristics of the target in pain modulate the observer's response. Second, from a conceptual perspective, physical or psychological pain is probably the most basic sign that a human being (but also non-human animals) needs help. Mapping how well, under what circumstances, and why we cognitively and affectively understand (or do not understand) this condition in others has remarkable implications for our altruistic and moral motivation.

As expected, empathic understanding of pain seems also to be modulated by group membership. In a functional magnetic resonance imaging (fMRI) study, Cheng and colleagues showed that "adopting the perspective of a Loved-one elicited greater activation in regions that belong to the pain matrix than adopting the perspective of a Stranger" (Cheng et al., 2010, p. 927). This confirms one of the most common experiences we have in our daily lives: we are better able to recognize the painful condition of someone we love than that of a stranger. Thus, if we accept Nichols and Batson's central ideas it seems that we will be more motivated to help and care for in-group members (same race, same sex, same age, loved ones, etc.) because we will be able to recognize their internal states better than those of out-group members.

While it would be wrong to claim that we are completely incapable of recognizing the emotional states of out-group members, especially negative ones, such as pain, it seems reasonable, and supported by empirical evidence, to claim that we must overcome some obstacles to achieve these results when it comes to the condition of out-group members, with no guarantee that we will be able to do so. In turn, this difficulty may increase the likelihood that we will help these people less if our motivation to help them depends directly on our empathic abilities. Thus cognitive empathy, whether basic or reenactive, appears to be a potentially unfair and immoral motivational guide to action.

What about affective empathy? When it comes to emotions, one could argue that we should rely on our affective skills and resources, specifically our ability to affectively resonate with or share the emotional states of others, as opposed to our ability to recognize and understand the other's state, which brings us back to Slote. However, this does not seem to solve the problems, since affective arousal, affective sharing, and affective empathy in general seem also inherently susceptible to biases of various kinds (de Vignemont & Singer, 2006).

The empathizers' *affective arousal* seems to be modulated by group membership. Specifically, studies show increased brain activation in areas related to pain when empathizers viewed members of their own race compared to members of another race. For example, Xu and colleagues found that, during fMRI scanning, "the empathic neural responses in the ACC [anterior cingulate cortex] decreased significantly" when Caucasian subjects observed Chinese faces being pierced by a needle compared to Caucasian faces receiving the same painful stimulus (Xu et al., 2009, p. 8525). The same result was found when Chinese empathizers viewed Caucasian faces in pain. Thus, same-race faces in pain elicited more affective arousal than different-race faces in pain.

Interestingly, the influence of racial categorization on emotional sharing appears to be at work even when observing other body parts, such as hands, receiving painful stimuli. In a study by Avenanti et al., sensorimotor contagion was higher for members of the same race (participants were white and black). In addition, the researchers also found "clear sensorimotor contagion (…) in response to the pain of stranger, very unfamiliar but not culturally grouped, individuals (violet models)" (Avenanti, Sirigu, and Aglioti 2010, p. 1021). The presence of sensorimotor contagion when observing a purple hand (a hand that was perceived as different but not of a particular race) and its absence when observing a culturally grouped hand (either black or white) is evidence of the influence of implicit and explicit racial biases (stereotypes and prejudices) on the ability to empathically share the pain of others. While dissimilarity was not sufficient to prevent sensorimotor contagion, racial biases appeared to be the core cause of the lack of sensorimotor contagion.

Moreover, the degree to which we share the emotions of others varies according to our "a priori attitudes toward the target group" (Echols and Correll 2011, p. 59). Again, this is particularly evident when observing the variation in affective arousal in response to others' expressions of pain. A priori attitudes such as judging the target's behavior toward the empathizer as fair or unfair (Singer et al., 2006) or attributing the cause of the target's pain to the target's behavior, e.g., blaming an AIDS patient for her disease (Decety et al., 2010), combined with other situational factors, such as the intensity of the pain or whether the pain is the result of treatment (Hein & Singer, 2008), modulate the degree to which empathizers share the target's painful state. As to be expected, the perceived fairness of the target increases affective sharing, whereas blaming the target for the cause of her pain or the therapeutic nature of the pain decreases affective arousal.

Cuteness is also a situational factor that can modulate affective sharing: the perceived cuteness of the target can increase or decrease how much and how deeply we share his or her feelings. Interestingly, this is also true for nonhuman animals: we tend to feel more affective empathy for animals we perceive as cute and more charismatic, such as mammals (Hayward et al., 2019). One of the reasons for this bias is that mammals, especially large ones, are more similar to us, which in a way confirms the pervasiveness of group membership modulation (Griffin et al., 2020).[4] The cuteness effect also appears to influence cognitive empathy. The physical attractiveness of the target has been shown to influence empathic accuracy (see Chapter 4): when the empathizer finds the target attractive, he or she increases attention and improves the ability to recognize and understand the other person's internal states, including pain or distress (Ickes et al., 1990; Ta & Ickes, 2017).

Another interesting modulating factor is the number of targets that affective empathy can "handle." When there is more than one target, especially when people are expected to help, experimental results have shown that agents down-regulate their emotional arousal, which in turn leads to lower motivation to help the people in need (Cameron & Payne, 2011). These findings are consistent with the well-known "identifiable victim effect," according to which identifiable victims "produce a greater empathic response, accompanied by a greater willingness to make personal sacrifices to provide aid" than statistical victims, i.e., a larger number of unidentifiable victims" (Jenni and Loewenstein 1997, p. 236). Needless to say, the smaller the number of victims, the easier it is for the empathizer to be emotionally aroused by them and be motivated to help them. This is problematic in larger-scale tragedies where it is difficult or impossible to identify large numbers of victims.

Finally, spatial and temporal proximities critically affect affective empathy. Hoffman called this phenomenon the "here and now bias" and argued that "because most empathy-arousing processes (at least the primitive, less cognitive ones) depend on immediate situational and personal cues, people are vulnerable to empathic bias in favor of victims who are present in the immediate situation" (Hoffman 2000, p. 197). In this respect, spatial proximity may explain a fairly common behavior that Hume recognized in his work on sympathy (Hume, 1739), i.e., we tend to care significantly more about the fate of people who are from our neighborhood, our city, and our country, even though we do not have a personal relationship with them. Similarly, temporal proximity seems to explain why it is so difficult, if not impossible, to share the

4 I have previously examined the limitations of cognitive and affective empathy (outlined in Chapters 4 and 5) in the context of moral motivation for environmental action. Specifically, I argued that both cognitive and affective empathy are too constrained in scope to effectively drive environmental behavior on a global scale. Consistent with the argument developed here in Part 3, I also proposed that phenomenological empathy – while lacking motivational capacity – functions as an epistemic tool for partially understanding other beings and the natural world. In this role, phenomenological empathy serves as a prerequisite for environmental engagement in epistemological terms alone, rather than as a motivational force (Stefanello, 2024a).

emotional states of future generations, people not yet born, regarding the catastrophic effects of the climate emergency.

Taken together, the evidence suggests that "[affective and cognitive] empathy is neither universal nor an automatic response" (Zaki and Cikara 2015, p. 471).[5] And yet, the more persistent proponent of empathy might argue that the biases of empathy alone do not prove that empathy cannot successfully be the sole or primary source for motivating altruistic and benevolent actions. For this claim to be true, one would still have to prove that recognizing, understanding, and sharing the emotions and mental states of in-group members (or those perceived as fair, cute, innocent, etc.) more deeply and better than those of out-group members leads to altruistic and benevolent actions that are directed only at that limited group of people, and thus cannot be the only or primary motivating reasons for our altruistic and moral actions in general.

From a conceptual standpoint, this is fairly straightforward: if our altruistic, benevolent, or moral actions are primarily or even exclusively motivated by affective sharing or by recognizing and understanding the other's emotional state, and if these sharing, recognizing, and understanding are strongly modulated by all sorts of biases, prejudices, stereotypes, situational contexts, individual factors, and so on, then our motivation will be equally biased and selective. Specifically, on one hand, it seems that empathy can be the source of motivating reasons for acting altruistically and/or morally *exclusively* toward those perceived as in-group members. On the other hand, empathy seems to motivate selfish and/or malevolent and immoral actions especially toward those perceived as out-group members. These, however, are two separate claims that deserve separate arguments.

Empirical evidence appears to support the first claim. For example, in one study, soccer fans showed an increase in anterior insula activation when observing fans of their own team in pain compared to fans of the opposing team. Most importantly, the difference in activation was also a predictor of empathic concern and motivation to reduce the other person's pain by enduring it oneself. Specifically, when observing fans of the opposing team in pain, activation of the nucleus accumbens was observed, which in turn predicted a decrease in motivation to help them (Hein et al., 2010). As Hein and colleagues pointed out, this study seems to prove that "the decision to help may not only

5 Note that "universal" here means that we can empathize with anyone, not that empathy is a universal characteristic of being human. According to the empirical studies presented here, the former does not seem to be true, while the latter is much more plausible. In this sense, following the phenomenological perspective, I will argue that empathy, as defined within this perspective, is an experience that we all have as human beings.

be determined by perceived group membership; it might also be influenced by the potential helper's attitude toward the in-group or out-group member" (Hein et al., 2010, p. 155). In this case, the target's soccer affiliation was sufficient to determine the empathizer's positive or negative attitude toward him or her.

Similarly, the perceived cuteness of the care receiver appears to influence not only the degree to which the caregiver shares the care receiver's pain, but also the level and quality of care. As Sherman and colleagues found, "prosocially oriented women responded to the subtle manipulation of cuteness (images of infants morphed to be more or less cute) with increased physical carefulness, as revealed by increased manual precision in a cursor tracing task" (Sherman et al., 2013, p. 155).[6] The cuter the target of empathy, the more motivated the empathizer will be, and the better the target will be cared for. The same goes for cognitive empathy: as shown above in the case of African American and Caucasian victims of Hurricane Katrina, better recognition and understanding of others' emotional states and internal conditions will lead to greater motivation to help them (Cuddy et al., 2007). Again, the problem is that our ability to recognize and understand the targets' internal states is modulated by both individual and situational factors, of which group membership is the most influential.

The second claim about empathy's ability to motivate immorality because of its narrow focus only on its target also appears to have empirical support. For example, as Batson and colleagues famously showed, in resource allocation situations, when instructed to empathize with the target, subjects "forsake justice in the interest of benefiting the person whom they felt empathy, even though they perceived doing so to be less moral and even though they knew this person's need was not as great as the need of others" (Batson et al., 1995, p. 1052).[7] The implications of these findings are quite significant: "Empathy-

6 Interestingly, the cuteness effect seems to be a determining factor only for women. This result is not as surprising as it might seem at first glance: "This finding makes sense, however, given that women have been shown to be highly sensitive to care-related cues (…) and are generally more responsive than men to children (…). It is possible that alternative care-related cues might work better in men. It is also possible that something unique to females (e.g., higher prenatal or circulating levels of female reproductive hormones) may be necessary to demonstrate this effect. Future research is needed to identify this critical gender-related factor" (Sherman et al. 2013, p. 156).

7 The concept of empathy adopted in the experiments is a combination of both cognitive and affective empathy. Subjects in the high-empathy condition were instructed to "*imagine how this student feels* about what is described. Try to imagine how it has affected his or her life and how he or she feels as a result" (First Experiment) (Batson et al., 1995, p. 1044) and "*imagine how the child who is interviewed feels about what has happened and how it has*

induced altruism and justice are two independent prosocial motives" and when they conflict, typically in the allocation of limited resources, empathy-based motivation can override justice-based motivation, leading to unfair actions (Batson et al., 1995, p. 1051), such as prioritizing helping someone just because they are the target of empathy while ignoring more deserving people who do not elicit empathy.

Decety and Yoder also support the idea that empathy and justice are two distinct motives: "The emotional fact of empathy (…) was not significantly correlated with justice either for oneself or for the other" and, thus, being empathetic does not seem to assure that the agent will act fairly (Decety & Yoder, 2016). Therefore, if empathy provides motivating reasons for our other-directed deliberative processes, there is no guarantee that we will end up acting morally. We may act altruistically, that is, we may increase the welfare of a particular individual, i.e., the target of our empathy, rather than our own. But this does not mean that we are acting morally, or more precisely, fairly. In the words of Paul Bloom, "empathy is a spotlight focusing on certain people in the here and now. This makes us care more about them, but it leaves us insensitive to the long-term consequences of our acts and blind as well to the sufferings of those we do not or cannot empathize with" (Bloom 2016, p. 9).

Recall that Slote considers empathy "the morally best of human motives" not in spite of its biases, but because of them (Slote 2005, p. 228; see also Chapter 3).[8] He claims that these biases, which he (conveniently) calls "preferences," are "morally justified" because they reflect moral distinctions that fit our intuitions. For example, our greater empathy for those close to us explains why it is permissible to prefer family to strangers. Indeed, "the same empathy that leads us to certain preferences or choices as agents also governs our empathic reactions of chill and warmth as spectators or contemplators of what (other) agents do" and this is because, following Kripke, he suggests that empathic approval/disapproval fixes the reference of moral concepts such as morally good or bad to non-subjective a priori moral properties, namely "our capacity for empathically feeling or reflecting what others (and, in particular, agents) feel," just as

---

affected this child's life. Try to feel the full impact of what this child has been through and how he or she feels as a result" (Second Experiment) (Batson et al., 1995, p. 1048).

8 Slote's claim about the monopoly of empathy when it comes to moral motivation depends directly on a qualitative claim. Moreover, contrary to Batson, Slote believes that morality is strongly linked to altruism: "It is a priori, I think, that morality depends on altruism, and I shall be arguing that anyone well acquainted with empathy in their own case and that of others can also see a priori that altruism and morality involve empathy" (Slote 2004, p. 18, footnote 6).

sensory experience fixes the reference of color concepts (Slote, 2010, pp. 62–64).

I find the assumption that empathic motives necessarily reflect our moral intuitions rather puzzling. Sure, being more empathically motivated to save your own child than a stranger in a burning building seems both morally justifiable and perfectly in line with our intuitive response. Conversely, if you are the head of an organ transplant committee, it is neither morally justifiable nor in line with our *moral* intuition to be empathically motivated to give your dying sister a life-saving organ transplant over another patient in her condition simply because she is your sister and her suffering will elicit an immensely stronger empathic response. Of course, we would want to choose our sister, but I think we would also intuitively recognize that this is not the moral thing to do. In other words, there are cases, some of which we explored above, in which empathic motivation can lead the agent to act immorally (e.g., to unfairly favor your relative or to discriminate against out-group members), and these actions violate some of our commonsense moral intuitions, such as that fairness is important in the allocation of limited resources or that all people are equal despite differences in race, gender, age, sexual orientation, and so on.

There is another more general point to be made about the connection between empathic motivation and immorality. In some circumstances, it is the *presence* of empathy, rather than its absence, that makes immoral actions possible. As Donise points out, this challenges Baron-Cohen's idea that it is the erosion of empathy that causes immorality (Donise, 2019). For example, people with psychopathological traits seem to be extremely skilled perspective takers: they use the information gathered through cognitive empathy to figure out how to better hurt, punish, and deceive their victims (Kennett, 2017; Marsh, 2014). Beyond the pathological realm, we all sometimes use cognitive empathy to achieve our own not-so-noble ends. When we are angry, we sometimes say things that we know will hurt the other person, and the ability to take the perspective of the target of our anger is crucial to understanding what that thing might be. Similarly, contrary to Slote's argument, affective empathy can also motivate immoral behavior, or at least does not always guarantee morality. Consider sadists: they do what they do precisely because they are able to, and indeed enjoy, feeling the other's pain, which, again *contra* Slote, suggests that vicarious suffering does not always lead to a desire to alleviate it.[9]

---

9 This point was famously and convincingly argued by Max Scheler (Scheler, 1913; see Chapter 8).

At the very least, everything discussed so far seems to weaken both the motivational monopoly and the normative claim about empathy: does empathy alone guarantee moral motivation, and should a phenomenon with these limitations provide normative and motivational grounds for our moral deliberative processes? I am inclined to say no. Empathy seems suspiciously "compatible" with actions that we would generally consider to range from problematic to downright immoral (Prinz 2011b, p. 221). As a matter of fact, *pace* Nichols, Baron-Cohen, and Slote, in some cases, when cognitive or affective empathy provides the motivating reasons for our other-directed deliberative process, we may end up committing immoral acts.

To be sure, I am not denying that empathy *sometimes* motivates moral action (Song 2015). This moderate version of the argument is surely more palatable, even to those who are skeptical of empathy, and manages to avoid some of the critiques of the motivational monopoly claim. At the same time, however, this way of framing the argument is far less powerful and, in the end, perhaps not worth all the attention that empathy has received in the literature. If the best we can grant empathy is that it "is *sometimes* epistemologically necessary for identifying the right action, that empathy is *sometimes* psychologically necessary for motivating the agent to perform the right action, and that empathy is *sometimes* necessary for the agent to be most morally praiseworthy for an action," then its role in moral motivation and morality, in general, is far less relevant (and interesting) than it might seem at a first glance (Masto 2015, p. 74, my emphasis).

I would argue, however, that the same is not true of the claim that empathy can sometimes motivate immoral actions. This is because avoiding immorality seems to take precedence over promoting morality, which can be justified if we accept that there is a deontic asymmetry between good and bad. Heyd articulated this asymmetry in the context of supererogation and suberogation: "(...) The good is open-ended in a way that the bad is not. The extremely good cannot be required, but the extremely bad (vicious) is the prime target of prohibition" (Heyd, 2019).[10] I think this applies to morally bad and good actions as well: in contrast to morally good actions, morally bad ones are not only less open-ended but, most importantly, must be the primary target of prohibition.[11] Although I cannot fully justify the asymmetry between good and bad here,

10 I am grateful to Simone Grigoletto for pointing out Heyd's reference.

11 Another way to frame this asymmetry is to refer to the Kantian distinction between perfect and imperfect duties. Perfect duties are moral rules that are absolute, unbending, and hold in all circumstances (e.g., do not harm others). The violation of a perfect duty is always morally impermissible because it always results in morally bad actions. Imperfect duties are less strict moral duties that allow some flexibility in how and when they are

my point is simply that we are and should be more concerned with potential sources of immorality than with potential sources of morality, which means that the attention to the potential immorality of empathy should trump the attention to the potential morality of empathy.

2 The Problematic Role of Affective Empathy in Moral Judgments

Accounts of moral judgment that rely on empathy share the same assumption as those that defend empathy-based moral motivation: in order to morally judge another person's action, the subject must either empathize with the other person's motive (affective empathy) or imaginatively adopt the other person's perspective in order to understand the other person's emotional response and action (a combination of affective and cognitive empathy). An example of the first type of account is (again) Slote's proposal. As noted (see Chapter 3), he argued that it is the feeling of warmth or chill generated by agential empathy (second-order empathy with the presence or absence with the first-order empathic concern of the agent) that constitutes approval or disapproval and, ultimately, the judgment of right and wrong.

Three aspects make this proposal particularly problematic. First, as Stueber has pointed out, the causal mechanism by which the empathic concern (or lack thereof) in the other person's motive is able to produce a feeling of warmth (or cold) in the observer (and future judge) of the action seems somewhat puzzling (Stueber, 2011). On one hand, since this is supposed to be an empirical claim, there is a problematic lack of empirical evidence supporting the existence and inner workings of this mechanism. In short, it is one thing to say that these feelings of warmth and cold are the result of agential empathy, and quite another to prove it empirically.

On the other hand, the introspective argument that Slote offers to justify this mechanism is not as straightforward as it might seem (Stueber, 2011). For introspective claims to have any normative weight – assuming that they can have it – they should meet, at least, some criteria. In particular, I adopt Horgan and Timmons's characterization of introspective judgments according to which "insofar as (i) one's own pertinent introspective phenomenological judgments arise from one's vivid experiential seemings, and (ii) such judgments are *widely shared by others in one's cultural milieu*, it is simpler to suppose that they arise in others similarly to how they arise in oneself – unless

fulfilled (e.g., duties of beneficence) as their violation does not necessarily result in immoral actions (Kant, 1785).

there is good reason to posit a trans-personal difference" (Horgan and Timmons 2022, p. 6, my emphasis).

In Slote's case, there seems to be good reason to argue that his introspective phenomenological judgment about the warmth-chill mechanism, to use Horgan and Timmons' terminology, is not as widely shared as he assumes. If this is true, then Slote's mechanism does not meet the second criterion and therefore cannot be automatically assumed to be present in others.

Let us start with *my* personal introspective experience: approval and disapproval are not always derived from a feeling of warmth and chill. Conversely, other feelings cause and accompany approval and disapproval and, ultimately, moral judgments. Consider, for example, the feeling of admiration. I often morally approve of actions because I feel admiration for them: I admire Martin Luther King's (MLK) courage and sense of justice in speaking out against segregation and racial discrimination, so I approve of his actions, and I judge those actions to be morally right.

I have reason to believe that I am not alone in relying on other emotional resources to guide approval and disapproval. Linda Zagzebski, for example, has famously argued for the centrality of admiration in her exemplarist moral theory, which is phenomenologically and qualitatively distinct from the feeling of warmth (Zagzebski, 2017). While it is true that admiration can sometimes present itself as a positive and uplifting feeling close to empathy-induced warmth, it is also true that admiration can consist of a painful feeling that arises when the admirer realizes how deficient he or she is in comparison to the admired person (Zagzebski, 2015). In spite of this painful feeling, the admiration and the resulting positive judgment of the admired person's actions are still present, which, according to Slote's thesis, should not be possible.[12] In other words, my admiration-based moral approval, which can manifest as either a positive or negative feeling, and my resulting moral judgment of MLK's actions are no less legitimate than those based on empathy.

A similar point can be made about disapproval: moral agents' disapproval seems to be triggered by a number of different emotions, not just by being chilled by the agent's lack of empathy. Anger tends to be a prominent emotion when it comes to moral disapproval. As D'Arms noted, "hot forms of blame from the anger family (indignation, resentment, and outrage are some familiar variants) seem to have as much claim to the name 'moral disapproval' as the

12 Note that Zagzebski clarified that in order for admiration to ground a judgment of admirability, the subject has to trust "the emotion [of admiration] upon reflection" (Zagzebski 2015, p. 209). In this sense, compared to Slote, Zagzebski implemented a corrective mechanism for the subject's emotional responses. I will return to this aspect at the end of this chapter.

chilly feelings that Slote foregrounds and seem, in any case, to be at least as prominent a species of moral reaction" (D'Arms 2011, p. 138).[13] This is entirely consistent with my personal introspective experience of moral disapproval: I feel profound outrage when I hear that yet another woman has been killed by her obsessive and stalking partner. I am not left cold by the killer's lack of empathic concern for his victim, I am angry at his behavior and at a society that has long been complacent about it. It is this anger, not the supposed feeling of coldness, combined with other non-emotional considerations, that grounds my moral disapproval and consequent moral judgments.

The above examples seem to attest that, even in the same cultural setting (e.g., Western context), the emotional states on which moral approval and disapproval are based are much more varied than simply being warmed or chilled by the motive of the other's action. In my view, this is enough to cast doubt on the commonality of the introspective experience of the warmth-chilled mechanism, which in turn should caution us against accepting Slote's normative claim.

Another related and problematic aspect of Slote's argument is that the sole criterion for approving or disapproving an action is the agent's empathic concern or lack thereof. Consider again the example of MLK: my admiration and consequent approval are not necessarily caused solely by the presence or absence of empathic concern in MLK's motivation to act. Would my admiration and consequent approval of MLK's actions disappear if I learned that he was not acting out of empathic concern, but only out of his rational belief in the fundamental equality of all human beings? Not only *would* it not disappear, it *should* not disappear. From a normative standpoint, it seems unjustifiable to judge MLK's actions as morally wrong (or not morally right) simply because the agent's motivation did not involve empathic concern.

Something similar applies to disapproval. Consider the white lie scenario: Suppose Pam's omission was motivated by empathic concern for Jim. So if Michael empathizes with her agential empathy, he should be warmed by Pam's empathic concern. According to Slote, this is enough to guarantee that Michael will approve of Pam's action and judge it to be morally right. But is this always the case? Why should Michael not judge Pam's decision to be morally wrong, even though her motive was empathic concern for Jim? The reality is that there are reasons (e.g., breach of trust) to disapprove of with-

13 Prinz made a similar point about admiration and anger. He argued that moral judgments are based on a variety of emotions such as anger, disgust, guilt, and admiration (Prinz, 2011a).

holding the truth from a friend, regardless of the fact that empathic concern was the agent's motive.

More generally, there are circumstances in which the agent's motives are completely irrelevant to moral approval or disapproval: for example, if I disapprove of the action of the obsessive ex-partner, I am not at all interested in what his motives were for harming his victim: I am not interested in whether he believed it was in her best interest to stay with him, or that he was saving her, or that he was seeking revenge for some wrong he had suffered. My anger, disapproval, and consequent moral judgment will and do arise regardless of the agent's motives, including empathic concern. In other words, the agent's motive is not always relevant, alternatively, is not the only relevant element for us to judge the moral status of their action. Note that the only exception to this is in cases of self-defense, where the agent's motive is crucial to judging the moral status of the action.

It follows that being warmed or chilled by the presence or absence of empathic concern seems neither necessary nor sufficient for moral approval or disapproval. On one hand, it is not necessary because either I can approve or disapprove of an action on the basis of some other emotional reaction (e.g., admiration or anger), which makes the warm-chill mechanism not as universally shared as it is supposed to be, or in certain cases I can approve or disapprove of an action without considering the agent's motives at all (e.g., the case of the obsessive ex-partner). To be sure, the agent's motives may sometimes be relevant, but they are not always normatively necessary for moral approval and disapproval. On the other hand, it is not sufficient because I can approve or disapprove of an action despite the presence or absence of empathic concern as the agent's motive, since an action that is not motivated by empathic concern can be morally right, and one that is motivated by empathic concern can still be morally wrong (e.g., MLK's actions and Pam's white lie, respectively).

It is worth noting that empathy biases cause the same, if not more, problems when it comes to moral judgments than when it comes to moral motivation. Even if we agree with Slote that moral approval and disapproval are indeed dependent on the empathically felt feeling of warmth or chill caused by agential empathy, we have no reason to believe that the ability to empathically feel warmth or chill would not be just as biased as affective empathy. If affective empathy is responsible for the feeling of warmth or chill that grounds moral approval or disapproval, then the presence or absence of this feeling would be subject to the same kinds of influences and modulations we discussed above.

It is likely that if the agent is perceived by the empathizer as an in-group member, it would be easier to be warmed by the motive of her action. As a result, it would be easier to morally approve of the actions of someone from our in-group, which in turn would lead to judging the in-group agent more favorably than the out-group agent. Conversely, if the agent is perceived by the empathizer as an out-group member, the ability to be empathically warmed by agential empathy would likely be impaired. Consequently, we would be more susceptible to being chilled by an out-group member's actions because we would be less able to empathically feel what those we perceive as different from us feel, including empathic concern as a source of motivation for their actions. Thus, even if an out-group member is acting out of empathic concern for another person, we may fail to recognize this and be chilled rather than warmed by the action, leading to moral disapproval and a morally negative judgment. Similarly, we may be mistakenly warmed by an in-group member's action, even if her motive is not empathic concern.

It seems much harder to justify the consequences of affective empathy biases for moral judgments than for moral motivation (although I have tried to show that they have highly problematic consequences there, too). It is one thing to justify the fact that we are motivationally biased toward those close to us, and quite another to say that we judge an action to be morally wrong simply because we are unable to empathically feel the other person's empathic concern because we perceive them to be a member of an out-group. While there are certain circumstances in which it is indeed moral to be more motivated to care for our loved ones because toward them we have special obligations, I would argue that there are no circumstances in which judging an action to be morally wrong on the basis of our biased empathic capacity is justified.

Consider the following case: Yichen, a middle-aged Chinese man, found a wallet full of money and decided to take it to the police station. When the owner of the wallet gets it back, he decides to give Yichen money as a reward. According to Slote, the observer should judge the moral status of Yichen's action based on whether she feels warmed or chilled by his motive. The problem is that because of the observer's negative prejudices and stereotypical beliefs about Chinese people, combined with the inherently biased nature of affective empathy and the mirroring mechanism on which it relies, she is unable to feel the warmth elicited by Yichen's empathic concern. On the contrary, she feels chilled by his lack of concern for the owner of the wallet, believing that he returned the wallet only because he wanted the reward. This will lead to moral disapproval and ultimately to a judgment that Yichen's action was morally wrong. Thus, there seems to be something troubling about the fact that the observer's moral judgment can be so easily and drastically modulated exclusively by our empathic ability to empathize with the agent's presence or absence of empathic concern, given how selective that ability appears to be.

Recall that to correct these problematic consequences, Kauppinen proposed to regulate empathic biases by adopting Smith's account of the impartial spectator (see Chapter 3): only by imaginatively placing oneself in the mental shoes of the impartial spectator can the observer up- or down-regulating her empathic response to the other's actions, depending on whether the agent is perceived as an in-group or out-group member (Kauppinen, 2014). This ideally regulated empathy should then lead to unbiased moral judgments. However, his solution is effective if and only if we are actually able to imaginatively adopt the perspective of the impartial spectator. But there are legitimate doubts about this.

The first very broad point concerns how biased and inaccurate perspective-taking and cognitive empathy can be (see Chapter 4). If empathizers can at best achieve a 35% accuracy rate when the target is the empathizer's partner, it seems unrealistic to ask the subject to imaginatively take the perspective of an ideal, i.e., not experientially known, spectator. Given the inherently flawed and limited nature of cognitive empathy, the chances of this very demanding mental operation achieving its goal seem slim. How can a partial and inaccurate phenomenon like cognitive empathy produce a result that is supposed to be impartial and accurate, like the impartial spectator's perspective?

To be sure, the issue is not so much that cognitive empathy can never achieve a less inaccurate and less partial result, but rather the degree to which this goal is realistically achievable. In other words, I do not think that the level of impartiality, i.e., total impartiality, that would make empathy a suitable normative source for moral judgment is as easily attainable as is sometimes thought. The problem with empathy as defined in the SD is that it is a tool that rarely seems appropriate for the task at hand, especially when compared to the available alternatives. In this sense, there seem to be better tools at our disposal for achieving a more impartial perspective when deliberating and making moral judgments. To be fair, Kauppinen himself seems to be aware of this, as he recognizes, following Smith, that principles, albeit formed on the basis of ideally regulated empathy, ground our moral judgments (Kauppinen 2014, p. 111; see Chapter 3).

Similarly, some proponents of empathy acknowledged that when it comes to deliberation, and especially moral deliberation, empathy is only one of many tools at our disposal. For example, Oxley argued that "since empathy's most important functions are epistemic, empathy alone is insufficient and undesirable as a sole moral criterion; empathy is a psychological experience, not a normative principle" (Oxley 2011, p. 6). Similarly, while Persson and Savulescu praised empathy's ability to motivate us to care for those in need, as imaginatively taking on the feelings of others' distress in a voluntary and controlled way motivates altruistic actions, they also recognized empathy's numerous biases (Persson & Savulescu, 2018). Accordingly, they proposed a similar solution to Kauppinen's: "By means of our reason we can counteract the fact that our empathy is spatio-temporally biased, unjustifiably discriminatory, and innumerate, and develop a more reflective empathy, though we would be hard put to overcome completely these shortcomings of our spontaneous empathy" (Persson and Savulescu 2018, p. 188).

While I sympathize with the appeal to reason and the warning about the inadequacy of empathy as the sole or even the best source of reasons for deliberation, I wonder again whether the role of empathy in moral judgments and morality in general has not been overstated. If everything that empathy does needs to be revised and corrected by reason, or is insufficient on its own, then its centrality to morality and deliberation seems greatly exaggerated. To be clear, I am not opposed to a rational corrective mechanism to counteract empathy's biases, as I am firmly convinced of how potentially dangerous they are when involved in our other-directed deliberative processes. My point is that if empathy's contribution to other-directed deliberation (either in the form of motivating or normative reasons) needs to be consistently revised or paired with multiple other resources and tools, then perhaps its centrality and overall role should be reconsidered. Before doing so (see Part 3), however, I need to consider in the next chapter the context in which the empathic relationship is embedded and how they influence each other.

CHAPTER 6

Issues with Empathy and Its Role in the Broader Context and in Our Relationships

The purpose of this chapter is to shed light on the problematic consequences of characterizing empathy as independent of the broader sociocultural, historical, political, and economic context in which it occurs, which is the default way in which the SD seems to understand the empathic phenomenon. In the first part, I will argue that this context has a profound effect on the empathic relationship and, consequently, on the other-directed deliberative processes in which empathy is involved. Not only can the broader context directly influence whether empathy will lead to problematic epistemic and moral outcomes, but it also appears to be responsible for revealing those outcomes. This is particularly true in asymmetrical relationships, which I will discuss in the second part of the chapter: empathy between privileged and non-privileged individuals can foster instances of epistemic injustice, and considering the broader context of these relationships can help reveal these epistemically unjust behaviors and their morally troubling consequences.

Despite some focus on its relational aspect, the interaction between the empathic relationship and its broader context has been grossly underdeveloped in the philosophical and psychological debate. The only exceptions are the hermeneutic and phenomenological approaches, and this, as I will discuss in the next section, gives these perspectives a valuable advantage over the SD of empathy (Pedersen, 2008; Throop & Zahavi, 2020). Outside of the philosophical debate, anthropological studies have also long focused on exploring this interaction (Rosaldo, 1984). For this reason, I will use anthropological considerations to frame my argument against the exclusion of the broader context from the SD definition of empathy and empathically based other-directed deliberation.

1 The Overlooked Influence of the Context on Empathy: Potential Immoral Outcomes

So far I have treated the empathizer and her target as if they were discrete entities whose relationship occurs in a void. I have done so because the SD of empathy rarely, if ever, refers to the context in which the empathic relation-

 | HTTPS://DOI.ORG/10.1163/9789004745360-008

ship is embedded. The implicit assumption seems to be that the empathic relationship and its epistemic, motivational, and normative contributions to our deliberative processes can be completely separated from the context in which it is situated. In some cases, ignoring the contextual aspect of empathy seems to be an attempt to address its partiality. After all, the basic idea behind all corrective mechanisms (e.g., Hume's general point of view or Smith's impartial spectator and related inspired accounts) is to adopt a perspective that, in order to be impartial, must filter out all information about the empathizer, including all influences of the specific context of the empathic relationship. However, this seems not only difficult to achieve but also potentially counterproductive: empathy and the empathic relationship are always rooted in a social, cultural, historical, economic, and political context, and if the influence of the context is deliberately ignored, empathy can lead to immoral and epistemically inaccurate outcomes, especially if it is used as the sole or most relevant epistemic, motivational, and normative source of our other-directed deliberative processes.[1]

In particular, the SD of empathy omits three constitutive elements of empathy: the subjective background of the target, the contextual background of both the empathizer and the target, and the broader context in which their relationship occurs. The absence of these aspects not only prevents the SD of empathy from achieving its goal, i.e., accurate insight into the other's inner world, but it simply makes the SD incompatible with the reality of empathizing with another person: being situated in a specific social, cultural, historical, economic, and political context is an ontological condition of every human being, including those involved in the empathic relationship.

This clearly echoes one of the fundamental tenets of the hermeneutic tradition: the idea of objective understanding, that is, free of any interference from the understanding subject, the object of understanding, and the context of that understanding, is a chimera. As Reidar Pedersen argues, "it is a historically situated subject that attempts to understand or empathize with another historically situated subject" (Pedersen 2008, p. 327). To eliminate the situatedness of the empathic subjects is to attempt, unsuccessfully, to erase a constitutive part of what it means to be a subject in a relationship, empathic, or otherwise.

1 As noted in Chapter 3, Stueber acknowledges the importance of contextual influence on reenactive empathy. However, he believes that this kind of imaginative perspective-taking can recognize its own limitations when it comes to this influence. I agree with the idea that empathy needs additional tools and that it can sometimes be responsible for signaling this need. However, as I will argue in the next section, it is empathy understood in phenomenological terms that is capable of doing this, rather than reenactive empathy (see Chapter 8).

The epistemic relevance of the context of the subjects involved is particularly relevant to cognitive empathy. Am I really empathically understanding what another person is thinking or feeling if I do not understand the broader socio-cultural, historical, and political context of that person and not just his or her specific condition? It does not seem enough to grasp the personal reasons for the other person's inner state, assuming that this is even possible (see Chapter 4), in order to gain an accurate understanding of it. This is because, on the one hand, contextual reasons may play a major role in the subject's situation and, on the other hand, individual reasons may be partly constituted or grounded in broader contextual reasons.

For example, it is not enough to understand that Indah, a teenage girl from Indonesia, is angry with her government and believes that adults do not care about the future of younger generations because of the climate emergency. To truly understand what she is thinking and feeling and, most importantly, why, we need to broaden our perspective. Indonesia is one of the most vulnerable countries when it comes to the catastrophic effects of climate change, and its high level of air pollution is responsible for 50% of the country's morbidity (Haryanto, 2018). Moreover, Indonesia is extremely vulnerable not only to the negative impacts of climate change, such as sea level rise, flooding, and storms, but also to its socioeconomic impacts, which are inherently intertwined: in Jakarta, for example, the areas most vulnerable to flooding due to sea level rise are the same areas with higher concentrations of low-income people (the northern and eastern parts of the city) (Firman et al., 2011).

More specifically, Indah and her family happen to come from the poorest and most polluted area in Jakarta: they already lost their home after the catastrophic flood in 2007, and her grandmother was diagnosed with terminal lung cancer (one of the most common air pollution-related diseases). Nothing seems to be changing, or changing as fast as it should. Policy implementation is slow or ineffective, and public discourse about young people's protests against climate change oscillates between paternalism and indifference. Simultaneously, it is important to consider not only the target's but also the empathizer's situated background and context: for example, whether the empathizer lives in Indonesia or in a Western country, or whether she is also a poor teenager or instead a wealthy 70-year-old, has a profound impact on the resulting empathic understanding. This contextual information is crucial for the accuracy of empathic understanding.

In this sense, empirical findings seem to confirm the influence of the cultural background on empathy. For instance, some studies suggest that an individualistic versus a collectivistic culture modulates the use and level of cognitive empathy (for a review, see Jami et al., 2023). In a study conducted by

Wu and Keysar, the authors found that the accuracy of cognitive empathy is influenced by the culture of the empathizer: "Chinese culture, which emphasizes interdependence, focuses attention on other people, whereas American culture, which emphasizes independence, focuses attention on the self. Consequently, compared with Americans, Chinese are better at solving perspective-taking problems, make fewer errors in assessing the intentions of another person, and are less distracted by their own private perspective" (Wu and Keysar 2007, p. 605).[2] Importantly, there appears to be some homogeneity in the level of use of cognitive empathy within the same type of culture (either individualistic or collectivistic), which will therefore be an obstacle in cases where an "individualistic" empathizer attempts to empathically understand a "collectivistic" target.[3]

At this point, the question is whether cognitive empathy, as imaginative perspective-taking, is capable of acquiring this kind of information via a simulative or re-enactive process. I am quite skeptical. Cognitive empathy, and we as empathizers, do not seem to have the epistemic "bandwidth" necessary to do so. Given the complexity and epistemically varied nature of contextual information, I am not sure that we as empathizers can imaginatively reproduce that context (e.g., the environmental crisis), as Smith himself and simulationist proponents argue.

In particular, my skepticism is motivated by two factors. On the one hand, the relevant information needed to reproduce and understand the other's situation in Smith's time was immensely less complex, both quantitatively and qualitatively, than what we would need today, and the climate emergency is a paradigmatic example of this. We now need a greater amount and a much

---

2 What the authors defined as perspective-taking is compatible with cognitive empathy in the SD of empathy.

3 The same seems true also for affective empathy: in another study, Chopik et al. found a correlation between higher levels of affective and overall empathy and collectivist countries, which they attribute to different parenting goals and styles: "East Asian parents teach their children to fear loneliness and isolation, whereas Western parents generally focus on teaching children the benefits of being independent and unique" (Chopik, O'Brien, and Konrath 2017, p. 10). Note that here are some conflicting findings on this point. For example, Cassels et al. found that the "Western sample reported greater levels of Empathic Concern and less Personal Distress when confronted with another person's negative emotional state, relative to [the] East Asian sample" (Cassels, Chan, and Chung 2010, p. 319). I am not, however, interested in discussing these inconsistencies or which specific culture modulates which aspect of the empathic relationship here, since I simply want to show that cultural context does affect empathy and that it would be conceptually and phenomenologically wrong to deny this phenomenon.

more varied kind of information to understand the other's situation with the level of detail advocated by proponents of ST. To be sure, I am aware that in ST accounts, the empathizer is usually asked to imaginatively reproduce only the information that is relevant to understanding the other's inner states. My point is precisely that the quantity and quality of relevant information, especially contextual information, has increased exponentially and continues to do so. This, on the other hand, forces us to focus once again on the limits of our imaginative resources, as they seem to be a crucial obstacle to the ability of cognitive empathy to actually achieve its goal, especially in situations where the contextual factors are particularly relevant, as discussed above.

To be sure, in arguing that cognitive empathy seems incapable of capturing this kind of information, I am not arguing that we need more or better cognitive empathy. Rather, there seem to be better tools at our disposal for doing so. Precisely because cognitive empathy seems unable to fully capture this information, it should not be considered the pinnacle of interpersonal understanding. Note that there is no contradiction here: when we use empathic understanding as a source for our deliberation, we should always be aware that the context of that understanding is extremely influential for accuracy, but that this contextual information cannot be obtained through cognitive empathy. The first claim acknowledges the influence of context, and the second claim acknowledges the limitations of cognitive empathy.

Importantly, it is not only the external contextual information that is necessary to understand others accurately and respectfully. When attempting to empathetically understand the other person's action, the agent's character should always be taken into account. Our actions, especially as moral agents, are better understood when placed in the larger context of our past actions and, ultimately, our overall character. This emerges clearly within a virtue ethics framework: in order to understand an action, but also its moral status, it is crucial to understand whether and how it is related to the agent's other actions and character.

For example, suppose we are trying to empathize with Indah and understand why she has joined a group of environmental activists who use civil disobedience as a strategy. Simulating her specific situation at the moment of her decision might give us only a very basic level of understanding: she cares about the environment, and she believes that this group will fight to protect it – assuming that the simulation-plus-projection routine would be able to overcome its biases and inaccuracies. However, our understanding of her decision would be much deeper if we took into account her development as a moral agent: in elementary school, she started recycling and taught her parents how to do it properly at home; in middle school, she spent her summers collecting trash on the beach; in high school, one of her teachers told her about Greta Thunberg and her style of protest, and she was fascinated by it; and so on.

The problem, however, is that it is already difficult to simulate another person's actions, so simulating their past actions and overall character borders on epistemic impossibility. As Goldie argued, the impossibility depends on the fact that the agent's character and past actions are part of the unconscious background against which the deliberative process unfolds. When Indah decides to join the group, her past actions and character traits are part of the unconscious background for her deliberation. Although Indah does not explicitly and consciously recall all of her past actions and character traits in relation to the specific deliberative process she is undertaking, they still implicitly influence it.

Thus, attempting to simulate the target's overall character can lead to the obstacles and pitfalls already discuss above (see Chapter 4): while the agent's character and overall life experience are crucial to understanding her actions, cognitive empathy as a simulation-plus-projection routine seems incapable of capturing them, leading the empathizer to a potentially inaccurate understanding of the other's actions that risks limiting the full scope of the other agent's agency.

Affective empathy is also influenced by the sociocultural context in which both the target and the empathizer find themselves. First and foremost, how we express our emotions is influenced by our sociocultural context. According to the dialect theory of Elfenbein, Hess, and colleagues, although there are prototypical expressions that cut across cultures, specific variations are also very common and depend on the target's sociocultural context. The dynamic between prototypical expressions and culturally based variations is comparable to the way languages work (Elfenbein, 2013; Elfenbein et al., 2007). For example, the Italian language has prototypical structures that remain unvaried, and at the same time has variations – called dialects – that depend on the specific geographical and cultural area of the speaker. The same goes for our emotional expressions: there are prototypical expressions that are mostly cross-cultural, but each culture has specific variations of these prototypical expressions.

Therefore, the cultural context of the target will play an important role in determining the specific way she will express her emotions (Keltner et al., 2019).[4] This can have implications for affective empathy, which aims to

4 The empirical results seem clear: "We documented systematic cultural accents for all of the emotions, and in 19 of 22 emotions, we observed unique cultural accents in every culture. About 25% of an individual's expression of a specific emotion resembled the emo-

share the other person's specific and individual emotional state. Relevantly, the emotions that are usually associated with social interactions, such as shame, envy, anger, and joy, are more likely to develop specific dialects than less socially involved emotions (Elfenbein et al., 2007; Keltner et al., 2019).

For example, the way Indah expresses her anger about the climate emergency and its consequences is influenced by her cultural upbringing and the specific emotional dialect she has adopted. Accordingly, belonging to the same culture as the target, and thus sharing the same emotional dialect, might allow the empathizer to have a better and deeper emotional recognition/understanding of the other's state. This adds another layer to the already discussed effects of group membership on emotional arousal (see Chapter 5): sharing or not sharing the same emotional dialect – and, more generally, having the same cultural background – seems to modulate affective empathy, thus reinforcing the in-group-out-group dynamic.

To be clear, I am not arguing that we are incapable of sharing the emotions of someone from a different culture, as this goes against our commonsense intersubjective experience and empirical evidence, given that culturally specific emotional dialects make up only a portion of our emotional expressions, while the remaining portion consists of prototypical expressions shared across cultures (Cordaro et al., 2018). My point is simply that when the empathizer and the target have different cultural backgrounds, affective empathy is more difficult, and in some cases impossible, to achieve. In particular, if it is achieved, the empathizer is likely to miss some relevant nuances in her target's emotional states. Therefore, it is a matter of ease and quality of the process.

In addition to the epistemically problematic consequences of ignoring the influence of the broader context, there are also specific ethical concerns that arise when this is the case. First, ignoring the context of the empathic relationship may make us unable to see the possible immoral consequences of empathy itself. I have already tried to show that there is no guarantee that cognitive or affective empathy will be used in a morally good way (see Chapter 5). Rather, cognitive and affective empathy can be useful tools for inflicting various kinds of suffering on other people, and in certain cases, I argue, it is precisely the sociocultural, historical, economic, and political context that allows us to see and judge whether the outcomes of our empathy-based other-directed deliberations are immoral.

---

tion-specific cultural dialect of that individual's locale. There is clearly cultural variation in emotional expression. These variations are neither isolated to specific emotions, nor to specific cultures, but a reliably observed, systematic and complex layer of behavior in the expression of emotion" (Cordaro et al. 2018, p. 13).

This aspect has been widely discussed in the anthropological literature. In particular, Bubandt and Willerslev, who defined empathy in a simulationist fashion as "the first-person imaginative projection, at once emotional and cognitive, of oneself into the perspective or situation of another" (Bubandt and Willerslev 2015, p. 5), argued that traditional accounts of empathy are to some extent and for the most part unidimensional because they ignore a fundamental and inescapable aspect of empathic understanding: the possibility of its misuse and abuse. In this regard, they argue that there is a specific type of empathy, namely "tactical empathy," which "is motivated by seduction, deception, manipulation, and violent intent" (Bubandt and Willerslev 2015, p. 6).

In particular, Bubandt and Willerslev used two ethnographic cases to show that empathy can sometimes be a tool to widen the gap between the empathizer and the others rather than to bridge it. For example, in one of the ethnographic cases, Muslim Indonesian political agitators forged a letter declaring an alleged Christian takeover of the region, which prompted some of the Muslim population to preemptively attack Christians in the area. As the authors argue, the fake letter worked because whoever wrote it performed a successful act of cognitive empathy, i.e., skillfully adopting the first-person perspective of a hypothetical Indonesian member of the Christian community willing to start a religious war to impose Christianity as the dominant religion. Without tactical empathy, the instigators would not have been able to effectively deceive readers, and they deliberately used tactical empathy to achieve this goal and actively harm their opponents.

There seems to be a "double movement of the imagination" in tactical empathy, in which the empathizer first assumes the other's perspective in order to achieve a kind of identification between the two perspectives, and then the empathizer interrupts and ultimately denies this identification in order to emphasize the incommensurability of the other's alterity (Bubandt and Willerslev 2015, p. 7). This double movement results in a radicalization, not a minimization, of the alterity of the target of empathy. In this sense, the ultimate goal of the political instigators was to deepen the distance between Muslims and Christians, to make the former believe that the latter was even more distant and different than they expected, thus confirming their worst paranoia and prejudices, leading to violence. This oscillation between the desire for identification and the exacerbation of alterity is reflected in the ambiguous nature of empathy. On the one hand, empathy can be a motivation and tool for good that can evoke concern, care, and protection for others. On the other hand, empathy can be a tool for harming others or misinterpreting their perspectives, thus triggering violence and dehumanization.

Crucially, in the ethnographic case, the misuse of empathy was only revealed by looking at and understanding the broader sociocultural context and its impact on it, since the empathic act itself (i.e., simulative perspective-taking) was successful, in the sense of being sufficiently accurate, and, unfortunately in this case, considered epistemically trustworthy by the Muslim population. This seems to hold true beyond this specific case: sometimes it is only the broader context in which the empathic act is embedded and shaped that can reveal whether or not empathy has been used for deceptive and ultimately immoral purposes.

A related second problematic implication of ignoring the cultural context of empathy is that the meaning of empathy itself can change depending on the culture. In this regard, Hollan has pointed out that in non-Western contexts, empathy is not by default understood as a force for good, as it is almost universally characterized in Western culture. For example, in the Pacific region, the Mayan culture of Mexico, and the Inuit of northern Canada view empathy as inherently problematic (Hollan, 2017). These cultures positively value a degree of opacity when it comes to the internal states of the subject, and empathy can threaten this desired privacy and inaccessibility. Accordingly, many people in Mayan and Inuit cultures are wary and reluctant to reveal their inner thoughts and feelings to others for fear that the empathizer will use this knowledge to hurt them and that this inaccurate empathic knowledge will be shared inappropriately with others, causing embarrassment and shame (Hollan 2012, p. 72).

Thus, it seems that empathy is not always required or valued in social interactions because the need to be understood is sometimes overridden by the desire to protect one's inner world from foreign access, even in Western contexts where it is usually characterized as valuable. Most importantly, "we need to recognize that the *kinds* of problems and situations people want recognized and understood and the *ways* in which they seek that recognition will be socially and culturally specific" (Hollan 2008, p. 484, my emphasis). In other words, empathy can and should manifest differently depending on the sociocultural context of the target.

It turns out that not everyone wants or needs empathy. Some people – because of their culture, social status, or simply individual differences and personal backgrounds – may prefer more discreet manifestations of empathy, or no empathy at all, than others, who instead desire explicit and more traditional ways of expressing empathy as defined in the SD. Grief is a good example of a situation that requires modulation of the empathic response based on various factors, especially cultural and personal background: not everyone grieves in the same way and, as a result, does not desire the same kind of empathic response.

Moreover, precisely because empathic relationships are influenced by the context in which they occur, all forms of empathy "are therefore implicated in the creation and maintenance of power relations, social structures, and identities" (Hollan 2017, p. 348). Consequently, group membership is not only shaped by perceived similarities (e.g., same gender, same race, and same age), but is also reinforced by culturally and socially determined relationships. Because empathy is higher and deeper between in-group members (e.g., people of the same socioeconomic class), it seems to be able to further consolidate existing relationships and memberships, while at the same time widening the gap with those who have less power and are thus considered outsiders (e.g., people of different socioeconomic status).

Ignoring the contextual nature of empathy has another implication: a lack of accountability for the messages of political leaders when it comes to the actions of citizens that reflect those messages. By characterizing empathy as an "individualized and decontextualized" phenomenon, we implicitly place all responsibility for its presence or absence on the individual subject, while failing to hold political and institutional actors accountable for the role they play in the behavior of individuals (Matthiesen and Klitmøller 2019, p. 188).

For example, when we are confronted with openly discriminatory and xenophobic attitudes toward migrants, the diagnosis should not be that the citizens who perpetrate such violations are merely deficient or incapable of empathy (Stefanello, 2021a). Not only have I already questioned the idea that the lack of empathy is in itself the source of immoral behavior (see Chapter 5), but the assumptions from which such xenophobic attitudes arise, consciously or unconsciously, are not the result of an inability to empathize with other people but are part of a precise "ideological position that has been increasingly legitimized in current political discourses" (Matthiesen and Klitmøller 2019, p. 189). In other words, there is a clear influence of political rhetoric and ideology on individual beliefs, emotional responses, and behaviors: racist behaviors are often simultaneously generated, encouraged, and legitimized by the larger political environment in which they occur.

On the one hand, those who engage in discriminatory behaviors and beliefs are often motivated by their affective empathy for a group of individuals who they believe are suffering as targets of discrimination. For example, racist attitudes toward migrants are often motivated by a misplaced fear that they will "steal" jobs from locals. This fear, in turn, is motivated and reinforced by the empathically shared suffering and concern of those who have actually lost their jobs and are struggling financially. In this case, the presence of empathy for those perceived as in-group members seems to be one of the motivating reasons for discriminatory behavior. On the other hand, the discriminatory outcomes of empathy also need to be contextualized: the "migrants-are-stealing-our-jobs" argument is justified and promoted on a much larger political scale than at the individual level. To ignore the political dimension within which such phenomena emerge and grow is to mistakenly devalue politics itself, its impact on public debate, and consequently on individual behavior.

All of this is to say that when empathy is involved in our other-directed deliberative processes, it does (and should) bring with it all of the above implications and considerations derived from the situated and embedded character of the empathic relationship. If we characterize empathy as independent of its broader context – as the SD posits – and use it as the sole or preferred source of our reasons in deliberation, we might end up with inaccurate beliefs and immoral actions.

Note that taking into account the broader context of empathy and its implications will exponentially complicate our deliberative processes, but I see this as a desirable by-product of this recognition: deciding what to believe about other people's inner states and what to do accordingly are complex epistemic and moral tasks. Any account of empathy that argues for its involvement in deliberation should welcome this call for complexity, and at the very least recognize that empathy cannot be the only viable source for exploring how this context affects both the other person's experience and the deliberative process itself.

2 Empathy, Asymmetrical Relationships, and Epistemic Injustice

Ignoring contextual influence can be particularly problematic in asymmetrical relationships. Consider, in particular, relationships between individuals where economic, social, and political power is unequally distributed. The unequal distribution may depend directly on the roles that the empathizer and the target occupy within the relationship (e.g., in the clinical relationship, the doctor inherently has more medical knowledge than the patient) and/or on the broader context, such as when the target belongs to already socially, politically, economically, and culturally marginalized groups. In this sense, individuals with more power – in whatever way that power is characterized (money, political and social, epistemic authority etc.) – can be considered privileged.

If we consider the empathizer and the target as separate from their context, and therefore from how power is unevenly distributed between them because of that context, we may fail to recognize the asymmetrical nature of this relationship. Consequently, empathy's inability to recognize the influence of this power asymmetry can turn it into a device for concealing and at the same time reinforcing the empathizer's exercise of power.

This is especially true in cases where epistemic power is asymmetrically distributed. Empathizers have the experiences of others at their disposal by default since they always have the power to modify them. When empathic other-directed theoretical deliberation is performed, the deliberator has control over the epistemic content of the other's experience: he has the power to misrepresent the other's experience, even when he is convinced that he has performed a successful act of cognitive empathy. This power is present in any case of empathic understanding, but it is stronger when the empathizer is privileged relative to his target, and the damage that can result from the misuse of this power is exponentially greater in asymmetrical relationships.

For example, a male empathizer might deliberate that the woman's account of her experience of sexual harassment at work is untrue and that she is lying to punish her boss for not promoting her (other-directed theoretical deliberation). The reason is that after empathizing with her, he did not understand why she did not report the incident immediately, or more precisely, he (inaccurately) understood that the incident was not serious enough for her to report it. He thinks or says things like, "the woman told me she was traumatized and scared, but she did not ask for help the day after the incident. If it were me, I would have told someone right away: when I was robbed last year, I did exactly that." Suppose further that this male empathizer happens to be the head of the human resources department, and on the basis of his empathic experience, while listening to the woman's testimony, he decides not to sanction the woman's boss (other-directed practical deliberation).

His act of empathy is not enough to convey to him why, given her emotional state and situation, she did not come forward immediately. To understand this, the empathizer must look at the sociocultural context of the target and of their relationship. The broader context tells us that, for complex reasons, men (and society at large) often do not believe women when they report sexual harassment or even assault because we tend to view men as epistemically more trustworthy and women as less reliable, especially when they accuse men of inappropriate behavior (Medina, 2012).

Empathy, precisely because it seems incapable of recognizing all of these aspects, can become the ideal ally both for obscuring these asymmetries and for attributing even more power to the already privileged empathizer. In particular, empathy can foster a specific epistemic vice, namely epistemic injustice, which in turn is responsible for further exacerbating these power imbalances. Miranda Fricker, who first characterized this vice, defines epistemic injustice as "a wrong done to someone specifically in their capacity as a knower" (Fricker 2007, p. 1). According to Fricker, it can manifest itself in two forms: testimonial injustice and hermeneutical injustice.

Testimonial injustice occurs when the testimony of a knower or group of knowers is deemed not worthy of epistemic credibility, not because of a lack of epistemic resources or skills, but because of some characteristics about them that trigger some kind of prejudice in the listener. The characteristics most likely to induce a biased attitude in the listener are those related to the identity of the knowers. As a solid body of empirical research confirms, the most common candidates are race, gender, age, and disability: we tend to trust a man's opinion more even if a woman has more or equal expertise on the matter (Hutchison, 2020), we assume that members of ethnic minorities are less trustworthy (Stanley et al., 2011), we are more skeptical of the testimony of the elderly, believing that they are less reliable not because they may have been diagnosed with dementia, but simply because of their advanced age (Levy & Macdonald, 2016), and we tend to partially, if not completely, exclude people with intellectual disabilities from the community of trustworthy knowers (Corrigan & Watson, 2002).

Hermeneutical injustice is caused by "a gap in collective interpretative resources" that prevents certain kinds of testimony from being adequately understood (Fricker 2007, p. 1). For example, prior to the concept of "systemic racism," the pervasiveness of racist attitudes toward African Americans in the United States was often unrecognized or misunderstood by non-black people (Chiao et al., 2008). Typically, the most targeted by this type of injustice are those who, for a variety of reasons, have unconventional ways of expressing themselves. Patients with mental illnesses are a perfect example of how the way they express themselves, combined with the listener's lack of adequate interpretive resources, leads to unfavorable credibility judgments (Carel & Kidd, 2014; Kidd & Carel, 2017).

Empathy can have a tendency to exacerbate epistemic injustice for two reasons. First, as Bailey herself observes, "empathy has the power to dramatically reshape one's willingness to trust others' testimony" (Bailey 2018, p. 149). This is because empathy plays a crucial role in making credibility judgments, across all kinds of relationships. According to Fricker, in order to formulate a credibility judgment, the hearer must perceive the speaker as trustworthy, and "this cognitive achievement is inevitably partly composed of an emotion: a feeling of trust" (Fricker 2007, p. 79). In addition to this specific feeling, the hearer's perception of the speaker's trustworthiness or lack thereof depends on what Fricker calls "a more general emotional engagement" that is crucially provided by empathy: "[the hearer] must empathize sufficiently with [the speaker] to be in a position to judge [the other's trustworthiness], and empathy typically carries some emotional charge" (Fricker 2007, p. 79). However, because the feeling of trust is so strongly dependent on the degree of empathy the listener feels for the speaker, the fact that empathy is so strongly modulated by group membership would seem to undermine the accuracy of the process by which trustworthiness is assigned (see Chapter 5).

Second, empathy seems to be especially responsible for fostering epistemic injustice in asymmetrical relationships. This is because privileged empathizers seem unable to see the difference between their condition and that of marginalized subjects. In this sense, privileged empathizers seem to be afflicted with a specific kind of *epistemic incompetence*, namely, the inability to see the inherently limited nature of their particular experience and how their privileges significantly distinguish them from those who have not enjoyed them (Liebow and Ades 2022, p. 532).

This inability is rooted in the implicit or explicit assumption that the broader context of the relationship is irrelevant, and relatedly, that the lived experience of the privileged person is the template against which all other experiences must be measured, compared, and ultimately understood. As a result, the privileged empathizer is unable to recognize that in an asymmetrical relationship, empathy can produce the exact opposite of what proponents of empathy hope for: by misrepresenting the target's perspective, the empathizer makes her feel, in Bailey's words, *not* humanly understood (Bailey 2020; see Chapter 3).

For example, the HR manager manifests this kind of behavior because he inaccurately understood through empathy the experience of the worker based on his personal experience as a man without considering the broader context of this event and his empathic act toward the worker. This has epistemically and morally problematic outcomes: when the HR manager challenges the woman's testimony by pointing out the supposed contradiction between her inner state (fear) and her action (delayed complaint) based on his personal experience, he unjustly mystifies and dismisses her testimony and at the same time humiliates her.

In his sense, some privileged empathizers approach the marginalized target's perspective as if it were completely transparent by virtue of their epistemic and sociopolitical power. However, this assumption has an almost paradoxical result since the assumed transparency and total accessibility renders the minds of the marginalized completely opaque, leaving only the empathizers' perspectives accessible. Janine Jones explained this paradox perfectly:

> It is nearly impossible to perceive or to know some other minds as minds within contexts of oppression. (…) The minds of members of oppressed groups are constructed as a priori knowable. The result is that such minds become a posteriori unknowable, or nearly so, to the dominant group who claims to know them
>
> JONES 2022, p. 86

Specifically, Jones argued that because black people in contexts of oppression are characterized by white people as fungible bodies devoid of rational minds when white empathizers attempt to empathize with them, black people's minds are seen as "open and empty for occupation and direction" by white people, who, it is posited, are the only ones who possess rational minds in the relationship (Jones 2022, p. 92). As a result, there seems to be both an epistemic failure, in that white people only have the illusion of accurately understanding black people's minds, and a moral failure, in that this approach to the empathic relationship risks further dehumanizing black people in contexts of oppression.

This conclusion is at odds with those who ascribe to empathy the ability to promote, rather than hinder, epistemic justice. According to Monika Betzler, for example, empathically understanding and sharing the other's condition is a way to legitimize that person's internal state and thus has a positive impact on the relationship between the empathizer and the target (Betzler, 2019). When empathy is successful, she argues, it enables the empathizer to respond appropriately to the other's condition, and responding appropriately to the other's situation requires that the empathizer first understand and then recognize the other as more than someone whose response to a given situation could have been the same as mine. This recognition is supposed to promote epistemic justice: "empathy is a way of providing testimonial justice to the target by affirming her evaluative perspective, as well as conveying to the target that she matters to the subject" (Betzler 2019, p. 147).

Crucially, as Betzler herself admits, this can only work if the empathizer can accurately understand and share the other's emotions. If this does not happen, the consequences are serious: "It is possible to empathize so inaccurately that a meaningful relationship is not created. It is easy to underestimate cultural, social, and personal contingencies that account for the different ways in which people perceive their environment" (Betzler 2019, p. 145). It follows that empathy is most likely to promote testimonial justice in relationships between subjects from the same sociocultural background who know each other well, that is, in intimate, non-asymmetrical relationships where the understanding is less likely to be inaccurate (see Chapter 4). If this is the case, however, I wonder how useful or appropriate it is to rely on empathy to provide testimonial justice, since it is most needed is in asymmetrical relationships with individuals who are often strangers and from different sociocultural backgrounds.

Two things to note here. First, when it comes to epistemic injustice, it does not seem to matter whether the privileged empathizer is well-intentioned: empathy can lead to epistemic injustice even when the empathizer is sincerely trying to understand the other person without explicit prejudice or ill intent. Thus, the privileged empathizer should be as aware as possible of his or her position of power and the potential epistemically and morally concerning consequences of that power when engaging in empathic relationships aimed at interpersonal understanding.

Second, I am not suggesting that empathy alone is responsible for epistemic injustice. Other phenomena contribute to this outcome. However, I think it is useful to focus on empathy because it is particularly difficult to identify as a potential catalyst for this kind of epistemic vice given the assumption about the inherent moral character of empathy that I have already tried to challenge (see Chapter 5). To be clear, I am not arguing that empathy is impossible in asymmetrical relationships, or that every instance of empathy leads to epistemically and morally unjust behavior. Rather, there seem to be inherent and structural reasons why empathy as defined by the SD is very likely to fall short in these relationships, which should caution us against choosing it as the primary source for our other-directed deliberative processes.

If we ignore this, the inclusion of empathy can potentially lead to two negative outcomes. On the one hand, empathy can limit the dissemination and acquisition of knowledge, which is epistemically harmful: if the privileged empathizer does not take into account that his credibility judgments may be biased because of empathy and does not acknowledge the unequal distribution of power, the target's testimony may at best be misinterpreted or at worst be excluded from the epistemic community altogether. This would leave the empathizer's empathically grasped account of the target's experience as the only available epistemic source in the target's experience and condition.

On the other hand, the involvement of empathy in asymmetrical relationships and related other-directed deliberation can also be morally problematic. If empathizers fail to understand that the inner world of the target will always remain, in some respects, beyond their epistemic reach, we will face what can be called the "colonization problem." It is precisely when the target's experience is seen as a kind of "territory to be conquered" that empathy becomes a tool that obscures the empathizer's exercise of power. In contrast, recognizing that marginalized individuals have greater knowledge and experience of their own conditions than privileged empathizers can return power to them (Garden, 2007; Stefanello, 2021b).

In conclusion, while it is true that the context in which the empathic relationship takes place has a crucial influence, it is equally important to point out that the cultural, social, historical, economic, and political differences between the empathizer and the target are not simply some temporary obstacles that the former will sooner or later overcome – perhaps simply by being more empathetic or more educated – or some kind of empirical data that they can take into account during the deliberative process. Instead, empathizers must find the right balance between the necessary understanding, though not achievable through empathy as defined in the SD, of the broader context of their targets and the empathic relationship, and the awareness that differences will never be eliminated or fully understood.

So far, I have discussed a definition of empathy, the SD, consisting of cognitive empathy, affective empathy, and sympathy. Based on this definition, I mapped three roles that empathy is thought to play in other-directed deliberation: an epistemic role, its role in the formation of moral judgments, and a motivational role. I have then taken all three components of the SD and shown how each of them can be problematic in fulfilling these roles and, in general, when they are involved in other-directed deliberation. It turns out that the involvement of the SD of empathy in deliberation has negative consequences, ranging from epistemic inaccuracies to immoral behavior.

If the results just presented are as troubling as they seem, one might be tempted to argue for the total exclusion of empathy from our deliberative practices. However, this would be not only impossible but counterproductive. Empathy plays an undeniable role in our lives, and thus in our deliberative processes. A more productive response to the questions discussed above might be to ask whether the SD is the only available definition of the empathic phenomenon, or whether there are other approaches that better capture what empathy actually is. I am convinced that the latter alternative is worth pursuing. Specifically, I believe that a phenomenological account of empathy may be able to better describe what the empathic phenomenon is and avoid or mitigate some of the dark sides of the SD of empathy. The next and final section of the book is devoted to articulating and defending this claim.

PART 3

A Different Road: Phenomenological Empathy as a Better Ally for Deliberation

CHAPTER 7

What Is Phenomenological Empathy?

The overall goal of Part 3 is to outline an account of empathy that I will call phenomenological empathy, inspired primarily by Stein's concept of empathy, and to show why this account is better equipped to deal with the criticisms leveled at the SD and why, given its epistemic and axiological role, it proves to be a better ally for our other-directed deliberative processes. To do so, I will first analyze how the nineteenth-century German aesthetic tradition developed the concept of *Einfühlung*, characterizing it as a specific aesthetic tool for appreciating works of art or nature. I will discuss Theodor Lipps's contribution to the debate in particular since he made *Einfühlung* a central concept in discussions of interpersonal understanding and social cognition. He did so by assigning empathy the task of understanding not only what others have produced, such as works of art, but also their interiority. Lipps's account proves especially relevant because it served as both a productive starting point and a critical target for the early phenomenological movement. The Göttingen Circle, in particular, engaged extensively with intersubjective experiences, developing sophisticated analyses of empathy alongside speech acts and collective intentionality.[1]

I will then discuss how Edmund Husserl understood the concept of *Einfühlung* throughout his work. He began working on the topic in 1905 and returned to it until the end of his career. Husserl's contributions to the phenomenological debate on empathy are invaluable. His seminal insight that empathy is the experience of foreign consciousness, graspable through the living body of another, albeit non-originarly, informs all subsequent discussions of the empathic phenomenon. This includes Edith Stein's account, on which my definition of empathy is mainly based. Although Husserl never presented his theory of empathy systematically, his insights provided Stein with crucial theoretical groundwork for developing her own distinctive contribution to the field. As I will discuss briefly, while her debt to Husserl's foundational insights remains undeniable, she advanced the discussion in significant ways. Rather than proposing an entirely new methodology, Stein refined and expanded

1 Members of the Göttingen Circle included Winthrop Bell, Rudolf Clemens, Hedwig Conrad-Martius, Fritz Frankfurter, Siegfried Hamburger, Erich Heinrich, Jean Héring, Heinrich Hoffman, Roman Ingarden, Alexandre Koyré, Hans Lipps, Dietrich Mahnke, Helmuth Plessner, Wilhelm Schapp, Kurt Stavenhagen, Edith Stein, and Alfred von Sybel. For a detailed account of the history and main theoretical contributions of the Circle, see Salice (Salice, 2025).

HTTPS://DOI.ORG/10.1163/9789004745360-009

Husserl's definition by articulating empathy's multilayered structure and clarifying its specific role within our broader intersubjective experience. This development proves essential to understanding empathy's full philosophical significance.

Given the centrality of Stein's account to this work, I will outline the salient aspects of her account of empathy as developed in *On the Problem of Empathy* (1917). I will largely follow the structure of her book, focusing first her critique of Lipps's account, on the essential features of empathy, then on its role in constituting the psycho-physical individual and finally on its role in constituting personhood. Importantly, I do not intend to provide a philosophical-historical analysis of Stein's work – or that of any other phenomenologists I refer to – or a complete reading guide to the text. Instead, my goal is to highlight Stein's innovative theoretical approach to empathy. Moreover, in the last two chapters, I will argue that Stein's theory more accurately captures our experience of empathizing with one another and poses fewer epistemic and moral challenges to our deliberative processes than the SD does.

My main focus will be *On the Problem of Empathy* because it offers a concise and systematic approach to empathy. Moreover, Stein's work stands out for its conceptual precision and linguistic clarity, making it an ideal entry point for readers unfamiliar with phenomenological methodology. Her distinctive contribution lies in her rigorous application of phenomenological analysis to the empathic phenomenon – a method she mastered under Husserl's guidance and employed consistently throughout her career. This ultimately allowed her to present a unique and innovative "philosophical anthropology," in which the phenomenological analysis of empathy reveals the constitution of human beings (Ales Bello, 2025, p. 54).

Finally, I will propose a tentative definition of phenomenological empathy or a phenomenological account of the empathic phenomenon. While Stein's account will be the main theoretical point of reference, the definition will also draw inspiration from other early and contemporary phenomenologists, as will become clear in the final chapters. Specifically, when developing this phenomenological account, I will focus on authors belonging to what is typically called classical phenomenology and their contemporary commentators. I will leave aside those associated with existential phenomenology such as Merleau-Ponty, Heidegger, and Levinas.[2] Although existential phenomenolo-

2 For a discussion of the empathic phenomenon in the works of Merleau-Ponty, Heidegger, and Levinas see, among many others, Ferencz, Magrì, and Thornton (Ferencz-Flatz, 2015; Magrì, 2018; Thornton 2024).

gists have made paramount contributions to the debate on the intersubjectivity, I will analyze the empathic phenomenon and its role in our deliberative processes using a realist phenomenological approach. Classical phenomenology's realist orientation – exemplified in Stein's work – emphasizes rigorous description and eidetic analysis of phenomena as immediately given in experience. This methodological commitment aligns precisely with this project's objective: understanding empathy's specific role in other-directed deliberative processes. Existential phenomenology, despite offering profound insights into lived experience, adopts an ontological approach that risks obscuring empathy's function as an experiential phenomenon with distinct epistemic and axiological dimensions. By contrast, the descriptive precision of classical phenomenology enables us to isolate and analyze empathy's particular contributions to moral and practical reasoning without losing sight of its experiential character.

1 Theodor Lipps and the Origin of the Concept of *Einfühlung*

Roughly in the same years as Hume and Smith, authors belonging to the German aesthetic tradition, particularly the Romantic tradition, began to use the term sympathy (*Sympathie*) to describe the way in which Man and Nature could become a unity (Nowak, 2011, p. 303). For instance, Johann Gottfried Herder (1744–1803) thought of sympathy as a means by which people could enjoy works of art:

> The more a limb signifies what it is supposed to signify, the more beautiful it is; and only inner sympathy [innere Sympathie], i.e., feeling and transposition of our whole human self into the form that has been explored by touch is teacher and indicator of beauty.
>
> HERDER, 1778, cited in JAHODA, 2005, p. 154

However, it was Robert Vischer (1847–1933) – son of Friedrich Theodor Vischer (1807–1887), whose work pioneered the use of *Einfühlung* in the context of aesthetics (F. T. von Vischer, 1846) – who first used the term *Einfühlung* in his doctoral dissertation (R. Vischer, 1873) to discuss the "psychological aspects of the appreciation of art" (Jahoda, 2005, p. 153). In particular, *Einfühlung*, which literally means "feeling into," was understood by Vischer as a specific affective response to works of art, that is when the spectator feels herself into the object. This "feeling into" consists of an "imaginary bodily perspective taking" (Ganczarek et al., 2018, p. 141), which involves imagining what it would be like to be part of that work of art (e.g., part of a painting) from an embodied and emotional standpoint.

The focus on the spectator instead of the artwork implies a fundamental change in aesthetic theory. For the first time, "(…) the emphasis is on the spectator's feelings toward the object" (Nowak, 2011, p. 304) and not on the beauty of artworks. In this sense, through both conscious and unconscious processes of perspective-taking, the viewer recognizes his or her similarities with the object and subsequently projects his or her inner states onto the work of art in order to assign meaning to it: "(…) The body, (…), objectifies itself in spatial forms. Thus it unconsciously projects its own bodily form – and with this also the soul – into the form of the object. From this I derived the notion that I call Einfühlung" (R. Vischer, 1873, p. 92, cited in Matravers, 2017, pp. 78–79).

Admittedly, Vischer's reflections on empathy have not received much attention in the contemporary debate, especially outside of aesthetics. The opposite fate was reserved for one of Vischer's contemporary authors: Theodor Lipps, who is considered the intellectual father of *Einfühlung*, not only for his contributions to aesthetics, but also – and most importantly for this work – for the epistemic role he assigned to *Einfühlung* in understanding other people's minds. It was from Lipps's work that the psychologist Edward Titchener first translated the German concept of *Einfühlung* into English with the newly coined term "empathy" (Titchener, 1909).[3] In this sense, his influence on the debate is rightly justified by the seminal conceptual shift he impressed on *Einfühlung*, namely "the move from empathy with objects to empathy with people" (Matravers, 2017, p. 80).

According to him, there are three different regions of knowledge, that is, we can know three different kinds of "objects" through three different tools. First, we can have knowledge of concrete things thanks to sensuous perception; second, we can have self-knowledge thanks to inner perception; third, we can have knowledge of other people (other I's) thanks to *Einfühlung* which, in *Leitfaden*, his version of a psychology textbook, he defines as "an objectivation of my experiences in an object which is distinct from me" (Lipps 1903a, p. 222). As Lipps wrote in his 1907 article *The Knowledge of Other Egos* (Lipps 1907, KOE from now on), *Einfühlung* answers the questions "How is it that I come to know of other individuals?" and of "sensations, representations, emotions, wishes, and thoughts which are not mine?" (KOE, p. 266).

---

3 Titchener coined the term "empathy" by merging two Greek words: *em* (*en*), meaning "in," and pathos, meaning "feeling," to translate the idea of "feeling into" present in the original German term.

Importantly, Lipps's empathy differs sharply from a competing popular way of answering these questions, namely the argument from analogy, whose intellectual father is considered to be none other than John Stuart Mill (Mill, 1865). According to this position, I can understand the other's mental and emotional states only because I can logically infer from my own experience what is going on in the other's mind by virtue of analogy. More specifically, in Lipps's words, "analogical inferences claim that, since I once found A and B together, also in new cases where I find A again I will think of the past B as existing, and not a fundamentally different B_1" (KOE, p. 273). So, to use Lipps's example, since I once found my angry face (A) and my anger (B) together, when I see someone else's angry face (A) again, I will think of my past anger as existing (B), i.e., I will think that since the other person is making an angry face, she is also angry (B), as I was when I made an angry face.

Lipps strongly criticized this way of characterizing interpersonal understanding, defining it as "totally absurd" (KOE, p. 266). As Timothy Burns and Marco Cavallaro have pointed out in the introduction to their 2018 English translation of KOE, Lipps's rejection of the argument from analogy consists broadly of three main criticisms. First, the argument from analogy does not explain how (and why) I should be able to understand that the physical expressions of my inner states are in fact related to (if not caused by) those inner states, and thus to those of the other person. The argument from analogy erroneously assumes that the subject will be able to infer the connection between the physical gesture – what Lipps called "optical gestures," i.e., its visible and physical manifestation observed from the third-person standpoint – and the kinesthetic gesture – i.e., how the gesture feels when lived first-personally by the subject – first and foremost in herself, and then, as a consequence, to grasp the other person's inner states (KOE, p. 276).

As Lipps skeptically argued, "if I am meant to infer from the fact that I perceive the facial image of the alien gesture the underlying emotion of anger, then I should have obtained a facial image of *my* gesture and have established the connection between it and my anger on the basis of perception" which – and this is the problem – does not happen since "I precisely *cannot* obtain this facial image from the observation of *my* face" (KOE, p. 268). In other words, the argument from analogy seems unable to justify its premise: it does not explain how the subject manages to put A and B together, i.e., how she can consciously identify her angry face as a result of her anger, which in turn casts some serious doubt on the ability to identify the other person's angry face as an indicator of her anger by analogy.

The only option would then be to obtain this facial image from the other person, which would require that we already know the other person's inner state. This brings Lipps to his second criticism: the argument from analogy fails precisely because "it presupposes what it intended to prove" (KOE, p. 263). For the subject to grasp the connection between his own A and B, he seems to first grasp the other person's connection between her facial expression and her inner state: I see the other's expression, and only then do I "look inward" into my experience. However, the understanding of the other's inner state is supposed to be based precisely on the connection between the facial expression and the subject's inner state.

More generally, in order to work, the argument from analogy must presuppose that the two subjects in the analogical relation are in fact similar: other people must have minds and bodies similar to the subject who is trying to understand them; otherwise the analogy is impossible. The problem is that this similarity is supposed to be the end goal of the argument from analogy, not its necessary starting point. It is because I have successfully deduced by analogy that the other person's expression indicates the same inner state as my own that I am able to recognize that person as having a mind like mine, functioning in the same way as mine. Thus, Lipps concluded that "I see bodies and bodily states together with their alterations. These bodies are not human bodies for my consciousness from the outset. Instead, they must become so *by virtue of the analogical inference*. (...) It is by means of this inference that the alien individual first comes into existence for me" (KOE, p. 269, my emphasis).

The third criticism concerns what Lipps saw as an unfixable weakness of the argument from analogy, namely the fact that the only thing this analogy can achieve is self-knowledge, not other-knowledge (KOE, p. 264). The reason is quite simple: there is no reason why what I end up grasping is the other person's happiness and not just my own. When I see the other person's smile, I will remember my past smile and the happiness associated with it, and that is the only epistemic content that the argument from analogy can provide, not that the other person's smile means that she is happy. In short, the other person's physical manifestations can initiate an analogical process that, at best, leads to an understanding of the subject's internal states associated with those physical manifestations. In Lipps's words (KOE, p. 270):

> In any case, the result is that process *'a'* [my angry face] is experientially connected to *my* anger and nothing else. I hope that everyone understands that my anger is something different from the anger of the other. Accordingly, literally all that the perception of process *'b'* [the other's angry face] can reproduce is the representation of *my* anger. I can be *reminded*, in this way, only of *my* anger that *I* felt on the occasion of perceiving this event.

Although the argument from analogy cannot guide us in understanding the interiority of others, but only our personal and present emotional state, this does not mean that Lipps thought the operation itself is impossible. On the contrary, understanding the mental life of others is so ingrained in what we are and do that Lipps characterized it in terms of an *instinct*. More specifically, he argued that "the instinct of empathy" is responsible for understanding the inner states of others as "a product of two factors. One is the instinct, or instinctive impulse, of the expression of life. The other is the instinct of imitation" (KOE, p. 276). Lipps immediately clarified that empathy, or any other tool for that matter, will not allow us to *perceive* the other person's inner state since "anger, friendliness, and sadness cannot be sensuously perceived" (KOE, p. 277). What happens via empathy is that "I experience, in me, the inner state that I see expressed in the other" (KOE, p. 280) through the combination of the two instincts mentioned above.

First and foremost, we all have an undeniable instinct to imitate other people's facial expressions, gestures, and overall physical manifestations, and Lipps cited the phenomenon of the contagious yawn as explicit evidence of this. When I see the other person making an angry face, with all the physical changes that implies, I have an instinct to imitate that face. It is not a conscious decision, it just happens.[4] Once this instinct of imitation is carried out, I am automatically reminded of my past experiences of, say, making an angry face, and by virtue of the instinct of expression, "I feel the tendency to call forth the same gesture. And the emotion that I naturally express in this gesture is bound up with it" (KOE, p. 280). In this sense, affective states and their physical manifestations and gestures are intimately connected: gestures embody the fulfillment of emotions. There is an instinctive and spontaneous tendency to express my emotions in my gestures precisely because there is this innate connection between my internal states and my external physical expressions (Lipps, 1907; Burns, 2022; Donise, 2024).

Lastly, in the final stage of the process, "I live through the tendency to expression again, but not as arising from my emotion, but rather as founded in the perception of the gesture in another's body" (KOE, p. 280). That is, I am able to recognize that the gesture and the emotion associated with it are not really mine, but belong to the other person, and because of this act of projection, I can understand that the other person is in fact experiencing a particular emotional state. Note that this process of attribution still occurs at an uncon-

4 In Lipps's words: "Now, by the grasping of another's gesture I immediately live through the tendency to produce the gesture" (KOE, p. 278).

scious level. However, the empathizer is able to recognize that even though he is experiencing the other person's emotional state in the first person, that state is not coming from his body, but from the other person's body (Donise 2024, p. 85).

But there is more. According to Lipps, when I empathize with another's emotional state, I am not only able to grasp it from an epistemic standpoint, i.e., understand that the other is angry, but I am also naturally inclined to share the same emotional state, i.e., to become angry myself. And I feel that anger not just in the sense of a recollected memory of that emotion, but I am experiencing that emotion first-personally in the present:

> According to Lipps, what happens is that when faced with the angry gestures of others, I am activated *in the first person* and therefore *re-experience* the internal state that I was in when I made those gestures myself.
>
> DONISE, 2024, p. 85, my emphasis

Thus, when there are no external or internal obstacles, empathy will instinctively and inevitably lead to emotional sharing: "The representing of the emotion in another's gesture, or the imagining into [*Hineindenken*] the same gesture, has become, then, an experience of the same, of co-feeling [*Mitfühlen*], of sympathy [*Sympathie*]" (KOE, p. 280).

Consequently, Lipps's mimetic theory of empathy is characterized by two peculiar features. On the one hand, because of this emotional sharing element, his account has been called a "model of actuality" since, through the mimetic process, the emotional state observed in the other person "become 'actually' present in my experience right now" rather than merely represented (Donise 2024, p. 87). On the other hand, in contrast to the analogical proposal, Lipps's account emphasizes the instinctive, unmediated, and emotional dimension of how we experience others that characterizes this process as not entirely cognitive in nature (Donise 2024, p. 89).

Note that the knowledge of other people's emotions is directly dependent on the inner life of the subject who performs this empathic grasp (Burns, 2022). While it is true that it is the other person's physical and facial gestures that trigger my imitative instinct, the empathic process is all internal to the empathizer's mind. For him, the empathizer certainly gains an understanding of the other person's inner life, but it is also undeniable that the activity of empathy itself belongs to the subject alone. In other words, nothing happens outside the empathizer except the initial input of encountering the other person's gestures and expressions.

A final influential aspect of Lipps's account of empathy is the distinction he made between positive and negative empathy. In *Leitfaden*, Lipps explained the empathic phenomenon in terms of the "inner participation" of the empathizer in the other person's inner state, which reaches its most "complete" or "full" manifestation when a complete "identification or oneness" between the empathizer's condition and that of the other is realized (Moran 2004, p. 281). This is because empathy, like all of our experiences, is naturally drawn toward fulfillment. This fulfillment is not always realized. Sometimes, empathy encounters obstacles that prevent it from actually achieving this completeness of experience and producing the identification between the subject's experience and the other person's experience. Lipps called this case negative empathy. The connection between empathy and fulfillment, and the fact that the latter is not always guaranteed, at least not fully, will be a crucial aspect of Stein's account of empathy, albeit in a very different conceptual framework.

2 The Concept of *Einfühlung* in Edmund Husserl

While Theodor Lipps's work on *Einfühlung* was undoubtedly groundbreaking, it was Edmund Husserl's phenomenological investigations of the empathic phenomenon that paved the way for all phenomenologists who followed, including Edith Stein. However, Husserl's starting point was Lipps's account, with which he agreed in its *pars destruens* but disagreed with its *pars construens.*[5] In particular, Husserl was sympathetic with Lipps's critique of the argument from analogy as he explicitly states the following: "Although I would not like to accept all that he says about empathy, I believe that *Lipps* was insofar on the right path as he vigorously struggled against the usual, and in fact, pitiful psychology of empathy" (Husserl, 1910–11, p. 83). In open contrast to the inferential and analogical account, in his winter lectures titled *Fundamental Problems of Phenomenology* (1910–1911), Husserl provides one of his first

5 As Kern points out, while "the only text concerning intersubjectivity that Husserl published during his lifetime was the French translation of his Cartesian Meditation in 1931." Nevertheless, intersubjectivity and empathy are pivotal themes throughout his work. Specifically, the first Husserlian manuscript addressing empathy, the fundamental notion in Husserl's phenomenology of intersubjectivity, date from 1905 to 1907. After 1905, Husserl worked on several manuscripts discussing empathy and access to others' inner sensations. Among the most influential are *Fundamental Problems of Phenomenology* and *Ideas II*, both of which were published posthumously (Kern, 2018, p. 11). For a detailed account of Husserl's discussion on intersubjectivity, see Kern (Kern, 2018).

and perhaps most concise definition of what empathy actually is and how it is supposed to operate. According to Kern, this text represents a "major development in Husserl's phenomenology of intersubjectivity" as it theorizes the "extension of the phenomenological reduction from egological subjectivity to intersubjectivity" (Kern, 2018, p. 12). In this sense, Husserl explicitly writes that empathy positively answers the question "do we ever arrive to an *other* phenomenological I?" since the empathic phenomenon consists of "a special form of empirical experience" of "the consciousness of the other I" (Husserl, 1910–11, p. 82).

However, and in this lies the critique of the "pitiful" – as he calls it – argument from analogy, in order for empathy to occur, there is no need to observe and then infer the other's inner state by virtue of an analogical reproduction of the other's inner state in the empathizer. This is because "when I feel empathy with your anger, I am myself not angry, not at all. Just as I am not angry when I imagine anger or merely recall it – unless, in the latter case, I become angry once again" (Husserl, 1910–11, p. 83). Rather, empathy is, like many other acts such as memory and imagination, a *presentification*, that is, one of those experiential – not inferential – acts whose objects are not present in-the-flesh here and now but allows for the understanding of the structure of the other's lived experience "through the recognition of the universality of the structure of experiences" (Ales Bello, 2025, p. 50).

More precisely, as Husserl himself strives to clarify in the Appendix VIII, empathy is "a kind of 'apperception' or, as we also may say, a kind of appresentation" (Husserl, 1910–11, p. 149). This means that, while I can directly experience the other's inner state without the need of inference or reasoning, the empathic act is "not a perception which gives the thing directly *in propria persona,* in the flesh, but a certain kind of quasi-perceptual awareness 'interwoven' (*verflochten*) with and founded on these perceptions" (Moran & Cohen, 2012, p. 97). This is also why Husserl claims that he would have preferred to use the expression "empathizing perception" to identify this specific experience of encountering another consciousness (Husserl, 1910–11, Appendix XI).

Importantly, the empathic perception is a peculiar act of perception which differs from the one directed at material things. This is because the empathic act is directed toward and it is able to apperceive "of what is 'interior', 'subjective', and what is 'by way of' externalizing expression" (Husserl, 1910–11, Appendix VIII, p. 150 as cited in Jardine, 2017, p. 155). In contrast to the perception of material objects of which further acts of perception can fulfill the empty presentification, the same cannot be said for empathic perception whose object, i.e., the foreign consciousness, cannot be perceived as an inanimate object would by changing one's position to gain a better vantage point. For Husserl, it follows that empathy necessarily consists only of "an 'incomplete' [perception], being constantly open, since of this human being there and, especially, of his interiority this perception expresses only a few things (…), whereas the rest remains indeterminately open" (Husserl, 1910–11, Appendix VIII, p. 150). The indeterminateness and openness of the empathic act, and thus of our ability to access the other's interiority, is perhaps one of the most insightful and fruitful intuitions in Husserl's discussion of empathy. This idea will permeate most, if not all, phenomenological accounts of empathy proposed after him, especially the one from Stein (see Chapter 9).

Precisely because the empathic perception has the interiority of the other person as its object, it is a distinctive kind of perceptual experience, "(…) in which others show up for us directly as expressive units whose bodily movements manifest and embody mindedness" (Jardine, 2017, p. 155). This is possible because both the other person and the subject are not merely physical entities devoid of intentionality, but rather are living bodies (*Leib*), i.e., "center[s] of sensorimotor responsiveness, through which I [the subject] am simultaneously aware of myself and others" (Magrì & McQueen, 2023, p. 89).

The theme of the living body is central to many of Husserl's works, from *Ideas II* to *Cartesian Meditations* (CM, from now on). Unlike the physical body (*Körper*), the living body comes with an inherent sense of ownership: this is my body and I have the capacity to control it. While I can perceive my body in the same way I can perceive other external objects, I am also always able to have "an inner sensuous awareness of it" (Moran & Cohen, 2012, p. 194). The pivotal contribution of empathy is its ability to allow me to experience others as having – or better yet, *being* – living bodies like mine, that is, the other is a body in which a consciousness is located and thus she is an experiencing, moving, reasoning, etc., body in the same way I am.

However, crucially, Husserl argues that the empathic experience of the other as a living body and, thus, of some aspects of the other's inner states, will never be given in an originary manner. The distinction between originarity (or primordiality) and non-originarity (or non-primordiality) is found in *Ideas I*, where Husserl explicitly refers to empathy as a non-originary experience: "We have originary experience of concrete physical things in 'external perception', but no longer in memory or in forward-regarding expectation; we have originary experience of ourself and of our states of consciousness in so-called internal or self-perception; not, however, of others and of their mental processes in 'empathy'" (Husserl, Ideas I, §1, p. 6). As we will see in the next part, Stein effectively develops this distinction, which is central to her account of empathy.

Throughout his works, Husserl develops different conceptual tools to express empathy's role and the peculiar relationship between one's apperception of one's own living body and the empathic apperception of another's living body. As early as his Winter Lessons, he employs the concept of "analogue" to highlight the similarity between how the other's living body and the subject's living body work. In particular, due to the analogical relationship between my living body and that of others, "we find the path to reach synthetically the otherness that is constituted, first, trough the knowledge of the body and then its reach to the soul," and yet "*the analogy is felt immediately*" and it is in any way conveyed by inferential reasoning (Ales Bello, 2025, p. 49, my emphasis).

Importantly, in keeping with the distinction between the originarity and non-originarity related to self- and other-experience of the living body, Husserl states that my experience and the other person's experience are separate and must remain so. In his words, "there is no channel linking the empathized stream to the stream in which the empathizing itself belongs" (Husserl, 1910–11, p. 85). Yet, these two experiences belong to the same "now," that is, my experience and the experience of the person I am empathizing with belong to the same temporal frame: "an act of empathy and the empathized act belong to the same time and they belong *to the same* time for *consciousness*" (Husserl, 1910–11, p. 85).

Although there is no direct connection between my "now" and the other's "now," this simultaneity grasped via empathy leads to the recognition that "each I-monad [is] in relation to each other" (Husserl, 1910–11, p. 86). Thus, it is empathy that enables us as subjects to experience others from our first-person point of view, that is, it allows us to grasp the inherent intersubjective character of our experience which, in turn, "plays a fundamental role in our constitution of both ourselves as objectively existing subjects, other experiencing subjects, and the objective spatio-temporal world" (Beyer, 2022).

In *Cartesian Meditation*, specifically the *Fifth Meditation*, the problem of empathy is further developed and analyzed with the ultimate goal of providing "a transcendental theory of intersubjective experience," which aims to reveal the constitutive intentional features of our awareness of others (Magrì & McQueen, 2023, p. 88). Through the transcendental reduction, we realize that inherent to the ego is other-directedness:[6] "*What is specifically peculiar*

6 On this point, Husserl emphasizes that in order to achieve the goal of transcendentally constituting other subjects a peculiar kind of epoché is needed. Specifically, one in which "we *disregard all constitutional effects of intentionality relating immediately or mediately to other subjectivity* and delimit first of all the total nexus of that actual and potential intentionality in which the ego constitutes *within himself a peculiar ownness*" (Husserl, CM, §44 p. 93).

to me as ego, my concrete being as a monad, purely in myself and for myself *with an exclusive ownness,* includes <my> every intentionality and therefore, in particular, the intentionality directed to what is other" (Husserl, CM, §44 p. 94). At the same time, we as egos are always and necessarily "experienceable by everyone," even when we abstract from their existence positing total "aloneness" (Husserl, CM, §44 p. 93).[7] In short, there is an inescapable relatedness "built in" our egos that put us in constitutive relationality with others. Even more precisely, as Moran and Cohen put it, "the transcendental ego is always and already constituted and constituting if it evolves in and within intersubjectivity" (Moran & Cohen, 2012, p. 102).[8]

As mentioned earlier, in the empathic act, the subject recognizes the other as a living body – that is, a psychophysical unit of body and soul – who is a center of intentionality and possesses and displays an inner life. This recognition is made possible by what Husserl calls "analogizing perception" which echoes the concept of "analogue" discussed above: "It is clear from the very beginning – states Husserl – that only a similarity connecting within my primordial sphere, that body over there with my body can serve as the motivational basis for the *'analogizing' apperception* of that body as another animate organism" (Husserl, CM, §50 p. 111).

In this sense, even though I cannot grasp the other as an animate organism directly, that is primordially,[9] I can do so through an analogy with my own animate organism. Note that Husserl reiterates that "it by no means follows that there would be an inference form analogy" since "apperception is not inference, not a thinking act" (Husserl, CM, §50 p. 111). Analogizing apperception and analogical inference are qualitatively different acts: the former is an

7 Here the full quote from Husserl: "If I 'abstract' (in the usual sense) from others, I 'alone' remain. But such abstraction is not radical; such aloneness in no respect alters the natural world-sense, 'experienceable by everyone', which attaches to the naturally understood Ego and would not be lost, even if a universal plague had left only me" (Husserl, CM, §44 p. 93).

8 Moran and Cohen's more extended comment and effective summary of this point: "The phenomenological reduction redirects the ego to itself, to its rapport with its own lived states but only by affirming an auto-a-perception of itself as both spatial and temporal, that is as both constituted by the temporal flux of its lived states and the spatiality of its *Leib* capable of co-existing with a multitude of bodies (*Körper*) and in which the ego is forced to recognize as and in itself a secondary sphere, that is a sphere in itself constituted by the *ego* as the *ego* but which is also given to the *ego* as foreign" (Moran & Cohen, 2012, p. 101–102).

9 In this clear passage of *CM*, Husserl reiterates this pivotal insight: "(…) the body over there, which is nevertheless apprehended as an animate organism, must have derived this sense by an apperceptive transfer from my animate organism, and done so in a manner that excludes an actually direct, and hence primordial, showing of the predicates belonging to an animate organism specifically, a showing of them in perception proper" (Husserl, CM, §50 pp. 110–111).

intuitive act and the latter is a theoretical process. This aligns Husserl with Lipps's rejection of the argument from analogy.

It is worth noting that every apperception is based on what Husserl calls a "primal instituting," or the process by which we acquire something – any kind of cultural acquisition – for the first time. For example, seeing a pair of scissors for the first time as a child, as Husserl mentions in *CM*. Once we have established the objective sense of something, we can perceive similar objects based on that initial perception, even though the present case differs from the original one in some ways. This "analogizing transfer" also occurs in empathy. Because I have established the objective sense of my own living body as a center of intentionality via self-perception, I can co-perceive others as having living bodies similar to mine.

Husserl famously used the concept of "Pairing (*Paarung*)" to "indicate the peculiar nature of that analogizing apprehension whereby a body within primordial sphere, being similar to my own animate body, becomes apprehended as likewise an animate organism" (Husserl, CM, §51 p. 112). In the context of empathy, pairing passively links the other's living body and their manifestations (e.g., gestures, facial expressions, and movements) with one's own through the analogizing transfer.[10] Crucially, pairing does not consist of an active synthesis – that is, an overt identification between the two subjects involved or a projection from the ego to the alter ego – rather, it is "a primal form of that passive synthesis which we designate as 'association'" (Husserl, CM, §51 p. 112).

This passive synthesis is mutual because both I and the other are always involved in the process, that is, we are always paired or given in a pairing. As Magrì and McQueen effectively summarize, "empathy represents a pre-reflective directedness to other-minded beings, who mirror my own being and whose situated experiences are irreducible to my self-experience. Such a structural, transcendental similarity between self and other provides the basis for relating to and exploring another's lived experience" (Magrì & McQueen, 2023, pp. 89–90).

Importantly, in §51 of *CM*, which is dedicated to pairing, Husserl poses perhaps the most consequential question in the debate on empathy: how are we able to recognize the other person as another living body and not merely a copy of ourselves when we empathize and apperceive the other through pairing? In answering this question, Husserl once again refers to the crucial distinction between the modes of givenness of self-experience and other-experience: "that none of the appropriated sense specific to an animate organism can become

10 Note that pairing is not "exclusively peculiar to this experience [i.e., empathy]," but it "is a *universal* phenomenon of the transcendental sphere" (CM, §51 p. 112).

actualized originarily in my primordial sphere" (Husserl, CM, §51 p. 113). Similarity yet difference: this productive tension between the self and the other permeates all phenomenological discussions of empathy and intersubjectivity. As we will see in the next two chapters, it is one of the most effective conceptual gains of the phenomenological approach to interpersonal understanding, compared to the SD-based accounts.

A final seminal contribution is the distinction between the natural and personalistic attitudes, which is closely related to the previously discussed distinction between *Körper* and *Leib*. In *Ideas II*, Husserl states that we can relate to the world and others in two distinct ways. The natural attitude is the default way in which we relate to the world daily, accepting its existence and manifestations without questioning them. A potential degeneration of this attitude is what Husserl calls the "naturalistic attitude," which exclusively engages with the world through an objectifying and reifying lens. This attitude is usually employed by the natural sciences (Husserl, Ideas II, § 49(e)). On the other hand, the personalistic attitude is characterized by Husserl in this *locus classicus* as follows: "The attitude we are always in when we live with one another, talk to one another, shake hands with another in greeting, or are related to another in love and aversion, in disposition and action, in discourse and discussion" (Husserl, Ideas II, § 49, p. 192). In other words, the personalistic attitude is the stance we – practically and non-theoretically – take toward other human beings when we relate to them as persons, or as living bodies. In contrast, the naturalistic attitude considers the other as merely a physical and material entity (*Körper*), which is measurable and exclusively located within the domain of causal powers and relations.

According to Husserl, "the naturalistic attitude is in fact subordinated to the personalistic, and the former only acquires [it] by means of an abstraction, or rather, by means of a kind of self-forgetfulness of the personal Ego" (Husserl, Ideas II, §49(e), p. 193). Thus, the personal attitude is how we pre-theoretically relate to others. In contrast, the naturalistic attitude must be explicitly pursued by the researcher through a kind of forgetting of her status and life as a person. As Husserl sums up, being a person means "to posit oneself as a person, to find oneself in, and to bring oneself into conscious relations with a 'surrounding world (*Umwelt*)'" (Husserl, Ideas II, § 49 (e), p. 193). Within the personalistic attitude, the other is also experienced as a person – that is, a living body in relation to a "surrounding world."[11]

11 The next chapter (see Section 8.3.1) discusses the crucial role of the concepts of *Umwelt* and horizon for the Husserlian account of empathy and his broader conception of intersubjectivity.

More importantly, the personalistic attitude allows one to understand another person's actions, expressions, and behavior as a result of their motivations and values through the empathic act.[12] According to Husserl, motivation governs and explains human actions because it coincides with "the lawfulness of the life of the spirit" or "personal life" (Husserl, Ideas II, §56, §54). Thus, to understand why an agent performed a specific act, had a particular thought, or an emotional reaction, we must examine their motivations and empathy is precisely the tool that allows us to do so: "I put myself in the place of the other subject, and by empathy I grasp what motivates him and how strongly it does so, with what power. And I learn to understand inwardly how he behaves, and how he would behave, under the influence of such and such motives, determining him with such and such force, i.e., I grasp what he is capable of and what is beyond him" (Husserl, Ideas II, §56 (d) p. 287).

It is precisely this empathically gained recognition within the personalistic attitude that enables respect for and understanding of the other as a person, revealing empathy's inherently ethical character. As Magrì and McQueen observe, "in this attitude, which is inspired by respect for the worth of individual persons, one attends to the affective qualities of another's environing world [an alternative translation of *'Umwelt'*] in different degrees of fulfilment, striving to comprehend the motives and dispositions that guide their character and behavior" (Magrì & McQueen, 2023, p. 94). This intimate connection between empathy, motivation, values, and personhood represents one of the most original and insightful dimensions of Stein's account of *Einfühlung*, as we will examine in the following discussion.

3 The Concept of *Einfühlung* in Edith Stein

Before turning to a detailed analysis of Edith Stein's account of empathy, it is worth highlighting some of the most significant moments of her life and career.[13] Stein, born on October 12, 1891, in Breslau, Germany (now Wroclaw, Poland), to a Jewish family, began her academic journey in 1911 at the University of Breslau, where she studied psychology and German for two years. How-

12 As Kern noted, Dilthey's connection between the personal or spiritual world and the concept of motivation was a crucial influence on Husserl's approach to discussing empathy and understanding others as persons (Kern, 2018, p. 12).

13 I am following Calcagno's biography of Stein (Calcagno, 2020). See also the "Edith Stein" entry in the Stanford Encyclopedia of Philosophy for a detailed biography (Szanto & Moran, 2024) and her biographical book titled *Life in a Jewish Family, 1891–1916* published posthumously in 1986 (Stein, 1986).

ever, she found the approach too positivistic and felt the need for a more complex and less psychologistic depiction of how the human mind operates.

This dissatisfaction, combined with her reading of Adolf Reinach and Husserl – particularly the first volume of *Logical Investigations* – prompted her move to Göttingen to explore the phenomenological method. In 1913, she enrolled at the University of Göttingen to study psychology and philosophy with a phenomenological focus. She attended Husserl's seminars and learned the phenomenological method under Reinach's guidance. Importantly, as Calcagno attests, "while studying, Stein also took part in the meetings of the Göttingen Philosophical Society and subsequently met other phenomenologists, including Hedwig Conrad-Martius, Theodor Conrad, Jean Héring, Max Scheler, Roman Ingarden, Alexandre Koyré, and Hans Lipps" (Calcagno, 2020, p. 626).

After attending Husserl's lectures on *Nature and Spirit*, she chose empathy as the topic of her dissertation, which she wrote from 1915 to 1916, under his supervision. In 1916, at Husserl's suggestion, she moved to Freiburg, where he had been appointed Professor of Philosophy, to complete her dissertation. Concurrently, between 1916 and 1918, Stein offered to be Husserl's assistant and contributed to the editing of *Ideas II*. However, she decided to interrupt their collaboration because she could not concentrate on her own research interests while continuing to edit Husserl's complex manuscripts and notes, and due to some personal and philosophical conflicts with him. Despite her considerable philosophical talents, academic teaching remained beyond reach for Stein, as prevailing sexism and anti-Semitism in the German university system prevented her from obtaining the *Habilitation* necessary for such positions.

A pivotal moment in Edith Stein's life occurred in 1922 when she converted to Christianity and embraced Catholicism, profoundly affecting her philosophical perspectives. That same year, she published *Philosophy of Psychology and the Humanities*, in which she discussed the foundations of the humanities in general and psychology in particular, emphasizing the interconnectedness of the individual and the larger community (Stein, 1922). She then entered the Discalced Carmelite Order in 1934, taking the name Sister Teresa Benedicta of the Cross.

After her conversion, she sought to integrate the insights of phenomenology with her faith, exploring the intersections between philosophy and theology, in works such as *Finite and Eternal Being. An Attempt at an Ascent to the Meaning of Being* (Stein, 1950) and *Act and Potency* (Stein, 1931). Tragically, with the rise of Nazi regime, Stein faced persecution because of her Jewish heritage. In 1942, she was arrested and deported to Auschwitz, where she and her sister were killed in the gas chambers.

Now, let us focus on her 1917 dissertation, *On the Problem of Empathy* (Stein 1917, PE from now on). Although the topic of empathy recurred throughout her work,[14] PE provides a systematic and detailed phenomenological analysis of the concept of *Einfühlung* in a clear and effective way. The original work consisted of four parts. Chapter 1, which was never published and is now lost, comprised a historical *excursus* of the literature on *Einfühlung* from Herder to Stein's contemporary thinkers. In Chapter 2, Stein focuses on the essence of the empathic phenomenon as opposed to other related but substantially different phenomena such as memory, expectation, and imagination. This allows her to show how her account differs from other competing theories such as Lipps's theory of oneness, the theory of imitation, the theory of association, and the theory of inference from analogy. She also refutes the theoretical proposal of Scheler by distinguishing empathy from sympathy or fellow-feeling. Chapter 3 deals with the constitution of the psycho-physical individual, which consists of the combination of soul and body. Finally, in Chapter 4, Stein discusses the role of empathy in understanding the mental (or spiritual) person and their as well as our own hierarchy of values.

3.1 *Stein's Original Contribution to Husserl's Account of Empathy*

Understanding Stein's account of empathy in PE requires considering its connection with Husserl's characterization of this phenomenon. First of all, she claims that she chose empathy as the topic of her dissertation to address what she considered an underdeveloped concept in Husserl's account of objectivity and, consequently, intersubjectivity. As she states in her autobiographical book (Stein 1986, p. 269, as cited in Magrì 2015, p. 132):

> Husserl in his course on *Nature and Spirit* had maintained that an objective external world can only be experienced intersubjectively (i.e., by a plurality of individual knowing subjects who are in a position to exchange information with each other); which means that such an experience presupposes other individuals. Husserl, following Theodor Lipps, named this experience "empathy" but did not explain what it consisted of. Here was a gap, which was worthwhile filling; I wanted to explain what empathy meant.

While Stein identified this lacuna in Husserl's approach, she simultaneously "acknowledges her debt to [him]: she draws from Husserl's method of research

14 For a detailed discussion of Edith Stein's philosophical production see Calcagno (Calcagno, 2007).

and conceptual tools, and this is very clear from the beginning of her text, which deals with the question of method retracing faithfully its stages as indicated by Husserl, ultimately dwelling on (…) the primary role of *Erlebnisse* [lived experience]" (Ales Bello, p. 52). Both her methodological commitment and her debt to Husserl become evident in the preface to *PE*, where she declares: "Of course, the statement of the problem and my method of work have grown entirely out of intellectual stimuli received from Professor Husserl so that in any case what I may claim as my 'mental property' in the following expositions is most questionable. Nevertheless, I can say that the results I now submit have been obtained by my own efforts. This I could no longer maintain if I now undertook changes" (PE, p. 3).

The consistency of her methodology with Husserl's approach, combined with her editorial work on *Ideas II*, initially led many scholars to question her dissertation's originality. For years, Stein was regarded either as merely one of Husserl's students who helped clarify his empathy theory or, more dismissively, as someone who simply reiterated his existing theorizations. However, as noted in her dissertation's foreword, she had neither read nor worked on *Ideas II* before completing her thesis, which explains the absence of references to that work (PE, p. 3). As Ales Bello rightly observes, "Stein's merits consists in having fully assimilated the phenomenological method and in being able to autonomously use it" (Ales Bello, 2025, p. 52). This assessment aligns with Husserl's own evaluation of her work, which he considered sufficiently original and high-quality that he contemplated "whether it will be possible to put this work in the Yearbook along with *Ideas*" (Stein 1986, p. 269, as cited in Ales Bello, 2025, p. 52).

Both Husserl's and Stein's testimonies thus confirm that *PE* represents an original and innovative contribution that remains coherent with Husserlian phenomenological method and core insights. In this regard, Calcagno argues persuasively that Stein's originality lies not in empathy's definition – which substantially aligns with Husserl's – but in her articulation of empathy's role and capabilities (Calcagno, 2020). According to his analysis, Stein's empathic phenomenon not only facilitates self- and other-understanding but also enables recognition that the other constitutes a person. Furthermore, it provides the epistemic foundation for "acquir[ing] knowledge in the human sciences (*Gestewissenschaften*)" (Calcagno 2020, p. 629).

These roles prove fundamentally interconnected: personhood involves specific activities, and empathy allows us "to grasp ourselves and others as persons and grants us access to uniquely human activities, such as our lived sense of history, religion, politics, and art" (Calcagno 2020, p. 629). While I will not examine empathy's foundational role in the human sciences, I will explore in detail the insight that every lived experience, including every empathic act, exists immediately and necessarily within a broader context partially constituted by and influenced by these inherently human activities. This insight provides empathy, as Stein defines it, with a significant advantage over the SD, as I will demonstrate in Chapters 8 and 9.

3.2 *Stein's Critique of Lipps and Other Competing Accounts of* Einfühlung

Let us begin our overview of Stein's account of *Einfühlung* by examining her critique of Lipps's and other alternative theories of empathy, which can be found in Chapter 2 of PE. According to Stein, there are two main problems with Lipps's account. First, she argued against Lipps's idea that empathy, in its most complete manifestation, consists of and results in a state of identification or oneness between the two selves. The source of this error lies in the fact that Lipps does not seem to recognize the fundamentally different mode of givenness between the experience of the empathizer and that of the other person to whom the empathic act is directed. In fact, "Lipps confuses the following two acts: (1) being drawn into the experience at first given objectively and fulfilling its implied tendencies with (2) the transition from non-primordial to primordial experience" (PE, p. 13). According to Stein, Lipps confuses experiencing that person's emotional state with having a primordial experience of it because of empathy.

For example, when I empathize with someone else's fear, I am not experiencing that fear primordially, that is, as given in the here and now, but I am always experiencing it non-primordially. I can primordially experience the fear of watching someone get bitten by a snake, but I cannot primordially experience the fear of that person getting bitten by a snake. When I empathize with the fear of another person, I primordially experience an empathized emotional state that is not and cannot be experienced by myself primordially. Its primordiality can be experienced only by the empathized subject who has lived those emotional states in her or his here and now. This does not mean that I cannot understand his or her fear. On the contrary, I can empathize with that fear, but the fear that I will experience as a result of the empathic act will not be given to me primordially (PE, p. 14).

The difference between the modes of givenness explains why Lipps's famous example of the spectator and the acrobat does not work. According to Lipps, when a spectator observes the acrobat performing his dangerous movements on the tightrope, he will internally imitate those movements and the affective states associated with them. This internal imitation will lead the spectator not only to experience the acrobat's inner state and movements first-personally but also to merge his self with that of the acrobat (Lipps 1903b, p. 122). Stein is determined to reject this depiction as an example of how empathy in its fullest form is not supposed to work (PE, p. 16):

> I am not one with the acrobat but only "at" him. I do not actually go through his motions but only *quasi*. Lipps also stresses, to be sure, that I do not outwardly go through his motions. But neither is what 'innerly' corresponds to the movements of the body, the experience that "I move," primordial; it is non-primordial for me. And in these non-primordial movements I feel led, accompanied, by his movements. Their primordiality is declared in my non-primordial movements which are only there for me in him (...).

It is perfectly possible to "surrender" to something – in this case, the acrobat's performance – but this does not mean that the subject will experience that thing primordially, nor will it result in "a dissolution of the 'I' in the object" – in this case, the dissolution of the spectator's 'I' in the acrobat's performance (PE, p. 17). Because the content of empathy will necessarily be non-primordial, even though the empathic act itself is primordially experienced by the subject, a condition of oneness between the selves involved in the empathic act will never be possible or attainable. As she concluded decisively: "Empathy is not a feeling of oneness" (PE, p. 17).

In this sense, empathy is able to grasp the experience of others precisely because it does not blur the boundaries between ourselves and those of other subjects. This is also clear in the case of the so-called "we" subject that arises when we experience the same emotional state over the same object (in Stein's example, the news that the fortress has fallen): "Not through the feeling of oneness, but through empathizing, do we experience others. The feeling of oneness and the enrichment of our own experience become possible through empathy" (PE, p. 17). In other words, for there to be oneness, empathy must come first: through empathy, we understand that the other person is in the same emotional state as we are, and then it is possible – but not necessary – to experience that feeling of oneness.

The second criticism has to do with the fact that Lipps's empathy is based on an act of imitation. According to Stein, when empathy is characterized as imitation, there is a gap between what empathy is supposed to explain, i.e., the foreign experience, and what it actually explains, i.e., the experience of the empathizer. If the gestures of the other person arouse in me the instinct to imitate them internally, which in turn leads me to express those experiences, then what results is not an understanding of the other person's experience, but rather "an experience of my own that arouses in me the foreign gestures witnessed" (PE, p. 22). As Stein pointed out, imitation merely "infects" us with the feelings of the other person, as in the case of contagious crying in children or when we are sad because someone close to us is upset.

She crucially pointed out that these acts of mirroring or motor mimicry "do not serve a cognitive function, (…) they do not announce a foreign experience to us as empathy does" (PE, p. 22) since even a mere wincing of pain can trigger our imitative instinct, but is not capable of arousing an emotion. Thus, the theory of imitation not only fails to explain what it promises, i.e., the foreign experience, but it also has weak, if any, explanatory power, since it transfers to us only those feelings that we experience first-personally as our own. The fact that these "transferred" feelings, as Stein called them, are experienced as one's own, and that their origin or source is fundamentally ignored, except as an initial trigger, explains why the theory of imitation is not able to successfully provide epistemically valuable information about other people's experiences, but only about the subject's (PE, p. 22).

Recognizing that much more could be said about the theory of imitation, Stein, for the sake of brevity, effectively summarized and adopted Scheler's criticisms of Lipps in his 1913 book *The Nature of Sympathy* (PE, p. 22). One of the four objections focused on the inadequacy of using the empathizer's past experience as a reference for empathy, since "we also understand experiences unfamiliar to us from our own earlier experience" (PE, p. 22). As Scheler argued, we can empathize with the terror of someone who is drawing without having had the same experience (Scheler, 1913, p. 11).[15] Another related objection concerns the fact that imitation does not seem to explain why "we also

15 For some, Scheler's criticism of Lipps' proposal misses the point since Lipps never claimed that the empathizer must have had the exact same experience of the other, but rather that she must have experienced the same emotions, even in different contexts. For instance, Donise raised this point: "Of course, to claim that I am activated on the basis of my experiences is not to claim that I am only able to 'feel' what I have actually experienced before. The example of the acrobat removes any possible doubt in this regard: in order to empathize with the acrobat, I certainly do not need to have had the experience of walking on a tightrope; otherwise, this would be a rather rare empathic reaction and circus performances would be very selective encounters. What I have experienced is loss of balance and vertigo while stumbling, riding a bicycle, or even just walking on an imaginary straight line or along the vanishing line between tiles as a child. Loss of balance is an experience that characterizes all of us bipedal human beings, which we would probably have no access to if we were crawling reptiles" (Donise 2024, p. 86). Note, however, that it is still possible that the empathizer has not (yet) experienced some emotions or inner states – perhaps because of age or a variety of other circumstances – and this would render her unable to perform the empathic act. Thus, Scheler's and Stein's criticism is still relevant.

understand expressions that we cannot imitate" such as a dog's wagging tail as an expression of joy (PE, p. 22). Moreover, since we can grasp "the inadequacy of an expression," this grasp cannot be the result of imitating that expression, otherwise, this recognition would be impossible (PE, p. 22). Finally, and perhaps most problematically, the theory of imitation is not logically sound because it "presupposes a grasping of expression as expression, exactly what it is to explain" (PE, p. 22). For imitation to be successful, the subject must have already grasped, albeit unconsciously, the other person's state. However, this should be the end goal of imitation, not its starting point. In order to imitate the other person's fear, I must have already grasped that she is experiencing fear.[16]

Lipps's account of *Einfühlung* is not the only theory of empathy that Stein rejected. In particular, she also broadly criticized any psychological approach to the problem of empathy because psychological analysis must always come after a phenomenological inquiry into the nature of the phenomenon (PE, p. 21).[17] A genetic-psychological approach to empathy that does not rely on phenomenology encounters a logical obstacle because "such investigation actually presupposes the being whose development it is seeking to ground – its essence as well as the existence, its 'what' as well as its 'that'" (PE, p. 21). Thus, since genetic psychology is unable to provide the nature and justification of the empathic phenomenon, this approach is not a valid method for investigating the nature of our experience of the other's consciousness. Note that Stein considers the inability to grasp the nature of empathy to be a common denominator of all the genetic theories of empathy that she criticizes. Accordingly, she concludes this section by stating that "before one can delineate the genesis of something, one must know what it is" (PE, p. 26). All non-phenomenological theories of empathy fail to do precisely just that.

Stein also challenged the theory of association. According to this theory, when a subject sees another person making a physical movement or facial expression, he or she remembers the internal state that in his or her experience caused that movement or expression, and by association understands that the other person is experiencing the same mental state. Crucially, the other person's internal state "[is] not given, but its existence is inferred" (PE, p. 24): the subject infers the other person's internal state on the basis of an "intuitive representation," i.e., an association between his or her own internal

16 Note that Stein's and Scheler's critique of Lipps's imitation-based account is surprisingly similar to his critique of the argument from analogy and its logically problematic structure.

17 In Stein's words: "Psychology is entirely bound to the results of phenomenology" (PE, p. 21).

state and the foreign one. The problem with this approach becomes clear when we consider that for Stein, empathy is "an experienced act, and it reaches its objects directly without representation" (PE, p. 24). In this sense, empathy consists in experiencing the experience of the other. There is no need for an associative or representational mechanism to grasp what the other person is experiencing.

A similar, albeit radicalized, concern is expressed by Stein against the theory of inference by analogy, which she strongly rejects following Lipps's critique. This theoretical approach is flawed because it completely ignores the experiential aspect of empathy and, more generally, what it means to interact with other human beings. In this regard, Stein commented that "this theory maintains that we see nothing around us but physical soulless and lifeless bodies" since the attribution of the other person's internal state is based entirely on an inferential process about the causal connection between the changes in my body and the resulting changes in my experience, which, once analogously recognized in others, I attribute to them (PE, p. 26).

As a result, the only outcome that inference by analogy can pursue is some form of probabilistic knowledge about the other's internal state whose explanatory value is consistent with that of the analogy and which ultimately remains to be proven. What Stein seems to be implying here, not so implicitly, is that the epistemic value of empathy, understood as the experience of others' experiences, is much higher than that of any of the competing theories presented so far.

3.3 *The Essence of the Empathic Act*

Let us now turn to the *pars construens* of Chapter 2. Stein begins with an example of an act of empathy: "A friend tells me that he has lost his brother and I become aware of his pain. What kind of awareness is this?" (PE, p. 7). Understanding the nature of this awareness is possible only through phenomenological reduction, that is, by looking at the essence of the phenomenon. After briefly explaining the method of her research, she compared empathy with other phenomena that might bear some resemblance to it and, thus, be confused with it.

First and foremost, Stein ruled out the possibility that empathy and external perception are the same phenomenon: while the empathic act is similar to a perceptual act (*Wahrnehmung*), in that both have direct access to their objects, i.e., *hic et nunc*, it differs from perception in that the internal state of others, unlike the objects of external perception, is never primordially made available to the empathizer. As she stated, "I can never get an 'orientation' where the pain itself is primordially given" (PE, p. 7).

As said, the distinction between primordial and non-primordial is tantamount to understanding the nature of *Einfühlung*: empathy is "an act which is primordial as present experience though non-primordial in content" (PE, p. 10). In this sense, empathy is similar to memory, expectation, or imagination: these acts share with empathy the different modes of givenness of the experiences they refer to. However, empathy differs from these phenomena in one crucial respect: "The subject of the empathized experience (...) is not the subject empathizing but another. (...) These two subjects are separate and not joined together, as previously, by a consciousness of sameness or a continuity of experience" (PE, p. 11).

In memory, the subject who remembers having experienced joy is the same as the subject who is remembered as being joyful, even though they are still separate in the act of remembering and the content of the remembered experience is primordially experienced only by the remembering subject. Expectation works in exactly the same way as memory. In the case of imagination, the subject doing the imagining is having a primordial experience, while the subject being imagined to be experiencing this imagined world is not primordial.

Unlike empathy, there is this continuity or "consciousness of sameness" between the subjects of memory, expectation, and imagination. In short, in memory, expectation, and imagination, the subject performing the act is the same as the subject being remembered, expected, or imagined. In empathy, the empathizer and the empathized subject are two different I's, otherwise it wouldn't be the act of understanding others, but only the act of understanding oneself, which was precisely one of the main problems with Lipps's account.

Stein's description of how empathy can be achieved clarifies the interplay between primordiality and non-primordiality. The empathic act consists of three different degrees that do not necessarily require completion. In the first degree ("the emergence of the experience"), the other's lived experience (*Erlebnis*) presents itself as an object emerging in the empathizer's perceptual field. When this happens, it is possible – although not necessary – that, in an attempt to understand another's inner state with greater clarity, one is pulled into that experience so that "[she is] now no longer turned to the content but to the object of it, [is] at the subject of the content in the original subject's place" (PE, p. 10). In the second degree of the empathic act ("the fulfilling explication"), the other's experience will no longer be a mere object for the empathizer. Finally, in the third degree ("the comprehensive objectification of the explained experience"), although the other's experience will become an object again, the empathizer will acquire a more detailed understanding of it.

At the first level of the empathic act, I directly grasp the emotional state of the other person by simply seeing his or her face. I see her smile, I grasp her joy, i.e., I grasp that she is joyful. However, I can (but do not have to) do more: I can try to gain a better understanding of her experience by paying attention to the object to which her emotional state is directed. I can pay attention to the source of her joy. Thus, in the second level of empathy, I let my focus be guided by the other person's intentional objects, which allows me to temporarily occupy the subject's experiential place. Note that what it means to be "in the original subject's place" plays a pivotal role in understanding how Stein's account of empathy differs from the SD as I will discuss it in detail in the next chapter (see Chapter 8). Finally, after the other person's inner experience (e.g., her joy) has been clarified for me, the other's experience will again become an object, but one about which I have gained much more knowledge.

At this point, Stein provided a definition of the empathic phenomenon as "a kind of act of perceiving *sui generis*" consisting of "the experience of foreign consciousness in general" (PE, p. 11), which echoes the definition of empathy in the *Foreword* as "the perceiving of foreign subjects and their [lived] experience" (PE, p. 3). The philosopher was also very explicit about the role and function of empathy: "This is how man grasps the psychic life of his fellow man" (PE, p. 11).

Strikingly, Stein noted that empathy is also the act by which humans can grasp God's inner states and commands, and, perhaps surprisingly, God can also grasp human life in this way.[18] However, while God can never be mistaken about what people experience, nor does He ever experience people's inner states as His own, "men are mistaken about each other's experiences" (PE, p. 12). This remark is interesting because it allows for the possibility of empathic error from the outset: part of what it means to understand each other is the possibility of misunderstanding each other. This is also consistent with the fact that people do not complete all three levels of the empathic process, but often stop at the most basic level, the emergence of the experience (e.g., the empathizer simply grasps that the other person is happy). Thus, part of what it means to understand each other is also the possibility of achieving only a superficial and basic understanding of each other.

At this point, after criticizing the other theories of empathy as discussed above (see Section 7.2.1), she compared her theory with Scheler's account, since, as she noted, it "deviates considerably from all discussed so far" (PE, p. 26), while also showing some similarities given their common phenomenological framework. Although "extremely seductive," Scheler's theory of empathy lacks clarity on one critical point: how is it possible – she asked – to distinguish one's own experience from that of others if, as Scheler does, we posit an undifferentiated stream of experience (PE, p. 27)? It is impossible, Stein

18 Note that Stein made these comments before her conversion to Catholicism in 1922.

argued, precisely because there is no such thing as a neutral stream of experience, since "every experience is by nature an 'I's' experience that cannot be separated phenomenally by the 'I' itself" (PE, p. 28). All the experiences that Scheler describes, despite his claim, are experiences that presuppose an "I" that is differentiated and separate from the "I" of the other person.

According to Stein, the source of Scheler's error lies in the fact that he "fails to recognize a pure 'I'," instead he takes the "I" to be a psychic individual (PE, p. 28). In other words, Scheler made a methodological error: to understand how we experience other minds, we must reflect on the experience of the pure "I" after phenomenological reduction, and not use reflection as a way to understand other consciousness. This is because, as Dahlstrom points out, "what is given in reflection are solely the experiences of the reflecting I – but not the others' experiences" (Dahlstrom 2021, p. 19). Thus, Stein argued that if we were to follow Scheler's account based on inner perception, we would end up experiencing our own experiences in reflection and not those of others (PE, p. 33):

> Just as our own individual is announced in our own perceived experiences, so the foreign individual is announced in empathized ones. But we also see that in one case there is a primordial, while in the other a non-primordial, givenness of the constituting experiences. If I experience a feeling as that of another, I have it given twice: once primordially as my own and once non-primordially in empathy as originally foreign. And precisely this non-primordiality of empathized experiences causes me to reject the general term "inner perception" for the grasping of our own and foreign experience.

3.4 *Empathy and the Psycho-physical Individual*

While an essential analysis of what empathy is must be the necessary starting point of any phenomenological investigation, in the remaining two chapters, Stein moves to a different kind of analysis, precisely a constitutional one. She investigates the constitution of the psycho-physical individual (Chapter 3) and the mental person, i.e., personhood (Chapter 4). Specifically, the goal is to elucidate how empathy contributes to the constitution of these two entities, that is, how empathy participates in bringing them together and in identifying them in experience (PE, p. 35).[19] And empathy seems to allow us to identify ourselves and others as psycho-physical individuals and persons.

---

19 In Stein's words: "We must treat empathy as a problem of constitution and answer the question of how the objects in the usual theories, such as the psycho-physical individual, personality, etc., arise within consciousness" (PE, p. 35).

Central to the analysis of the constitution of the psycho-physical individual is the concept of the living body (*Leib*), which we already saw as central for Husserl's discussion. After stating that, contrary to Lipps's position, the pure "I" is already individuated from the beginning rather only in opposition to the other's I, and rather that it is only "illuminated" in the encounter with another self, Stein argued that the "division between soul and body was an artificial one, for the soul is always necessarily a soul in a body" (PE, p. 38). The point now is to clarify what this body is and "how and as what it is given to us" (PE, p. 38).

Stein emphasized the special way in which the body is given in consciousness: the givenness of the body cannot be compared to the way other physical objects are given to us. Moreover, there is a certain elusiveness about the body: unlike other physical objects, the body is never fully given to us because there is no way in which we can grasp all of its sides simultaneously. She compared it to the moon: "It would withhold its back side with more stubbornness than the moon and invite me to continually consider it from new sides. Yet as soon as I am about to carry out its invitation, it hides these sides from me" (PE, p. 38).

Crucially, the body is inescapable for the subject: there is no hiding from the body. While I can distance myself from physical objects and completely remove them from my field of experience, I cannot do the same with my body: "For even if we shut our eyes tightly and stretch out our arms, in fact allowing no limb to contact another so that we can neither touch nor see our physical body, even then we are not rid of it. Even then it stands there inescapably in full embodiment (hence the name), and we find ourselves bound to it perpetually" (PE, p. 39).

In this sense, our body is always a living body that is not merely the object of outer perception – as when we observe the body as a mere physical entity (*Körper*) – but is the unity of body and soul and the "zero point of orientation" (PE, p. 40). Both my bodily sensations (such as pressure, pain, or cold) and my body parts (such as limbs, head, and torso), although "close" to my body, are separate from it. However, they are not as distant as other physical objects (such as a stone) might be. Thus, the living body cannot be externally perceived as physical objects are, nor can the outer world be bodily perceived as the living body is (PE, p. 40). Conversely, the living body is "constituted in a two-fold manner as a sensed (bodily perceived) living body and as an outwardly perceived physical body of the outer world. And in this doubled givenness it is experienced as the same. Therefore, it has a location in outer space and fills up a portion of this space" (PE, p. 40).

As Stein pointed out, the living body can also move in the space in which it is located. Most importantly, our living body can also move in our imagination. Since I can actually move around my room and move the objects in it (e.g., I can move the chair and get up from the table), I can also imagine myself doing these things. When I imagine these movements, something peculiar happens: there is a doubling of the "I." On the one hand, the real living body remains in the same position and does not move, but, on the other hand, my imagined "I" has performed the imagined actions: "Thus my 'I' has been doubled, and, even though the real 'I' cannot be released from its body, there is at least the possibility of 'slipping out of one's skin' in fancy" (PE, p. 44).

This doubling mechanism – which will be relevant to empathy – highlights a crucial characteristic of our living body, namely that it cannot exist without an "I," while the opposite is not always true, since the self without the body is possible, as we have seen in the case of the imaginary "I" moving in space. The reason for this is that "the living body is essentially constituted through sensations; sensations are real constituents of consciousness and, as such, belong to the 'I'" (PE, p. 44). Without the "I" there are no sensations, and therefore no living body.

Given the important role that sensations play in the living body, Stein offered a taxonomy of feelings that focuses on their relationship to the living body. She distinguished five types of feelings that will be relevant to empathy when discussing the constitution of the *foreign* psycho-physical individual and the person (see Section 3.5 and Section 4.4, respectively).[20] First, "*sensations of feeling or sensual feelings*" are a type of sensation that is felt directly by the living body, such as "the agony of a sensual pain" (PE, p. 45). Second, "*general feelings*" pervade all parts of the body, all its movements and thoughts, without being confined to any particular part. While the pain of a tooth is a sensual feeling, the feeling of being worn out is a general feeling that pertains to the whole body. Third, "*moods*," claimed Stein, "are 'general feelings' of a non-somatic nature" (PE, p. 45). They are similar to general feelings because they do not involve a specific part of the body, but they are different from them because they do not have bodily manifestations (PE, p. 46). Fourth, *mental feelings*, such as happiness or sadness, have a phenomenal quality, although they are not "body-bound" (PE, p. 46). These emotions are directed toward the world and are capable of revealing values. Fifth, *sentiments*, such as love and hate, that Stein discussed in Chapter 4 (PE, p. 92) are other-directed and they reveal the value of a person.

After discussing this taxonomy, Stein reiterates that feelings are accompanied by somatic manifestations and that these manifestations are the result of

20 See also Chapter 9 for an in-depth discussion of this taxonomy in relation to values.

these feelings. Thus, when our legs tremble with fear, that trembling is caused by the feeling of fear. Importantly, this causal relationship between feelings and their somatic manifestations only concerns the physical body, not the living body. This is another reason for Stein's criticism of Lipps's account, according to which it is only by imitating the physical manifestations of the other person's feelings that it is possible to grasp their inner states. This is incorrect because the causal relationship that would guarantee the success of the operation exists only between the physical manifestations and the *Körper*.

As Stein stated, "the relationship of feeling to expression is completely different from that of feeling to the appearance of physical accompaniment" (PE, p. 48). Blushing is not the causal consequence of feeling shame; rather, the feeling of shame is released in blushing. In this sense, the expressions of feeling, such as blushing, consist of their unloaded energy. More precisely, expressions of feelings are the *symbols* of those feelings, which means that their expressions are inherent in them: being ashamed is given in blushing (Vendrell Ferran 2015, p. 499).[21] In short, "since phenomena of expression appear as the outpouring of feelings, they are simultaneously the expression of the psychic characteristics they announce" (PE, p. 50).

Finally, feelings have a specific function, which is "to release or motivate volitions and actions" (PE, p. 48), but it should be noted that actions do not result causally from feelings. Rather, there is a motivational relationship between feelings and the actions they initiate, which allows the "I" to act freely and creatively, something that would be impossible within a mere causal relationship.

The previous discussion (first part of Chapter 3) allowed Stein to propose the definition of the psycho-physical individual as an inseparable unity of soul and body, which has "fields of sensation, is localized at the zero point of orientation of the outer world, moves voluntarily (…), is the field of expression of the experiences of its 'I' and the instrument of the 'I's' will" (PE, p. 53) and can be perceived as such. This definition is necessary for her next step, that is, how the *foreign* psycho-physical individual is constituted for us since the fact that we – I and all the other Is – possess a perceivable body is the *conditio sine qua non* for the existence of empathy. More specifically, it is our awareness of our body as both a living body and a physical body that makes empathy possible (PE, p. 54).

21 Following Husserl, Stein argued that "symbol means that in something perceived there is something else and, indeed, we co-grasp something psychic in it" (PE, p. 71). This definition is also found in Lipps, which Stein took as evidence of a direct influence of Husserl on Lipps's work.

However, there is a significant difference between how we can perceive our own body and how we can perceive the body of another person. Our bodily perceptions are primordially given to us and at the same time "co-given" (*Miterleben*) with our perceptions of physical objects. Similarly, the sides of our body that are not seen are primordially co-given to us, since other perceptions can fulfill these expectations, despite the fact that not all sides are given simultaneously. In contrast, this kind of fulfillment is not possible when it comes to others and their foreign living bodies: "I can neither bring them [foreign fields of sensation] to primordial givenness to myself in progressive outer perception nor in the transition to bodily perception" (PE, p. 53). Instead, the only way to grasp the living bodies of other people is through "empathic representation" (PE, p. 53).

Despite this difference, empathic representation is only possible because we can perceive our own physical body, and thus the foreign body, as more than just another inanimate object in space. As Stein pointed out, when my hand is on the table, I do not perceive it as I perceive the book next to it. My hand exerts pressure on the table and can be more relaxed or more rigid. And I can co-primordially "see" all of these sensations. And when a foreign hand is presented to me, "if I follow out the tendencies to fulfillment in this 'co-grasping', my hand is moved (not in reality, but 'as if') to the place of the foreign one" (PE, p. 54). As a result, through empathy, I can "feel with" the sensations of the other person's hand. And yet, during this process of empathy, there is no confusion as to whom these sensations belong to: everything that empathy brings to light is always marked as foreign and distinct from our own sensations. Stein called this empathic representation "sensual empathy" in the sense of "sensing-in" the other person's sensations (PE, p. 54).

Sensual empathy is based not only on the fact that our body is simultaneously a physical and living entity but also on our ability to ascribe different qualities to it in our imagination while maintaining its type unchanged. In this sense, what Stein called imaginative doubling can be a kind of precursor to sensual empathy: the fact that I can imaginatively change the size of my hand is what allows me to empathize with other people's hands that have different qualities and characteristics from mine. If this were not the case, I, say, an adult woman, would not be able to empathize with the hands of men and children because of their different characteristics. Instead, "my physical body and its members are not given as a fixed type, but as an accidental realization of a type that is variable within definite limits" (PE, p. 54).

To be clear, it is also possible to empathize with bodies that belong to a completely different type than my own as in the case of a dog's paw. However, this will result in a lesser degree of empathic fulfillment: I will be able to grasp the dog's pain, but other movements or sensations specific to the body type will be largely excluded. Thus, there is a direct proportionality between body type and degree of empathic fulfillment: the closer the other person's body is in type to mine, the higher the degree of empathic fulfillment will be. In this context, the concept of "analogizing" is explained as the ability and possibility to grasp a "familiar type" (PE, p. 55) in the other person's body.[22]

Empathizing with another psycho-physical individual and grasping their body as a living body has two fundamental consequences. On the one hand, since the other's body is in itself a zero point of orientation, "I obtain a new image of the spatial world and a new zero point of orientation" in the sense that I co-primordially, thus non-primordially in content, grasp the other's bodily sensations and orientation while still primordially holding my orientation and sensations (PE, p. 57). On the other hand, by virtue of this new image of the spatial world in which the body of the other individual is a zero point of orientation, I realize that my living body is not the *only* zero point of orientation, but one among many others (PE, p. 58). It is only through empathy that I can recognize that my living body is only one among other physical bodies, and that only I can primordially perceive my body as a living body, just as only others can primordially perceive their bodies as living bodies.

Most importantly, sensual empathy allows me to see that the world I experience through my body is not the world as it is, that is, the world is "independent of my perception" because empathy takes me outside the limits of my individual self and its bodily perception (PE, p. 59). Following Husserl and Royce, Stein concluded that "empathy as the basis of intersubjective experience becomes the condition of possible knowledge of the existing outer world" (PE, p. 60). In other words, empathy is responsible both for grasping others as psycho-physical individuals like me, albeit always non-primordially, and for the possibility of an understanding of the world we share with them (see Chapter 9).

Moreover, empathy allows us not only to grasp the spontaneous and voluntary movements of others and interpret them as alive, i.e., as movements belonging to a living body, but also to co-see the general feelings of others. These feelings, such as aging, health, and apathy, can be co-seen in other people's movements because they permeate all parts of the body. Therefore, we can see that the other person is apathetic by looking at the way he walks, talks, and moves (PE, pp. 63–64). In this sense, empathy is responsible for making visible the causal relationships between the others' internal states and their

22 This notion is similar to Husserl's concept of "associative pairing" (Husserl 1931, §50).

physical manifestations. Following Stein's examples, we can understand that the other person's hand is in pain because she has smashed it with a hammer, or we can see that the child's tantrums are the result of her tiredness after running around all afternoon. In all of these cases, empathizing with the other's movements or general feelings allows me to see them and also to grasp their place within the larger causal relationships that connect the psychic and the physical.

Through empathy also it is possible to grasp the other person's feelings: as our own expressions of feelings are symbols of those feelings, the other person's expressions of feelings are at one with her feelings. Thus, when we empathize with the other person's expressions of feelings, we are grasping those very feelings. If I empathize with the other person's blushing, I am grasping his shame. Note, however, that if I want to empathize with other people's feelings, I need more than the first degree of the empathic process. The first degree of co-perceiving the other's movements and general feelings as manifestations of the psychic life of the foreign living body is sufficient only to make me aware that the other has a feeling. If I really want to grasp the other's feelings, I need the second degree of empathy, that is, the empathic process in which I am guided by the other person's intentional objects. In addition, I will also need another kind of empathic act, namely mental process, which Stein will define in the next chapter (see Section 7.2.4).

This is because, as already mentioned, the expression of feelings and those feelings are not governed by a causal relationship, as are sensations and general feelings. Rather, "there is a different relationship between shame and blushing than between exertion and blushing," namely the former is motivational and the latter is causal (PE, p. 77). The causal relationship follows the if...then structure (e.g., if I run, then I will blush), while in the motivational relationship, "the proceeding of one experience from another is experienced in purest immanence without the detour over the object sphere" (e.g., the proceeding from shame to blushing is immanently experienced in the blushing itself) (PE, p. 78). Because of its immanence and experiential nature, the motivational relation is far more intelligible than the causal relation, because what connects the components of the relation can be experienced (e.g., the connection between blushing and shame can be experienced, hence its intelligibility). In this sense, "I understand an expression, while I can merely bring a sensation to givenness" (PE, p. 78).

The fact that expressions of others are intelligible means not only that the empathizer can understand the inner life of the other person through these expressions but also that these same expressions can help the empathizer correct potential errors in empathic acts. Again, Stein emphasized that empathy is not immune to errors and inaccuracies, or what she called "deceptions" (PE, p. 80). The empathizer can check the accuracy of her empathic acts on the basis of the other person's expressions, and if there is a mismatch between the empathized feeling and the other person's expression, she can correct it.

The core idea is that empathy is able to reveal the meaning and motivational context of the other person's expressions, and because it can grasp their motivational relationship, the empathizer can both correct, clarify, or interpret the other's ambiguous or unfamiliar internal states (e.g., the other is blushing out of anger, not shame) (PE, pp. 78–79). According to Stein, we can even go a step further, because by empathizing with the meaning and motivational context of the other's expression, we grasp not only the singular feeling but also "a habitual attribute," that is, we can grasp the other's character (e.g., we can grasp not only that the other is feeling shame right now, but also that she is consistently prone to shame given her shy temperament).

Finally, empathy has another function: it gives us a better understanding of ourselves by deepening or correcting our self-knowledge. By empathizing with the other person's empathic acts directed at me, I see myself as the other person sees me. This "empathic feedback" from the other person allows me to uncover some self-deceptions that I might otherwise have accepted and to illuminate some blind spots about my interiority by comparing my primordial inner perception with my empathic act of the other's empathic act toward me. In Stein's words: "It is possible for another to 'judge me more accurately' than I judge myself and give me clarity about myself. For example, he notices that I look around me for approval as I show kindness, while I myself think I am acting out of pure generosity" (PE, p. 82).

3.5 *Empathy and the Mental Person*

According to Stein, empathy is capable of disclosing something more than what happens in the realm of physical nature, that is, the movements, sensations, and general feelings of psycho-physical individuals. In fact, as she noted at the beginning of Chapter 4, when we grasp the feelings of others through empathy, we are already entering another realm, that is the mental one, because it is in feelings that "the world of values" is constituted: "In joy the subject has something joyous facing him, in fright something frightening, in fear something threatening. Even moods have their objective correlate. For him who is cheerful, the world is baptized in a rosy glow; for him who is depressed in black. And all this is co-given with acts of feeling as belonging to them" (PE, pp. 83–84). Thus, through expressions of feelings "the mind 'becom[es] visible' in the living body" (PE, p. 84).

As said, while causality is the law of the psychophysical world, motivation is the law of mental life and helps us define what a mental subject is. The mental subject, i.e., the person, exists in a mental context that is intelligible precisely because the person's mental acts form a meaningful whole ordered by a motivational structure. In contrast, psychophysical causality lacks this structure. It follows that empathizing with one context or another, depending on their different structures, will result in different empathic acts aimed at different objects: on the one hand, "empathic comprehension of mental contexts" and, on the other hand, "empathic grasping of psychic contexts" (PE, p. 88). As said, since feelings are mental acts, they follow the motivational structure, that is, they have a specific meaning that motivates, in the sense of limits, how this feeling can be expressed. The fact that the expression of a feeling is not infinite or arbitrary indicates that mental acts depend on rational laws and, consequently, that the person is also subject to these laws and "its experiences are intelligibly related" (PE, p. 89).[23]

In this sense, the ultimate goal of the final chapter is to explore the constitution of the person – and not merely the subject – in the emotions and, ultimately, how empathy can contribute to comprehending the foreign person overall. Note that Chapters 3 and 4 have a similar structure: first, Stein determined the constitution of the subject at the individual level and then she explained the role of empathy in grasping or comprehending the foreign entity (the foreign psycho-physical individual and the foreign person, respectively).

Precisely to characterize the person, Stein reintroduced the taxonomy of affective states already discussed in Chapter 3. This time, however, she focused on the last two affective phenomena, feelings, and sentiments because they are the only ones capable of revealing the person's world of values. While feelings, as already discussed, are directed toward the world, sentiments are other-directed and disclose their personal values. Sensations, general feelings, and moods, on the other hand, are incapable of doing so because they relate only to the most superficial layers of the personality, whereas feelings and sentiments issue directly from the deeper level of the "I." Specifically, in sensations (e.g., sensing the light), there is no self-experience as they have nothing to do with the "I." In contrast, general feelings and moods have a special status because they do not come from either the surface or the depth of the "I," but simply "fill it entirely" without, however, bringing anything of that I to givenness (PE, p. 91).

23 Note that this claim implies some form of value realism and objectivity of values. I will discuss this point in Chapter 9.

Crucially, feelings issue from the self and are related to two specific elements, namely knowledge and values. First, Stein argued that to have a feeling about something, the subject must know about that thing. In this sense, knowledge precedes and is necessary for feeling: if I am afraid of snakes, I must know what a snake is and that there are snakes around me. Second, these feelings based on knowledge have the crucial function of revealing "essential relationships among the hierarchy of felt values, the depth classification of value feelings, and the level classification of the person exposed in these" (PE, p. 92).[24] Stein's example of this "axiological disclosing ability" of feelings is particularly effective: the feeling of anger over the loss of a bracelet belongs to a more superficial level of the ego than the loss of the same bracelet received as a gift from a loved one. For the same reason, the pain caused by the loss of that loved one would come from an even deeper level of "I" than those feelings of anger. Since there is a correlation between a felt value and the strata of our personality, "every time we advance in the value realm, we also make acquisitions in the realm of our own personality" (PE, p. 92).

Interestingly, according to Stein, it is possible to formulate right and wrong judgments about the person's value hierarchy grasped via empathy precisely because of the rationality of the mental context governed by motivation: if the suffering of losing one's wealth reaches the deepest level of one's personality and, therefore, wealth is felt to be the most important value, then the judgment "he feels 'irrational'" is legitimized precisely by the fact that he has subverted the correct (i.e., rational) value hierarchy (PE, p. 92).

Sentiments are also capable of reaching and revealing the deeper levels of personality. Unlike feelings, however, they are always directed toward other people, and specifically toward their value. For instance, "in the act of love, we have a grasping or an intending of the value of a person" (PE, p. 92). We do value the other person unconditionally and not because of some particular feature or her actions. To love the other person for no reason other than because she is, in fact, that person is not only directed toward her value but also expresses the deepest level of our personality and discloses the highest value in our hierarchy.

Stein concluded this section by clarifying that feelings are not only inherently related to the various layers of the personality, but that they also have

---

24 In the note on page 92, Stein referenced Scheler's *Formalism in Ethics and Non-formal Ethics of Values* in regards to the concept of the hierarchy of values (Scheler, 1916). In Chapter 9, I will discuss Stein's claim regarding the cognitive role of emotions and her value theory.

four important characteristics that make them particularly revelatory of our inner life. Each feeling has not only a specific depth but also a reach, duration, and intensity (PE, pp. 94–97). Feelings not only have different depths in relation to the personality level from which they come, they can also have different ranges in each of these personality levels. They can fill the personality level from which they come more or less, depending on their "mood component." The more the mood component is present, the greater the reach of the feeling. For example, anxiety can be more or less pervasive depending on how focused the anxiety is on its object: a less focused anxiety will be more spread out across the personality level and will be more like an anxious mood. In addition, the feelings may last longer or be more limited in time, and they may be more or less intense.

Stein's detailed characterization of the nature of the person's emotional life is crucial to show how the person and the world of values are intertwined and, most importantly, that this connection can be grasped through the expressions of that emotional life. As she noted in a crucial passage of her work, this is of the utmost importance for empathy and the constitution of the foreign person (PE, pp. 98–99):

> As my own person is constituted in primordial mental acts, so the foreign person is constituted in empathically experienced acts. I experience his every action as proceeding from a will and this, in turn, from a feeling. Simultaneously with this, I am given a level of his person and a range of values in principle experienceable by him. This, in turn, meaningfully motivates the expectation of future possible volitions and actions.

While sensual empathy is concerned with the basic level of constitution and with grasping the causal context of the psycho-physical individual, a more complex and complete empathic act, i.e., mental empathy, directed toward the other person's feelings and sentiments is able to comprehend some aspect of the other person's personality and values. Thus, when we empathize with the actions and expressions in the other's living body, we are able to gain "a glimpse into the kernel of the person" (PE, p. 99).

As this formulation suggests, for Stein there is a core in the person that remains stable despite the undeniable influence of the circumstances to which the person is exposed. It is possible, as the image of the glimpse implies, to *partially* grasp this core via empathy. This unchangeable core is called "personal structure" and has a peculiar function because it "marks off a range of possibilities of variation within which the person's real distinctiveness can be developed" based on the specific influences and circumstances that affect the person's growth and nature (PE, p. 100).[25] This variation within limits is able to take into account both the influence of the environment on the person's hierarchy of values and, ultimately, on her actions, as well as the recognition of a stable core from which the personality can unfold, again more or less completely, depending on circumstances such as empirical contingencies (e.g., illness) or social context (e.g., not meeting a person worthy of love) (PE, p. 101).

This raises the question of the depth to which one person can empathize with another, given the differences in their "experiential structures," determined by, among other things, their ethnicity, gender, age, socioeconomic status, and so on. On the one hand, the fact that there is this unchanging core in every person makes it theoretically possible to empathize with all the experiences of the other person. In this sense, as soon as I empathize with someone and grasp a value, I am immediately aware of being in the presence of a person whose experiences are intelligible and coherently organized within a motivational context (PE, p. 104).

On the other hand, because of our different experiential structures, there are some limits to the extent of the intelligibility of these foreign experiences. However, this never leads to complete unintelligibility, since "I can still have [these experiences] in the manner of empty presentation" (PE, p. 104): I can understand the other's experience as the result of his value hierarchy even though I do not possess the corresponding value experience and thus the corresponding motivational context. For example, in empathizing with the other person's feeling of excitement about buying an expensive sports car, I understand that the other person values the pursuit of material wealth, even though wealth is not at the top of my value hierarchy and I have never felt excited about driving, much less owning, an expensive sports car. Empathizing with this kind of experience will always remain an incomplete act since I will not be able to fully attribute to the other person a motivational context and a level of personality that I do not possess.

Moreover, similar to sensual empathy, empathizing with people with different experiential structures has the important role of enhancing our self-knowledge and fostering self-evaluation by comparing what we do or do not have in common with them in terms of values and motivations (PE, p. 105). Thus, if it is true that understanding is always possible between individuals who are persons, it is also true that there are limits to this understanding given

25 She quotes Dilthey on the "significance of the milieu for the character" (PE, p. 100). Stein provides a more detailed discussion of Dilthey's account of the concept of type in the next section (PE, pp. 102–105). I discuss Stein's approach to this concept in Chapter 8.

the differences between people, and if we fail to recognize these differences and "take the self as the standard, we lock ourselves into the prison of our individuality," which in turn leads to the falsification of the other person's experience (PE, p. 105).

4 A (Tentative) Definition of Phenomenological Empathy

Before showing how phenomenological empathy differs significantly from the SD of empathy, it is necessary to provide a tentative definition of its main features. This is intended to be a stepping stone to a more articulated and nuanced account of phenomenological empathy that will hopefully emerge at the end of Part 3. I will use the term "phenomenological empathy" to refer to the specific way of describing and understanding the empathic phenomenon that is inspired by a phenomenological approach and, in particular, by Stein's account. In this sense, I will argue that what the SD has called cognitive and affective empathy are in fact distinct phenomena that are not what empathy actually is.

In contrast, the classical phenomenological tradition, represented by thinkers such as Husserl, Stein, and Scheler (see Chapter 8) posits that empathy involves a primordial experience of others' consciousness which is not primordial in content. This experience does not entail imaginative perspective-taking (cognitive empathy), affective sharing (affective empathy), or concern for others' well-being (sympathy). To be clear, I am not proposing a "new kind" of empathy. The term "phenomenological empathy" – or alternatively, "the phenomenology of empathy" – refers to the phenomenological analysis and description of experientially grasping foreign consciousness.[26] This represents what I consider the only faithful description of empathy's true nature. The phenomenological analysis provides the sole conceptually and phenomenologically sound account of empathy, as the SD tradition fundamentally mislabels distinct phenomena as empathy (see Chapter 8). Specifically, my account of phenomenological empathy is largely Steinian while proposing some differences or modifications as well as drawing on contemporary Steinian scholarship. Here are the main features of my account:

---

26 For brevity's sake, I will use the expression "phenomenological empathy" rather than "the phenomenology of empathy," but I understand them to be synonymous as they refer to how the phenomenological approach describes empathy. I am grateful to the anonymous reviewer who encouraged me to clarify this point and suggested the term "the phenomenology of empathy."

- First, phenomenological empathy is characterized as an *experience* not as a skill or an emotion in itself. Specifically, I will define it as a quasi-perceptual and quasi-immaginative grasp of the other's experience. While phenomenological empathy is capable of achieving a specific epistemic goal and therefore has an instrumental quality, and while it is certainly an experience of internal states, among which emotions and feelings are prominent, it is at its core an experiential act. Crucially, in its most basic manifestation, what Stein called the first level, phenomenological empathy is always "on." Unlike the processes defined in the SD, from a phenomenological point of view, empathizing with others and the world we all share is an ongoing activity that cannot be turned on and off.
- Second, phenomenological empathy cannot be reduced to imaginative perspective-taking, simulation-plus-projection, affective matching, affective sharing, or concern for the other well-being. In other words, phenomenological empathy is not the same as cognitive empathy, affective empathy, or sympathy. To be clear, a phenomenological approach to empathy does not argue that these phenomena do not exist. The point is that they are not what empathy consists of.
- Third, phenomenological empathy has two goals: on the one hand, to experience others as *living bodies* that are the fields in which their interiority is expressed, and on the other hand, to experience the other individual as a person, i.e., as a *bearer of values* whose hierarchy is expressed through his or her emotional reactions to others and life events.
- Fourth, these two goals reflect the role of phenomenological empathy in our lives and, more specifically, in the deliberative process. Empathy has a fundamental *epistemic function* because it allows the empathizer to grasp the inner states of the other individual. This is both crucial for interpersonal understanding and the precondition for objective knowledge of the world we share. Empathy also performs an *axiological function* by disclosing that the other person's actions, emotional reactions, and decisions are always embedded within a motivational framework structured by their hierarchically ordered values.
- Fifth, phenomenological empathy is a *multilayered experience* because the empathizer can achieve different levels of understanding depending on which level of the empathic act she completes. The more the empathizer is willing to be guided by the other's experience, the deeper her understanding will be. This explains why empathic understanding can vary in accuracy and overall complexity. Not only are there different degrees of empathy, according to which the empathizer can choose to either only grasp that the other is in a certain state or to try to understand her inten-

tional object further by following the other's intentionality. But there are also two different characterizations of the empathic act, depending on which internal state of the other subject is being grasped, and thus which level of his or her personality is being targeted. Importantly, I will not use Stein's terminology of "sensual empathy" and "mental empathy" to indicate these two characterizations since they could be interpreted as reintroducing a distinction between an affective and a cognitive kind of empathy, which is instead one of the crucial differences between the phenomenological account of empathy I am defending here and the SD. Instead, I will use the term *expressive empathy* to refer to experiencing the other as a living body, and the term *personal empathy* to refer to experiencing the other as a person. To be clear, these concepts are not meant to convey that there are two distinct empathic acts or phenomena, but rather that phenomenological empathy is a single complex and multifaceted phenomenon that includes different degrees and levels. It can simultaneously apprehend various expressions and states of the other person, including affective states in all their manifestations, cognitive states, volitional states, and axiological states. Nor do I intend to propose an alternative way of translating Stein's original concepts; rather, this choice is meant to signal that while my account is strongly inspired by Stein's proposal, it does not perfectly overlap, especially when it comes to the extent to which personal empathy can grasp the other's values compared to Stein's mental empathy.

- Sixth, although phenomenological empathy in its fullest manifestation can sometimes achieve a deep understanding of another person, it provides only a *partial* grasp of their inner world. The phenomenological approach thus recognizes the fundamental impossibility of complete interpersonal transparency. Total understanding would dissolve *otherness* itself, rendering the other as comprehensible as we are to ourselves – a conceptual impossibility that would eliminate the very alterity that defines interpersonal relations. However, acknowledging this limitation does not negate the possibility of interpersonal understanding altogether. On the contrary, phenomenological empathy's experiential nature makes it – at least in its basic form – an inherent feature of embodied personhood. Thus, understanding others as living bodies and persons like ourselves constitutes a fundamental activity intrinsic to our experience of the world and interpersonal relations.
- Seventh, phenomenological empathy seems by design to be equipped to deal with its potential shortcomings. Far from being perfect, it does not guarantee an error-free result: inaccuracies and biases can and do occur. However, because of this awareness, and because its epistemic scope is

already more limited than that of the SD, the empathizer can also engage in damage control. In this sense, the pervasiveness of empathic experience allows the empathizer to adjust and correct the understanding gained through empathy, thanks to empathy itself, which signals when the previous empathic act was flawed by empathizing again with the other person.
- Eighth, the phenomenological account of empathy recognizes the need to expand the subject's toolbox for interpersonal understanding. While acknowledging the existence of a fixed core within each person, the phenomenological approach also recognizes that the historical, socio-cultural, and political context in which that person develops and lives significantly influences the empathizer, the target of the empathic act, and the empathic process itself. Crucially, the phenomenological account remains aware that empathy alone cannot achieve comprehensive interpersonal understanding, and that additional sources of knowledge and complementary tools are necessary.

Here I have only sketched in broad strokes what phenomenological empathy entails. In the next chapter, I will expand on this account by demonstrating that it might resolve some of the problems that plague the SD approach to empathy, precisely because the phenomenological framework is fundamentally different from the latter. In the final chapter, I will show how and why phenomenological empathy appears to be a better ally for other-directed deliberation than the SD approach.

CHAPTER 8

Does Phenomenology Resolve Empathy's Problems in Deliberation?

It is now time to test my central hypothesis, namely that by changing the definition of empathy, we might be able to solve or at least mitigate some of the problems that the SD of empathy seems to face when involved in other-directed deliberation. To do this, I will first have to show how and why phenomenological empathy differs from cognitive empathy and affective empathy, understood as imaginative perspective-taking on the one hand and affective sharing on the other. I will also show how a phenomenologically informed account of empathy recognizes the centrality of the contextual aspect of the empathic relationship, which has often been overlooked by the SD. I will then argue that, because of these fundamental differences between the two ways of conceptualizing the empathic phenomenon, the phenomenological approach seems to have an advantage over accounts based on the SD in both the epistemic and the moral domains.

To be sure, I am not trying to deny the existence of phenomena like imaginative perspective-taking and affective sharing, or that we do not use them in our epistemic and moral lives. That would be absurd and completely counterintuitive. Instead, I will suggest that what the SD of empathy defines as empathy is not what the empathic phenomenon actually consists of, rather the SD merely refers to related but distinct phenomena that we experience and use in our interactions with others. In contrast, a phenomenological account of empathy seems to better capture not only the specificity of the empathic act but also what we experience when we actually empathize with others. As I will argue repeatedly, it is crucial to label these phenomena correctly since how we define them affects their role in our deliberative processes.

1 A Possible Solution to Cognitive Empathy's Problems

In Chapter 4, I argued that cognitive empathy, defined as a form of imaginative perspective-taking usually characterized as a simulation-plus-projection routine, may not be the best option for achieving its supposed epistemic role in other-directed deliberation, i.e., reproducing and understanding the reasons for the other's behavior. There are three reasons for this. First, cognitive empa-

 | HTTPS://DOI.ORG/10.1163/9789004745360-010

thy in its most basic forms does not seem to be able to guarantee the recognition of like-mindedness as it is supposed to do. Second, cognitive empathy seems to be prone to inaccuracies due to its biased nature. Third, cognitive empathy is likely to threaten the agency of the person to whom the empathy is directed.

In what follows, I will first try to show that phenomenological empathy is fundamentally different from cognitive empathy since it does not involve any form of mirroring, simulation-plus-projection, or first-person perspective-taking, but is a *quasi-perceptual and quasi-imaginative grasp* of the other's expressions and inner states as expressed in the foreign living body, which also allows the empathizer to grasp the other as a person, i.e., as a bearer of motives and values. Because of this crucial difference, phenomenological empathy seems to be better able to deal with the set of problems encountered by cognitive empathy, i.e., it seems to be able to guarantee the recognition of the embodied mindedness of others, to mitigate the dangers of inaccurate empathic understanding, and to respect the agency of others.

1.1 *Cognitive Biases and Inaccuracy in Phenomenological Empathy*

Cognitive biases permeate every aspect of cognitive empathy, and in general, cognitive empathy seems to be less effective and accurate than it is thought to be. First, while basic empathy is supposed to be responsible for recognizing others as like-minded through mirroring mechanisms, it seems unable to always guarantee the attribution of like-mindedness to other agents based solely on the activation of MNs.[1] Second, the activation of reenactive empathy is also not without its own concerns, since whether the other person is deemed worthy of empathic perspective-taking is not automatic and seems to be granted on the basis of biased considerations. Third, based on a solid body of empirical evidence, high-level empathy appears to be biased toward the most accessible information, i.e., a person's salient characteristics such as age, race, and gender. It also suffers from the so-called "diversity problem," which is the projection of the empathizer's internal state onto the internal state of the other person because the former underestimates the differences between the two. Finally, high-level empathy has proven not to be the best tool at our disposal for interpersonal understanding, given its surprisingly low score on accuracy (see Chapter 4).

---

1 I use the concepts of basic empathy and reenactive empathy from Stueber's account (see Chapter 3) but everything I say can also be applied to mirroring empathy and reconstructive empathy from Goldman's account (see Chapter 1).

Phenomenological empathy seems able to solve the first problem effectively. In contrast to basic empathy, it seems able to recognize like-mindedness in others. More precisely, it is able to guarantee not only a mere attribution of like-mindedness to others, but a more poignant recognition of the fact that what is presented to me in an act of empathy is a living body, i.e., not merely a physical body that moves or displays some gestures and facial expressions. Experiencing the other as a living body means that "we experience the other's bodily gestures and movements as intrinsically embodying mindedness, as movements lived through by someone; we see them as movements which the other purposively achieves or involuntary suffers, which bring her perceptual world into ever new orientations, or as the manifestations of her affects" (Jardine & Szanto, 2017, p. 90).

The recognition of embodied mindedness does not rely on the recognition of the goal-directed nature of other people's actions gained through mirroring, as in low-level empathy. This recognition depends directly on the nature of our body, which presents itself not as a physical object that can perform goal-directed actions – recall the industrial robot picking up a cup (see Chapter 4) – but as "a field of expressions for [our] experiences" (Scheler, 1913, p. 10). Another person's laughter or cry is not simply an outward modification of the physical body, but it expresses a part of her inner life, specifically happiness or sadness. As Scheler, like Stein (see Chapter 7), famously claimed: "It is *in* the blush that we perceive shame, *in* the laughter joy" (Scheler, 1913, p. 10).

In other words, not only is the performance of goal-directed actions not sufficient to assign like-mindedness, but also the recognition of like-mindedness itself is not sufficient to describe the kind of recognition we achieve in empathy. In the empathic encounter with the other, understood in terms of phenomenological empathy, we immediately recognize the other as a living body, that is, as an expressive unity of physical and mental, bodily and psychic.

Phenomenological empathy differs from basic empathy not only in what it can (or cannot) accomplish but also in *how* it accomplishes it. Whereas basic empathy is supposed to attribute like-mindedness based on mirroring and the spontaneous activation of MNs, phenomenological empathy is a *quasi-perceptual* activity that does *not* involve mirroring or imitation. Although not perfectly overlapping, as Jardine and Szanto summarized, phenomenological empathy and perception share three features. First, just as perception *directly* perceives its object, empathy *directly* perceives that the other person is smiling happily. To be sure, the point is not to equate the intentional object of perception and empathy since the former is a physical entity, while the latter a living body. Rather, the focus is on the "directness" of both experiences: there is no need for mediation in order to perceive that a cat is crossing the street or that the person in front of me on the bus is smiling. Both the cat and the grinning person appear directly to us, and we are "immediately acquainted" with these two, albeit radically different, intentional objects (Jardine & Szanto, 2017, p. 89).

Second, perception and empathy have an epistemic role because they "provide a *prima facie* justificatory basis for our (perceptual [or empathic]) judgments" (Jardine & Szanto, 2017, p. 89). If, as a result of my perceptual act and my empathic act, I believe that there is a cat crossing the street and that the person in front of me on the bus is smiling, my beliefs would be *prima facie* justified. In other words, perceptual and empathic acts are capable of providing *some* knowledge to the subject who performs them. Understanding the quality and accuracy of the epistemic content provided by empathy will be crucial to understanding the role of empathy in deliberation (see Chapter 9). For now, suffice it to say that phenomenological empathy is capable of achieving two epistemically related goals: the recognition of the other as a living body and, related to this, a *prima facie* justification that the other is experiencing something (e.g., amusement or happiness).

The final and third characteristic that perception and empathy share is that they both grasp their intentional object perspectively, that is, only certain aspects are directly perceivable while others are momentarily or inherently precluded. This is phenomenologically true for both physical objects and other people since some features of physical objects are not directly perceivable or not all at the same time, just as some aspects of the other person's embodied mindedness will not be perceivable. Crucially, as Jardine and Szanto note, to say that some aspect of the other person's living body is not directly perceivable does not mean that the other person's living body itself is not perceptible. Indeed, it would be counterintuitive and phenomenologically incorrect to argue that because I cannot directly perceive one side of the cat's tail, my direct perception of that particular cat and cats in general is not possible. Similarly, the fact that phenomenological empathy does not directly perceive every aspect of the other person's grinning face does not mean that the other person's living body is completely unperceivable.

However, as discussed above, the perspectival character of perception and empathy are quite different. It is precisely this difference that highlights the imperfection of the analogy between these two acts, hence the "quasi" in the "quasi-perceptual" characterization. As Stein – as well as Husserl – reminds us, empathy and perception are similar because their intentional objects are "present in the here and now" since they are both experiential acts that directly acquaint us with their intentional objects and produce some kind of knowledge (Stein, PE, p. 7). But while perception can in principle bring to givenness the sides of the physical objects, albeit in apperception, empathy cannot do the same. Some aspects of the other person's inner world will never be directly perceivable, no matter what the subject tries. In this sense, the other's inner world is simultaneously available and unavailable to us, or rather, different aspects are available with different degrees of depth, and some of them are completely inaccessible (see Chapter 9).

One might object that the mirroring process underlying basic empathy could also be characterized as experiential and perceptual. After all, I see another person perform a goal-directed action or make a facial expression, and my perception of that action or expression activates the MNS' circuits. While it is undeniable that it is a perceptual act that triggers the activation of the mirroring process, it does not follow that the mirroring process itself is perceptual and, at the same time, that the supposed recognition of like-mindedness is carried out by a perceptual act. Rather, after its initial triggering, the mirroring process has nothing to do with the perception of the other person's bodily movements or expressions. Once initiated, the mirroring process belongs to the realm of the neurophysiological rather than the experiential or perceptual.

Moreover, the supposed attribution of like-mindedness is not the direct result of an act of perception. According to accounts of basic or mirroring empathy, the intermediate step of mirroring is essential – in the sense that it is the *conditio sine qua non* – for this recognition to occur. In contrast, phenomenological empathy, especially at its first level, consists entirely of a quasi-perceptual acquaintance with the living body of the other, and it is precisely through this perception of the other that the empathizer obtains a direct and immediate recognition of the other subject as a living body, without the need for any mediating step such as mirroring or imitation. In short, the attribution of like-mindedness does not seem to depend on mirroring mechanism.

One of the main consequences of the quasi-perceptual nature of empathy is that recognizing the embodied mindedness of others is a built-in feature of our life experience because what allows me to recognize others as experiencing living bodies, i.e., phenomenological empathy, is not something that I have to actively turn on or off when I encounter others. Rather, every time we encounter another person, we empathize with her, that is, we recognize her as a someone with an embodied mind who is experiencing something. The idea that empathy is always "on" when it comes to our interpersonal interactions echoes the idea that perception is also always "on" when it comes to our conscious lives. Incidentally, this is also why, unlike the SD, my phenomenological account of empathy is not a success definition since it is impossible for it to fail in its first-degree ability to recognize the other as such.

Excluding the need to mirror the other's facial expressions, gestures, or goal-directed actions from the empathic act seems to give phenomenological empathy a specific advantage over cognitive empathy. As empirical evidence suggests, the decision whether it is worthwhile to initiate a more effortful simulation process (reenactive or reconstructive empathy) is strongly influenced by group membership. Reduced activation of mirroring networks between subjects perceived as belonging to different groups seems to be responsible for a decrease in basic empathy and consequently for a decrease in engagement in reenactive empathy. However, if empathy does not require any kind of mirroring activity, then the fact that mirroring is biased does not seem to be relevant either for recognizing the other's embodied mindedness or for judging whether to engage in higher-level forms of simulation.

Two caveats. First of all, the fact that phenomenological empathy does not have to deal with the biases that affect mirroring does not mean that every time we empathize with someone we have to achieve a particularly deep empathic grasp of the other person, nor does it mean that phenomenological empathy is completely immune to bias or prejudice of any kind. While phenomenological empathy guarantees the recognition of the other as a living body and not just as a physical entity, it does not guarantee that for every act of experiential empathy (e.g., seeing the other person grinning happily at her phone on the bus) there will be an instance of personal empathy (e.g., grasping the other person's feelings as located within her motivational context).

In some cases, there is also an obstacle within experiential empathy. There may be a "structural" impossibility in fulfilling the expectations of the first degree of experiential empathy, either because the empathizer and the other living being belong to different species, as in the case of humans and animals (recall the reference to a dog's wagging tail), or because the empathizer has not experienced what she is trying to empathize with, as in the case of a child trying to empathize with an adult or a non-colorblind person trying to understand the experience of being colorblind (Stein, PE, p. 80). This gap, however, does not prevent a very superficial form of understanding of the foreign experience and still allows for the recognition of embodied mindedness (of a different kind in the case of the dog, which is still a living being, although not a person) (Svenaeus, 2018, p. 749).

Beyond these specific instances, as Stein reminded us, "people do not always go through all degrees but are often satisfied with one of the lower ones" (PE, p. 11). When, through experiential empathy, I grasp that the other person on the bus is grinning and that, by letting her intentional object guide my focus, she is grinning at her phone screen, or more specifically, because of something on her phone screen, I can be satisfied and stop my empathic act. I do not need to empathically grasp what she is looking at or reading on her phone, or how that makes her feel (e.g., she might be grinning sarcastically or she might be sincerely amused by the content on her screen), or how that feeling and its object fit into her broader motivational context.

According to Stein's account, the kind (sensual or mental empathy or, in my account, experiential or personal empathy) and depth of the empathic act (first degree only or up to third degree) depend on *what kind of experience* the other person is going through. Sensual feelings, general feelings, and moods require experiential empathy while emotions and sentiments require personal empathy. There is a correlation between the depth of the affective states that the other person is experiencing and the depth of the empathic act. The more the affective state expresses deeper layers of the personality, the more the empathic act will target the motivational and axiological context of the person. Thus, the empathic act can be modulated in relation to its depth which is understood both epistemically and axiologically. While experiential empathy can only reveal a certain amount and type of epistemically valuable information, personal empathy can reveal a deeper and specific type of information, namely, part of the other person's motivational and axiological context.

This raises an important challenge for Stein's account and for phenomenological empathy in general: is mental empathy the only instance in which we grant personhood to the other individual? In other words, is it only when I empathize with the other person for the purpose of revealing his or her motivational and axiological context, and not merely his or her psychophysical dimension, that I recognize him or her as a person? I will address this issue in the next chapter (see Chapter 9). For now, suffice it to say that phenomenological empathy, because of its quasi-perceptual nature, seems capable of providing a basic recognition of others as living bodies with motivations and values.

Thus, while in the case of reconstructive empathy, the subject's willingness to engage in simulation sometimes depends on its ability to mirror the other's expressions; in the phenomenological approach, it is the other's state that calls for the specific kind of empathic engagement. It is also true that the empathizer can choose how far the empathic act goes since in both experiential and personal empathy, the empathizer can stop at the first degree. However, I am not trying to argue that phenomenological empathy is completely free of all forms of prejudice or bias, which brings me to the second caveat, namely, that it is quite possible that the empathizer's willingness to be guided by the intentional objects of the other person could be influenced by biased evaluations.

It may well be that because I hold racist beliefs and the person in front of me is of a different ethnicity, I am unwilling to follow her intentional objects and thus understand her causal and/or motivational context better. For example, I can empathically grasp that the Black person in front of me is angry, but I can refuse to focus on her intentional objects, i.e., the fact that she is protesting police brutality. While this is undoubtedly problematic, especially in terms of empathy's involvement in other-directed deliberation, in phenomenological empathy, as opposed to cognitive empathy, the influence of biases seems to intervene at a later and more explicit stage of the empathic process, which could lead to greater awareness on the part of the subject and thus easier mitigation.

Although this remains to be proven empirically, from a purely speculative and phenomenological point of view, it makes sense to say that the obstacles to our willingness to follow the other's intentional object and to understand more of the other's motivational context seem less implicit and therefore more recognizable. Because it does not rely on neurophysiological mechanisms, the subject engaging in phenomenological empathy may be more aware of the reason why she is unwilling to focus on the other's intentional objects. For example, if the racist empathizer pays close attention to her empathic acts, she might uncover the following reasoning: I empathetically understand that the black person in front of me is angry, but I do not care – both affectively and epistemically – about the reason for her anger or what kind of value hierarchy this rage reveals. Awareness may not be enough to solve this problem, but it at least makes it visible and, unlike mirroring, more open to questioning.

Despite this potential advantage of phenomenological empathy over cognitive empathy, it has been suggested that phenomenological empathy, precisely because of its quasi-perceptual nature, may fail to address some of its biased outcomes. As Janine Jones has argued, empathic failures "may begin in perceptual encounters" (Jones, 2022, p. 89). For example, she recounted what police officer Darren Wilson said in 2014 after he shot and killed Michael Brown, an 18-year-old black man, in Ferguson, Missouri. Wilson said that he "felt like a five-year-old holding on to Hulk Hogan" when he grabbed Brown and that when Brown looked at him, he "had the most intense aggressive face. The only way [to] describe it, it looks like a demon" (Jones, 2022, p. 89).

However, Wilson's description of his own body ("I felt like a five-year-old") seems to contrast with his physical characteristics, as the police officer is 6'2" and weighs 195 pounds. Thus, the officer's perception of his body seems to be linked to his perception of Brown's body, which he perceived as much stronger and larger than his own. In other words, Wilson perceived Brown's body as monstrous in size, which in turn justified the attribution of aggressiveness, his feelings of fear, and ultimately the killing. The point is that perception, and therefore empathy as a quasi-perceptual act, can be mistaken, and one of the sources of error is the preconceived notions that the perceiver/empathizer has about the other person. Because I believe that black men are aggressive and dangerous, in my empathic encounter with one, I am likely to perceive his physical gestures and postures as expressions of anger and, as a result, feel a justified sense of danger. Consequently, as Jones makes clear, "being able to perceive black people in the world is a reasonable requirement for being able to empathically imagine them" (Jones, 2022, p. 89). In this sense, it seems difficult to deny that prejudices and biased beliefs can influence the way we perceive others and, as a consequence, pollute the outcome of the perception-based empathic act.

A preliminary answer would be to intervene at the level of prejudices and biased beliefs, which should allow for less distorted perception and consequently a less problematic empathic act. Of course, this should also be effective in reducing the biases associated with mirroring: through debiasing strategies, the empathizer might be less inclined to see the other as an out-group member, thus increasing the perceived similarity between them and favoring mirroring and simulation. However, as noted above, there is a relevant difference between phenomenological and mirroring empathy: in the latter, cognitive biases and prejudices modulate the activation of mirroring circuits, whereas in the former, no activation is required because the empathic act is always ongoing. Because of this difference, phenomenological empathy may be more open to correction.

In this regard, Stein explicitly asserted that empathic deception can and does occur, but that empathy has within itself the tools to correct it, or more precisely, is itself the way to correct these errors. It is quite possible that the first act of empathy may result in a biased outcome, but it is through a subsequent act of empathy that the empathizer can recognize this error and then attempt to correct it. As Jardine points out, "as with our perceptual experience of material objects, empathic perception contains its own immanent standard of correctness, in such a way that our initial grasp of the other's subjective life can be confirmed or disconfirmed through the ongoing course of empathic perception" (Jardine, 2015, p. 577).

According to this mechanism, there will always be something that signals to the empathizer that her initial attempt to grasp the other's inner state was not successful, and that these signals can only be grasped through another act of empathy. This certainly captures a phenomenologically true aspect of the empathic experience, namely its iterative nature. It is quite common to make several attempts at empathizing not only to correct possible mistakes but also to gain a deeper and more complete understanding of the other's state.

One could still argue that if the empathizer holds biased beliefs, then every one of her acts of empathy will lead to a biased outcome. No matter how many times Officer Wilson tried, he would always have perceived Brown as bigger, stronger, and more aggressive than he was. However, I am not entirely sure that this would be the case. I tentatively believe that if Officer Wilson had the time to engage in repeated acts of empathy, he would have been able to at least mitigate his erroneous and biased empathic outcome. To me, this sounds plausible because Officer Wilson may have misread Brown's facial expressions and bodily gestures, i.e., the first degree of an act of experiential empathy, which, as said, is always ongoing and open to repetition. In an environment perceived as calm and free of danger, Officer Wilson might have noticed that his and Brown's bodies were not as different in size and weight as he initially perceived, and that the expression on Brown's face was not one of anger or aggression, but of fear.

To be clear, this would not mean that Officer Wilson's biases would go away, that he would be less prejudiced against black people in his daily life, or even that he would have refrained from tragically shooting Brown. It would only mean that this specific act of empathy would have been less biased and more accurate, even if only slightly and after repeated attempts.

As discussed in Chapter 4, cognitive biases and their impact on accuracy levels have problematic implications not only for basic empathy and our willingness to engage in reenactive empathy but also for the outcome of reenactive empathy itself. Empirical evidence suggests that cognitive empathy relies heavily on two strategies, depending on the degree of perceived similarity between the empathizer and her target. The more the empathizer perceives the target as similar, the more she will engage in introspection and projection, whereas the more the empathizer perceives the target as different, the more she will rely on stereotypical characterizations. Both of these strategies are likely to lead to an inaccurate understanding of the other person, which in itself may reinforce or be a source of bias.

Unlike reenactive empathy, phenomenological empathy does not seem to be particularly susceptible to either of these problems. The central reason for this is that it is fundamentally different from reenactive empathy. Whereas the latter involves a process of imitation, simulation, and reenactment of the other's internal states and deliberative process, the former eschews all of these forms of mediation in favor of a direct quasi-perceptual grasp of the other's internal states and a decentering of the empathizer to follow the other's intentional objects.

First, phenomenological empathy has nothing to do with imitation. Stein made this abundantly clear in her critique of Lipps's account of empathy (Stein, PE, pp. 21–23; see Chapter 7). Eliminating the need for imitation in empathy means that the empathizer does not need to use her own past experience as a template for understanding the other's inner states. When imitation is required, the more the other's experience is perceived as dissimilar, the more the empathizer will rely on stereotypical inferences about others and their experiences. For an imitation-based account, a lack of prior knowledge about those perceived as dissimilar and their experiences is an obstacle that must be overcome in order to carry out the empathic process, and the only way to do so is either to mistakenly assume that others are more like us than they are, or to appeal to stereotypical information about them.

Conversely, phenomenological empathy, despite its reliance on a specific kind of contextual knowledge that may include some stereotypical aspects, i.e., typification (see Section 8.3.1), functions differently. On the one hand, the empathizer has direct access to the other's expressions through the quasi-perceptual grasp of the other's living body, and on the other hand, the empathizer decenters herself in order to focus on the other's experience. The key difference is that in phenomenological empathy, stereotypical cues are never the primary source of information upon which the empathic process is built. Rather, it aims to refine any form of stereotypical knowledge that serves as a starting point, not an end point.

Moreover, phenomenological empathy is not a simulation-plus-projection process. This is forcefully and clearly stated by Stein in her under-discussed critique of Adam Smith's sympathy (Stein, PE, p. 14):

> If, as in memory, we put ourselves in the place of the foreign "I" and suppress it while we surround ourselves with its situation, we have one of these situations of "appropriate" experience. If we then again concede to the foreign "I" its place and ascribe this experience to him, we gain a knowledge of his experience. (According to Adam Smith, this is how foreign experience is given.) (...) We could call this surrogate for empathy an "assumption" but not empathy itself.

In phenomenological empathy, there is no place for introspection and its subsequent projection onto the other. For this reason, the imposition of one's own lived experience on the other, and the consequent mystification, at least in part, of the other's perspective, seems less likely in Stein's conception of empathy because the other is no longer a blank screen onto which one's own interiority can be projected. By decentering myself as an empathizer and opening the experiential space to the other's experience and intentionality, I bracket my interiority and follow the other's inner world. This mechanism should be able to avoid Gallagher's diversity problem and first-person bias by allowing an understanding, albeit always partial, of the other's interiority rather than mine. Similarly, it should avoid all of the shortcomings of our introspective and simulation abilities that Maibom pointed out since these processes are not involved in phenomenological empathy (see Chapter 4).

To reiterate, I am not saying that we never use introspection-plus-projection or simulation-plus-projection mechanisms in interpersonal understanding, because we very much do. My central claim is that we must not mislabel these mental acts: they are not acts of empathy. When we empathize with other people, we are doing something different than internally imitating their state and simulating their situation on the basis of our prior experience.

Finally, it remains to be seen whether phenomenological empathy has an advantage over reenactive empathy in terms of accuracy. To address this question, it is crucial to analyze more closely what happens in second-degree phenomenological empathy and what it means for the empathizer to be guided by the intentional objects of the other person. This discussion will allow me to show how phenomenological empathy differs from imitation, simulation, and perspective-taking. The status of the second degree of the empathic act is also closely related to the problem of agency in cognitive empathy. I will discuss both of these issues below.

1.2 *The Problem of Agency in Phenomenological Empathy*

Following Goldie's argument, I have argued that a specific form of high-level empathy, namely other-oriented perspective-taking, which consists of imaginatively taking the other person's perspective as if one were that person, is conceptually incompatible with not limiting the other person's full agency. Ignoring this incompatibility leads, on the one hand, to an inaccurate understanding of the other person's condition and deliberative process and, on the other hand, to an erosion of the other person's status as a rational agent, which is ethically problematic. In contrast, I will to argue that phenomenological empathy seems better equipped to deal with respecting the other's agency and avoiding both the epistemic and ethical pitfalls of cognitive empathy.

First and foremost, phenomenological empathy is not concerned with the problematic implications of shifting the epistemic status – from unconscious to conscious – of some elements of the target's deliberative process in the empathizer's simulated deliberation. There are two related reasons for this: on the one hand, phenomenological empathy does not aim to understand and ultimately predict the reasons behind the other's deliberative process by reproducing it, and on the other hand, it does not consist of an imaginative act. In this sense, the *goal* and *method* of phenomenological empathy differ substantially from those of other-oriented perspective-taking.

This is worth pointing out because we usually tend to think of empathy, regardless of its specific characterization, as aimed at understanding the other. While this seems to be true in very general terms, there are crucial differences. Other-directed perspective-taking aims to replicate the other's deliberative process, and the success of this operation is characterized by the empathizer's ability to predict the outcome of the other's deliberative process. Thus, understanding the reasons for the other's actions or inner state seems to have a distinctly utilitarian purpose. Phenomenological empathy, on the other hand, aims to understand the other, first by recognizing the other as a psychophysical individual who is also a bearer of motives and values, and second by grasping, with varying degrees of depth and detail, the specific affective and mental states of the other. However, this is not something we do in order to better predict and thus respond to the actions of others. It is a state in which we find ourselves. It is a modality in which we experience others, ourselves, and the world we share.

Moreover, other-oriented perspective-taking and phenomenological empathy achieve their goals in distinctly different ways because they are qualitatively different activities. Other-oriented perspective-taking is an imaginative act of simulation, whereas phenomenological empathy does not involve imagination or simulation. Specifically, in the second degree of the empathic act, especially in instances of personal empathy, the other person's feeling or sentiment guides my focus and allows me to be "at the subject of the content in the original subject's place" which is a very different experience than imaginatively putting oneself in the other person's situation while being the other person (Stein, PE, p. 10). The empathizer does not attempt to become the other person while taking the other's exact place in the experience. Instead, the empathizer remains herself and follows the intentionality of the other without the need to substitute the other's self. As Calcagno effectively puts is, in the second degree of the empathic act, I as the empathizer "stand in the other's place, not as identical with that subject, but as myself" (Calcagno, 2014, p. 35).

While it is true that when the empathizer engages in the second and third degrees of personal empathy, "we are dealing not merely with a perception of the other as an embodied and experiencing subject, but a presentification (*Vergegenwärtigung*) of her experiences with their objective correlates" (Jardine, 2015, p. 577), and while there may be a similarity between imagination and the second degree of empathy, it is also true that this empathic act remains distinct from imagination and memory.

Specifically, in contrast to imagination and memory, second-degree empathy requires "a form of self-displacement (*Hineinversetzen*)" that aims to leave room for the other's intentionality, which the empathizer can bring to givenness, albeit always in a non-primordial way, after following the other's intentional object (Jardine, 2015, p. 580). In this sense, while imagination is concerned with presentifying modifications of *oneself*, empathy is directed toward the foreign experience because it "is a distinctive form of other-directed intentionality, (…), which allows foreign experiences to disclose themselves as foreign rather than as own" (Zahavi, 2014a, p. 138).

Second-degree empathy, especially in personal empathy, involves something more than first-degree empathy. While the former is a quasi-perceptual act, the latter seems to also require what we can call a *cognitive component* in order to decenter and follow the other's intentionality. It does not follow, however, that empathy can be characterized as mediated because of this cognitive component since it is still quasi-perceptual, nor, most importantly, that this cognitive component must coincide with imagination. As Dullstein points out, Stein neatly separates empathy from imagination: "Empathy is, according to [Stein's] descriptions, less active than imagination. Stein uses terms such as 'being drawn into' and 'being guided by' in order to make it clear that an empathized mental state is – in contrast to a phantasm – not experienced as something we come up with. It is not experienced as being the result of one's own considerations, but rather as something that is objectively given" (Dullstein, 2013, p. 346).

For this reason, we might say that phenomenological empathy, especially in its second degree, is not only quasi-perceptual, but also *quasi-imaginative*, in the sense that it is similar to imagination, but it is not imagination. In short, second-degree empathy does not involve imagination in the sense that one does not have to imagine the other's situation in order to understand it. Rather, it involves a more unmediated, though partially cognitive, experiential understanding of the other's intentionality.

In contrast to this interpretation, some scholars have argued for the involvement of a specific kind of imaginative act in second-degree empathy. Fredrik Svenaeus, for example, argues that "in the second step of Stein's model we view the transformation of something merely perception-like into something that is also imagination-like, proceeding through the third step to something that is perception-with-imagination-like" (Svenaeus, 2016. p. 237). While I agree with him that in empathy we have an interplay between different experiential acts, I would argue that we must not forget the uniqueness of the empathic experience, which is not simply a mixture of perception and imagination, as this would come dangerously close to what the SD of empathy has called cognitive empathy, i.e., mirroring plus perspective-taking. To me, a more faithful way to characterize phenomenological empathy (and Stein's account) would be to say that empathy is a combination of quasi-perception and quasi-imagination. In this sense, empathy is not merely a particular kind of perception or imagination, as the terms "perception-like" and "imagination-like" suggest, but an experiential act *sui generis*.

Interestingly, even in cases where the imaginative character of second-degree empathy is recognized, it has nothing to do with the kind of imaginative process involved in other-oriented perspective-taking or simulation more generally. As Elisa Magrì points out: "In empathy, we are receptive not only to what is present, but we also (and on a more fundamental level) respond to the implied tendencies of a given situation. In doing so, a certain degree of imaginative projection is required, which is, however, different from simulating" (Magrì, 2015, pp. 12–13). If I understand Magrì correctly, in the kind of imagination she has in mind, there is no recreation of the other's state in the empathizer's mind, nor any attempt at prediction, that is, there is no other-oriented perspective-taking.

While I am still not convinced that second-degree empathy, strictly speaking, requires any kind of imagination in order to unfold, I believe that the type Magrì proposes is still able to avoid Goldie's criticism. In this sense, there seems to be no disagreement about the fact that in phenomenological empathy the empathizer does not attempt to take the first-person standpoint of the other by simulating their perspective. Even in Summa's reading of Stein's second degree of empathy as based on what she called "central imagining", first-person perspective-taking is characterized not only as distinct from simulation but also as always dependent on the "as if" condition: "In this moment [the fulfilling explication], I do not imagine that the other is seeing this or that, but rather try to figure out what s/he is seeing (and how s/he is seeing this) as if I were seeing the same from his/her position" (Summa, 2017, p. 98). While acknowledging a form of perspective-taking in empathy, Summa denies the possibility of doing so while *actually* being the other person.

In any case, first-person perspective-taking seems impossible within a phenomenological framework because of the irreducible distinction between the modes of givenness of the primordiality of first-person experience and the non-primordiality of empathic experience. Thus, in the phenomenological approach, I do not try to be the other person or to experience their experience from their point of view. Rather, I allow my intentionality to be drawn and guided by the other's intentionality while remaining myself and maintaining my point of view: I make room for the other's point of view without losing mine. Trying to be the other would not only be structurally impossible, it would also be pointless because in order to empathize I do not need to become the other or give up my own point of view. At the same time, this does not mean that I am merely following my own intentionality and projecting it into the other's interiority since I am experiencing self-displacement and my focus is being guided by the other's intentionality.

The peculiar aim of phenomenological empathy and the specificity of its nature seem to prove that there is no conceptual incompatibility between this account of empathy and the full-fledged agency involved in deliberation, base cases excluded. Since phenomenological empathy does not reproduce or simulate the other's condition from her first-person standpoint, the consequent risk of assigning a different epistemic status to some elements of the other's deliberative process, and thus of limiting the other's full agency, seems to be avoided. This has positive consequences on both the epistemic and ethical levels. On the one hand, it reduces the potential inaccuracy resulting from misrepresenting the reasons behind the other's deliberative process, and on the other hand, it seems to better avoid the risk of diminishing the other's status as a rational agent.

Two caveats. First, my claim that phenomenological empathy appears to be more accurate than other-directed perspective-taking is made on a purely conceptual basis, as it is meant to represent a possible solution to Goldie's critique, which is made on a conceptual basis as well. Empirical evidence is needed to prove that phenomenological empathy is capable of providing higher levels of empathic accuracy (Ickes, 1993). Second, in saying that phenomenological empathy is more accurate than cognitive empathy, I do not mean to imply that a phenomenologically informed empathic act is capable of *fully* grasping the other's experience nor is it immune to deception and inaccuracy *tout court*.

On the contrary, precisely because phenomenological empathy does not presuppose any first-person access to the other's experience through imaginative perspective-taking, the impossibility of reproducing the other's experience, let alone fully grasping it, is one of its default features. As Zahavi effectively summarizes, "empathy (…) is an experience which rather than eliminating the difference between self-experience and other-experience takes the asymmetry to be a necessary and persisting existential fact" (Zahavi, 2014a, p. 138). Empathy will never be able to transform other-experience into self-experience, that is, the kind of epistemic content provided in other-experience will always be significantly less accurate and deep than that accessed in self-experience (see Chapter 9). Thus, phenomenological empathy provides an understanding that will inevitably be incomplete, but with a higher chance of being accurate – conceptually speaking – than perspective-taking.

In addition to these epistemic advantages, the conceptual compatibility of phenomenological empathy with a full notion of agency also seems less likely to undermine the other person's status as a rational agent since the risk of reducing or mischaracterizing the other person's reasons for her actions and decisions should be mitigated by this more accurate and simultaneously less ambitious epistemic outcome. This seems clear in instances of personal empathy that are capable of revealing the specific action or inner state as situated in a broader motivational context rather than as the result of an isolated instance, a mindless reflex, or a completely obscure reaction. This should ensure, at least conceptually, that the other's status as a rational agent, i.e., someone whose decisions depend directly on his or her deliberative process, is less likely to be denied. At the same time, personal empathy never assumes that the motivational context of the other person can be fully revealed, certainly not by other-oriented perspective-taking, nor even by decentering and following the other's intentionality.

2 A Possible Solution to Affective Empathy's Problems

In Chapter 5, I challenged the assumption that empathy as defined in the SD is capable of providing motivational and normative grounds for our other-directed deliberative processes and guiding our moral judgments about the actions of others. In particular, I argued that recognizing, understanding, and sharing others' emotions, especially negative ones, do not necessarily, always, or automatically lead to moral motivation or to justifiable moral judgments about others' actions. On the contrary, I have tried to show that when empathy as defined in the SD does play these roles, its biased nature makes it highly susceptible to, and compatible with, motivating immoral outcomes and unjustified moral judgments. I focused particularly on affective empathy, understood as affective sharing, because it is often argued that sharing the distress of others – even more than merely recognizing or understanding it – is a powerful, if not the most powerful, force of altruistic and/or moral motivation in our lives. Because of its limitations, I then suggested that the centrality of empathy in morality should be revised.

My overall goal here is to show that phenomenological empathy seems to be able to avoid these problems almost entirely. The reason for this is twofold. On the one hand, it has nothing to do with affective sharing and thus does not have to worry about its shortcomings, and on the other hand, in the phenomenological approach, empathy is not only distinct from sympathy, but it does not play a foundational role in morality.

2.1 *Phenomenological Empathy and the Problem of Affective Biases*

One of the features that drastically distinguishes phenomenological empathy from affective empathy is the fact that affective sharing is not necessary to achieve the former. Both experiential empathy and personal empathy do not require the empathizer to feel what the other person is feeling in order to understand it. Moreover, the phenomenological approach denies the possibility of affective isomorphism altogether. Consequently, our inability to impartially share the emotions of others without being influenced by our biases and prejudices does not seem to be a problem that a phenomenological account of empathy needs to solve.

For a phenomenological account of empathy, a total sameness of the emotional states of the subjects, both in terms of the nature of the emotions and their intensity, is not only unnecessary but impossible. More specifically, by introducing a distinction between primordiality and non-primordiality, Stein argued that the empathized state will never have the same kind of givenness as that of the other (see Chapter 7). Thus, even if the two subjects are experiencing the same internal state, they are not in a state of isomorphism because their internal states are *essentially* different in terms of their mode of givenness. In other words, in a phenomenologically characterized act of empathy, even if the empathizer is experiencing an empathized affective state that belongs to the same "family" of the other person's state (e.g., the primordial joy of the target and the non-primordial joy of the empathizer), the isomorphic condition is not and cannot be satisfied.

As Íngrid Vendrell Ferran points out, while it is true that in certain cases "there are not two contents, just one," this content is "felt by two different subjects" with a different mode of givenness (Vendrell Ferran, 2015, p. 486). Note that a separate but related reason for rejecting isomorphism is the specular rejection, *contra* Lipps, of the possibility of a fusion between the selves of the subjects involved in the empathic relationship. Precisely because the two selves remain separate throughout the empathic act, the idea of an isomorphic state seems conceptually and phenomenologically implausible.

For this reason, phenomenological empathy must be distinguished from emotional contagion (*Gefühlsansteckung*). In emotional contagion, the feeling of the other person "overflows me" and becomes mine, as when I am sad and want to be cheered up by a happy person (Stein, PE, p. 23). Note that, however, I am not primordially experiencing the other person, hence, there is no isomorphism between my emotional condition and his: he is experiencing primordially his joy and I am experiencing primordially *my* joy as a result of being unwillingly infected by his joy. This is precisely why, according to Stein, what Lipps was actually describing in his work was emotional contagion, not empathy. Crucially, in emotional contagion there is no grasping, no epistemic access to the other person's emotional state: "The difference between grasping and taking over a feeling is clearly apparent" (Stein, PE, p. 23).

Even a more moderate version of isomorphism, namely affective sharing, is regarded by a phenomenological account of empathy as a phenomenon distinct from empathy and as an unnecessary condition for the empathic act. Empathy does not require affective sharing because my intentional object need not be the same as that of the other person with whom I empathize. When I empathize with my friend's fear, my intentional object is her fear, not the snake she is attending to and is afraid of, which means that I do not feel my friend's fear of the snake, and therefore do not share it in order to understand it (Zahavi & Overgaard, 2011, p. 8).

Beyond the difference in the intentionality of the two acts, it seems both conceptually and phenomenologically incorrect that sharing the other's emotions is crucial for empathy. There are many instances in which we can perfectly understand what the other person is feeling without being in that particular emotional state, or while in an entirely different emotional state. Consider Zahavi's effective examples of these cases: I can understand that my child is afraid of the monster under the bed without being afraid myself; similarly, I can understand a stranger's anger and not only not be angry myself, but experience fear instead (Zahavi, 2014a, p. 132).

The rejection of affective sharing as necessary for phenomenological empathy is uncontroversial as far as the first degree is concerned. If I have empathized with, i.e., quasi-perceived, the other's pain (experiential empathy) or fear (personal empathy), I need not actually be in pain or fear myself. However, when it comes to the second degree of empathy, some interpreters of Stein's work claim that affective empathy is necessary. For example, Svenaeus argues *contra* Zahavi that "such situations, in which the empathizer proceeds from step-one to step-two sensual empathy, do demand that the empathizer feels herself into the feelings of the empathee by having the same *sort* of feeling that the empathee has but in the co-original way" (Svenaeus, 2018, p. 751). Along the same lines, Dullstein claims that "to a certain extent, Stein endorses in this second phase the isomorphism-condition" that she later characterized as a form of "inner resonance between the empathizer and her target" (Dullstein, 2013, p. 345).

As for the involvement of the imagination, whether affective sharing is seen as part of the second degree of empathy depends on how one understands the double movement of decentering and following the other's intentionality. Following the other's intentionality does not seem to require affective sharing, especially if we agree on its quasi-imaginative rather than simulative character. As Magrì emphasizes, "if I am feeling led by the other, I am not pretending to have the same state as the other. Indeed, in order to experience empathy one is not required to go through the same experience as the other" (Magrì, 2015, p. 16). Moreover, in instances of personal empathy, the scope of the second degree seems to be broader than it appears if we consider that affective sharing is necessarily involved. In the fuller and deeper instances of personal empathy, the empathizer can grasp the intentional and motivational context of the other person. In this sense, by suggesting that being in the same emotional state as the other is necessary to achieve this kind of understanding, we may end up trivializing the goal of phenomenological empathy.

Again, as their different goals suggest, phenomenological empathy is *essentially* different from isomorphism and emotional contagion, so that even positing a more moderate requirement such as affective sharing may muddy the waters and problematically collapse these phenomena. Finally, I think that Stein's relentless critique of Lipps's account is an important, if not definitive, indication of how we should interpret what happens in the second degree. The idea of having to feel what the other is feeling while following her intentionality seems dangerously close to Lipps's imitation mechanism, even taking into account the different modes of givenness.

Importantly, the exclusion of affective sharing from empathy does not mean that empathy is an emotionless experience. When we empathize with someone else, we certainly have emotions. In particular, we often have an emotional response to the emotional state of the other person with whom we have empathized, which may also be a "close relative" of the empathized emotions (e.g., feeling proud of our child's excitement about a good grade in school). The point is that the act of sharing need not be present. Zahavi effectively clarifies the distinction: "It might well be that the emotions we perceive in others induce emotional resonances and action tendencies in our own bodies and that these responses then feed into and influence the way we apprehend the other, but there is a decisive difference between acknowledging this and defending the view that our understanding of the other's emotion requires us to have that very emotion ourselves" (Zahavi, 2014a, p. 132).

I do not need to feel pain in my arm or experience loneliness after the end of a marriage to understand that my friend is in pain because of an injury to his arm or that he feels lonely after his recent divorce. Especially if the other person is a loved one, I may be distressed by his pain or fearful for his mental well-being, or in the case of a stranger, I may experience a superficial sense of unease or emotional discomfort after understanding his condition, but I do not have to feel what he is feeling. In other words, just because we do not (have to) share the other person's emotional state does not mean that we are not having an emotional experience when we empathize in the phenomenological sense. This should answer Svenaeus's objection to Zahavi: rejecting the need for affective sharing does not deny the emotional aspect of the empathic experience (Svenaeus, 2016).

To reiterate, I am not suggesting that we never experience emotional contagion or some version of affective sharing, but rather that we avoid mislabeling these phenomena: they are not empathy. This distinction would seem to mitigate the potentially distorting influences that an account of empathy understood through the phenomenological approach might suffer when involved in our other-directed deliberative processes, especially the moral ones. There is, however, an even more fundamental issue to be addressed when it comes to empathy and its role in morality. As I will discuss next, according to a phenomenological approach, empathy (and sympathy) is no guarantee of morality, especially when it comes to motivating the empathizer to act morally or guiding her in formulating moral judgments.

2.2 *Phenomenological Empathy, Moral Motivation, and Moral Judgments*

One of the crucial differences between a phenomenological approach and the SD is that, according to the former, empathy is not directly involved in motivating altruistic and/or moral actions or in formulating moral judgments, while according to the latter, cognitive empathy and especially affective empathy play a prominent role in morality, if not directly, as in Baron-Cohen's and Slote's proposals, then at least as a cause of sympathy, which is then responsible for moral motivation and judgments, as in Batson's and Nichols's accounts (see Chapter 5). While the SD also tends to distinguish between (cognitive and affective) empathy and sympathy, ambiguity remains about how these phenomena relate to each other. Phenomenology, by contrast, appears better equipped to define these as distinct and separate phenomena.

Although Stein did not spend much time articulating this difference, it is nonetheless very clear in her work. In the section entitled *Empathy and Fellow Feeling*, she argued that "sympathized and empathized joy need not necessarily be the same in content at all. (They are certainly not the same in respect to quality, since one is a primordial and the other a non-primordial experience)" (Stein, PE, p. 14). Both the content and the mode of givenness of the two acts are different. Whereas in the case of empathy, the content of the act is the joy of the other person, which is not primordially given, in the case of sympathy the act is directed at the same object, in our case, the successful examination of a friend, which causes an emotional state in the other person and another primordially experienced emotional reaction in the sympathizer.

The difference is also highlighted when we look at the more literal translation of the terms: empathy as "feeling-*in*-the-other" (*Einfühlung*) and sympathy as "feeling-*with*-the-other" (*Mitfühlen*) where the different prepositions effectively show the essential difference between these two acts. As an empathizer, I grasp the other's joy over her successful exam whereas, as a sympathizer, I am joyful with my joyful friend over her academic achievement. From the start, Husserl himself recognized that, despite their resemblance, these two phenomena must be distinguished. He refers to empathy as an "intuitive illustration" that can result in a feeling with the other that is not, however, a sympathetic feeling: "If someone, right before my eyes, burns or cuts himself, or else when he gets news of something that I overhear, which results in his emotional suffering, etc., we feel immediately with him (in a feeling-with that is not, in the usual, completely different sense, feeling-with, sympathy) – or at least so it seems" (Husserl, 1910–11, p. 151). Michael Andrews also effectively highlights the distinction between empathy and sympathy as follows: "Unlike sympathy, which constitutes a 'shared emotion' or 'shared perception' with one or many others, empathy affords no such simulacrum. Empathy, as opposed to sympathy, constitutes an experience of distinction between 'I' and Other" (Andrews, 2022, p. 238). The peculiarity of the empathic experience is precisely its ability to allow us to grasp and relate to the other person without ever collapsing two selves.

Given this *essential* difference between empathy and sympathy, their respective roles in morality must be clearly differentiated. As John Drummond points out, "empathy grasps the other as experiencing grief over this loss, a loss to which I, along with the empathized subject, primarily direct my attention. In sympathizing with the other, however, I do not merely recognize the other's grief; I have an affective reaction to that recognition. In sympathy I direct my attention not merely to the loss but to the grieving subject as someone about whose well-being I care" (Drummond, 2022, p. 354).

In feeling *with* the other's grief, my focus is not purely epistemic, as it was in empathy, but it becomes, if not fully moral, at least altruistic.[2] In sympathy, I feel with the other because I am concerned for the other well-being. Importantly, this concern is expressed in an emotional response to the other's condition: I feel sadness for my depressed, recently divorced friend. However, for

2 See the distinction between morality and altruism discussed in Section 1.3.2.

sympathy to occur, it is not necessary to feel the same emotion as the other person, nor is it necessary for the other person's emotion to be negative. I can sympathize with my depressed friend over her recent divorce by being worried, or I can sympathize with my friend's academic achievement by feeling proud. Note that sympathy is qualitatively different from the emotional reactions that Zahavi discussed in cases of empathy. If I empathically grasp a stranger's anger and react with fear, I am not sympathizing with the stranger because I do not care about his well-being (in this case, quite the opposite: I care about my own safety).

In contrast to sympathy, empathy has the specifically epistemic goal of grasping the other's inner states in order to understand them. In empathizing with the other's joy or sorrow, our only goal is to grasp experientially the other's inner state and, in the second degree, the intentional object to which it is directed. There is no need or place for care or concern in the empathic act. Thus, due to its epistemic nature, the empathic act in the phenomenological approach has generally been considered either completely devoid of any moral valence or not directly involved in morality (Zahavi, 2008; Zahavi & Rochat, 2015; for a contrasting view see Andrews, 2022).

When it comes to sympathy, it is the element of *concern* or *care* for the target that makes its potential contribution to morality more apparent. In particular, sympathy seems, at least conceptually, well suited to motivate the subject to act altruistically, in the sense of acting to promote the other's, rather than our own, welfare. By being concerned about the other person's well-being, I am likely to be more motivated to perform caring acts toward that person. For example, I might decide to drive my depressed friend to her therapy sessions, or I might decide to give my friend money to pay for her graduate course that she would otherwise not be able to attend.

Within the phenomenological framework, it is crucial to recognize that sympathy does not necessarily entail the *actual performance* of altruistic actions toward another person. Concern for another's welfare may exist independently of concrete altruistic behavior. While the SD approach to empathy acknowledges this theoretical possibility, it treats such instances as rare exceptions. Most SD-based accounts assume that sympathy reliably leads to altruistic and moral action on the part of the sympathizer. The phenomenological approach, by contrast, more effectively distinguishes between the sympathetic experience itself and its potential – yet never inevitable – behavioral manifestations.

Before discussing how the relationship between phenomenological empathy and sympathy is conceptualized, let me first question, from a phenomenological perspective, the idea that there is a necessary implication between sympathy and morality, i.e., that any sympathetic action will coincide with a moral action. In this sense, even Drummond, a proponent of the ethical valence of sympathy from a phenomenological perspective, recognized the possible egoistic and immoral outcomes of this phenomenon: "sympathy – he noted – also runs the risk of motivating paternalistic or even oppressive actions" (Drummond, 2022, p. 356; see also Chapter 9).

Because of our concern for the other's well-being, we may be motivated to limit or deny his or her autonomy and agency over choices that we perceive as potentially harmful. Consider the case of a friend who is emotionally burned out because of a toxic work environment. I sympathize with her and am concerned and worried about her situation. She tells me that she wants to quit. However, the next week, in an anxious phone call, she tells me that she has decided not to follow through with her decision. Motivated by my sympathetic concern, I told her that if she did not quit her job, I would never speak to her again. Although motivated by genuine sympathy for her, my emotional blackmail can be considered an immoral act because I am not respecting her autonomy to choose freely what she thinks is the best course of action. It seems that sympathy alone is not only insufficient to guarantee a moral outcome, but can also be responsible for immorality.

There are still two aspects that need to be addressed. On the one hand, I need to clarify how the phenomenological approach frames the relationship between empathy and sympathy, and on the other, I need to discuss the critique that Classical Phenomenology, and Max Scheler in particular, makes of the contribution of an empathic phenomenon understood as affective sharing or perspective-taking to morality. First and foremost, the phenomenological approach seems to deny a necessary causal relationship between phenomenological empathy and sympathy since the epistemic grasping of the other's experience does not automatically lead to an emotional response and consequent care for that person. Our everyday experience corroborates this distinction: we frequently recognize others' suffering without necessarily caring about their plight.

This does not exclude the possibility that phenomenological empathy can sometimes function as a "cognitive basis" for sympathy, as in the case of my academically gifted or depressed friend (Drummond, 2022, p. 355). Thus, the fact that empathically grasping the other's joy or sadness can provide the epistemic basis for developing sympathy is perfectly possible, both phenomenologically and conceptually, as long as we do not collapse the two acts. The key point is that a phenomenological approach to empathy recognizes that its relation to sympathy is contingent and never inevitable. This seems consistent both with the critique of accounts that assign a crucial role to cognitive and affective empathy and sympathy in morality as well as with the suggestion made in Chapter 5 that the role of empathy in morality may have been overstated and that a more moderate reframing of the issue might be useful.

Crucially, the phenomenological framework explicitly critiques the ethical relevance of both affective and cognitive empathy. While Stein did not directly address the issue, Scheler, to whom she referred when discussing sympathy (Stein, PE, p. 14), devoted Chapter 1 of his *Nature of Sympathy* to a critique of the so-called "ethics of sympathy" (Scheler, 1913, p. 5), namely Hume's and Smith's accounts, which characterized empathy as a fundamental element of morality. Scheler's critique is particularly relevant because it clearly shows why the phenomenological approach is an alternative to the SD-based accounts such as those of Slote and Nichols, which assign to affective empathy, inspired by Hume's sympathy, and to cognitive empathy, inspired by Smith's sympathy, the roles of motivating moral action and formulating moral judgments, respectively.

Interestingly, Scheler's main goal in his work was to argue that it is impossible to ground morality solely on shared feelings. Instead, he contended that love is the fundamental phenomenon that can provide a basis for our moral lives. To this end, he first provides a taxonomy of shared feelings, aiming to "identify the structural laws governing emotional life" via this phenomenological, i.e., eidetic, analysis (Moran, 2004, p. 283). Specifically, he distinguished five kinds of shared feelings which, notably, are all involuntary in nature (Davis & Steinbock, 2024). The first is *feeling with one another* (*Miteinanderfühlen*) which refers to two or more people feeling the exact same emotion together, such as parents sharing the joy or suffering related to their child. The second kind is *vicarious feeling* (*Nachfühlen*) which consists of grasping another's feeling from a distance, without actually experiencing that feeling oneself. This is a prerequisite for recognizing others' emotions, including for empathizing with them. The third is *fellow feeling* (*Mitgefühl*): it involves an intentional feeling directed toward the other person. When someone is in pain, I not only grasp or comprehend their pain but also feel for them. In other words, I have a feeling oriented toward them and their situation. The key distinction is that, in fellow feeling, my feeling is not exactly the same as the other person's feeling. A clear separation remains between my feelings and the feelings of others that I feel for. For example, if my friend is grieving, I don't necessarily feel grief myself, but I may feel sadness, compassion, or concern for them in their state of grief. In other words, it is an affective reaction to the other's condition and can be understood as a combination of affective empathy and sympathy.

Fourth is *psychic contagion*, or emotional contagion (*Gefühlansteckung*), which refers to the experience of being overtaken by and losing oneself in the collective feeling or mood of a group. This can be positive, such as the festive atmosphere of a pub, or negative, such as panic in a crowd. In these instances, individual identities merge into a "we." Finally, *identification* (*Einsfühlung*) is an extreme form of psychic contagion in which one completely loses one's "I" and inhabits the other's experience as if it were one's own, with no distance remaining (e.g., in mystical experiences).

First of all, Scheler demonstrates that sharing another's feelings presupposes an understanding of their experiences. He further argues that fellow feeling cannot guarantee moral action because the mere sharing of emotions remains disconnected from the axiological domain. As he observes: emotional sharing "in all its possible forms is in principle blind to value" (Scheler, 1913, p. 5). Unlike fellow feeling, love engages with values directly – we can simultaneously love someone while regretting their moral failings. This capacity makes love, rather than empathetic sharing, the proper foundation for moral life (Moran, 2024, p. 285).

To see why fellow feeling cannot play this role, it is enough to consider the fact that sharing the pleasure of inflicting pain on another person cannot be considered moral. In contrast, as he explained, "the sharing of another's pleasure can only be moral when the latter *is itself moral*, and warranted by the value-situation which evokes it" (Scheler, 1913, p. 5). it follows that because of the value-blindness of affective empathy and sympathy, or as he called it fellow feeling, there is no guarantee that sharing the other's emotional state will result in a moral action. Since the act of sharing the other's pain has no moral value in itself, taking affective empathy as the privileged motivational source of our moral other-directed deliberation implies the possibility of immoral outcomes.

In his second critique, Scheler targeted the Smithian thesis according to which we can formulate moral judgments only by imaginatively taking the impartial spectator's perspective. Scheler rejected Smith's view entirely by providing the counterexample of "the whole class of ethical judgments we pass upon ourselves" (Scheler, 1913, p. 6). When we judge the moral status of our own actions, there is no need for cognitive empathy: it seems quite far from our inner experience to claim that when we judge our actions to be immoral it is because of the internalized viewpoint of some "social authority" or impartial spectator (Scheler, 1913, p. 6). While there is no denying that how others judge us influences our own judgments, it is also true that cognitive empathy does not seem to be involved in how we judge our own actions. That process is much more direct and unmediated.

As Dermot Moran effectively summarized, in Scheler's account, empathy or sympathy cannot be the basis for morality because "one must already recognize the moral feeling as good and morally worthy before sympathizing with it"

(Moran, 2004, p. 185). In other words, both affective and cognitive empathy as well as sympathy can play a role in motivating moral action and formulating moral judgments, but they can play only a secondary role because I must already recognize the action as moral or judge the action as immoral with tools or processes that are not empathic before I can either share the other's emotional state and be moved by it to act or imaginatively take the other's perspective to justify my judgment. Thus, neither affective nor cognitive empathy can be primarily responsible for our moral motivation and judgments.

Although Scheler argued that genuine fellow feeling is distinct from complete identification or fusion with another person, he acknowledged that "a minimum of undifferentiated identification" is necessary for our most fundamental awareness that another being is alive (Scheler, 1913, p. 31). According to him, this primitive form of identification not only underlies recognizing animate movement but also the simplest instances of vicarious feeling, fellow feeling itself and the capacity for intersubjective understanding between minds (Moran, 2004, p. 288). Importantly, Scheler did not locate such identification in the domains of bodily sensations or spiritual consciousness but rather in an intermediate "vital consciousness" realm encompassing emotions, instincts, and drives. Furthermore, in contrast to Husserl and Stein, Scheler believed that the other's status as a person is not directly graspable through their living body; rather, it is grasped spiritually. For example, works of art can make us aware of their authors without having any experience of their living bodies since we recognize personhood based on "the signs of spiritual activity" of the other person (Moran, 2004, p. 289).

Crucially, as Calcagno argues, Stein rightly rejected the notion that any such identification could be constitutive of community (Calcagno, 2017). Based on her analysis of the individuated living body, Stein argued that the sphere of "ownness" – the irreducible first-personal givenness of the psyche-spiritual unity of the person – prevents any total dissolution of the self into the collective, or, as Stein will call it, community.[3] Even though intense emotional expe-

3 The concept of community is particularly relevant to Stein's philosophy, especially in *Philosophy of Psychology and the Humanities* (Stein, 1922), in which she begins to develop her influential social ontology. As Calcagno (Calcagno, 2014) discusses in detail, this aspect of Stein's philosophical approach is particularly original and innovative compared to other competing accounts, such as Scheler's. However, I will not discuss this aspect of her proposal here, since my focus is on the empathic relationship between two subjects. Following Calcagno's reading, I will only briefly highlight the core aspects of her notion of community (2020, pp. 631–633): Stein delineates three forms of sociality: community (the most intense form of togetherness and solidarity), society (a collectivity oriented around a shared goal), and the mass (a loose association based on imitation). In order to experience community, subjects must be able to distinguish individual affectivity from collective affectivity. Reason

riences may temporarily de-focus one's sense of individuation, for Stein, this ownness remains the fundamental ground of all experience and cannot and should not be dissolved.

So far, I have argued that phenomenological empathy and sympathy are two qualitatively different acts, that sympathy does not always guarantee moral outcomes, that the relationship between phenomenological empathy and sympathy is not causally necessary – although phenomenological empathy may sometimes be a precursor to sympathy – and, finally, that, according to a phenomenological approach, cognitive and affective empathy are not predictive of moral motivation or a condition for formulating moral judgments. Donise summed up the complicated relationship between empathy, sympathy, and morality nicely:

> Once we have acquired knowledge of the other's feelings, we come to the really relevant question for ethics: deciding what to do with them. The mere feeling we call 'empathy' does not determine the direction or morality of the action to which it gives rise. (…) But even at the level of 'sympathy', (…) the connection with ethics shows its limits and proves not always functional. Sympathizing (…) can also be directed towards experiences that have nothing ethical about them: for example, a mother will easily sympathize with the inner states of her son, even if the son is a criminal.
>
> DONISE, 2019, pp. 249–250, my translation

Because of these considerations, a phenomenological approach seems less vulnerable to the shortcomings of cognitive and affective empathy in morality since it is already well aware of their potential compatibility with immorality and thus does not assign them a foundational role in morality.

What remains to be explored is what happens when we use phenomenological empathy for our other-directed moral deliberations. There seem to be two possibilities, both of which are compatible with the basic distinction between empathy and sympathy, and thus with the claim that phenomenological empathy does not in itself have moral valence or a foundational role in morality.

First, one might argue that phenomenological empathy can make a specifically epistemic contribution to morality: the information gained through

---

and other intellectual capacities are also necessary to understand the concept of the "we." Underpinning this account of community is Stein's view that empathy is the foundational act for gaining not only knowledge of oneself and the other person, but also of community and spiritual objects created through human will, reason, and freedom.

empathy can constitute motivating reasons and contribute to the formulation of moral judgments in other-directed deliberation. Second, one might also ask whether the recognition of others as embodied and minded persons provided by phenomenological empathy can contribute to, or be a precondition for, our other-directed deliberative processes, and whether this might be in tension with the epistemic character of empathy. The next chapter is devoted precisely to discussing the role that phenomenological empathy plays in other-directed deliberation in general, and moral other-directed deliberation in particular. But first, we need to see whether the phenomenological approach is able to address the relationships between empathy and the context in which it is situated.

3 A Possible Solution to Empathy's Contextual Problems

In Chapter 6, I argued that despite the focus of some accounts on the relational aspect of empathy, the SD of empathy largely ignores the impact of the context in which the empathic relationship unfolds, and that this can be problematic from both an epistemic and a moral standpoint. This is because the broader context of both the empathizer and the target of empathy is crucial to gaining an accurate understanding of the other's inner states. Moreover, this context is also essential to understanding whether the empathic relationship might lead to morally problematic consequences, such as in cases of asymmetrical relationships where empathy might exacerbate epistemically unjust dynamics.

In what follows, I will try to show why a phenomenologically informed understanding of empathy might be better suited to deal with these problems. Not only is this approach more aware of the context in which empathic acts take place, but it is also aware that empathy alone would never be able to understand this context satisfactorily, which can contribute to mitigate possible instances of epistemic injustice.

3.1 *Phenomenological Empathy, the Influence of the Context, and Epistemic Injustice*

In contrast to the SD, the phenomenological approach presupposes by its very definition that empathy and the subjects involved in it are irrevocably enmeshed in a context. Specifically, the influence of the context, both in terms of the immediate context of the subjects, their character, and the broader socio-cultural context, is recognized as inescapable. This becomes clear when we consider the notion of "horizon." According to Husserl, Stein, and fundamentally all authors belonging to the phenomenological tradition, objects are never perceived in a vacuum but always "against a background (*Hintergrund*) and in the midst of a 'surrounding world' (*Umwelt*) of other objects, and also of other living bodies which are also other persons, animals, and so on" (Moran & Cohen, 2012, p. 147). In other words, everything or everyone we experience is "intertwined and permeated with an intentional empty horizon" (Husserl, *Hua* XI 5–6).

It follows that by enriching our understanding of the context in which they are situated, it is possible to achieve a more determinate experience of the objects or other living bodies. This is also true for the lived experiences of the subjects since every lived experience "has a past that fades into an indeterminate horizon of the past and similarly it has one of the future" (Moran & Cohen, 2012, pp. 147–148).[4] Every experience of any object – physical objects, people, animals, etc. – presupposes and depends on the horizon in which it is situated. In this sense, the notion of horizon can be characterized as "a system of references" (Moran & Cohen, 2012, p. 147). Crucially, this system of references can be characterized as "subjective and individual," as in the case of the character of the subject, or as "shared," as in the case of the historical and sociocultural context. Husserl explicitly linked the possibility of being a person and being experienced as such by others to the existence of this common world: "We could not be persons for the other persons if, in a community, in the intentional relatedness of our lives, we did not have before us a common world; correlatively speaking, the one is not constituted without the other" (Husserl, *Hua IV*, p. 191, as cited in Kern, 2018, p. 45). Thus, mutual recognition of personhood – also a central theme for Stein (see Chapter 9) – is predicated on sharing a common horizon, "the social backdrop against which intersubjective encounters take place" (Magrì & McQueen, 2023, p. 96). The notion of horizon, which is incredibly more complex than what I can discuss here,[5] sheds light on the key fact that embeddedness and situatedness are constitutive features of our experience, including empathic experience, and one of the tenants of any phenomenological account. As Zahavi points out, "when we encounter others, we encounter them in a shared world, and our understanding of each other takes place in a specific context and situation" (Zahavi, 2014b, p. 163). Conversely, other accounts of empathy, especially those that rely heavily on empirical evidence to define the empathic phenomenon, tend to

4 Husserl referred to this aspect of experience in terms of "inner horizons" (Moran & Cohen, 2012, p. 147).

5 For an introductory discussion on the concept of horizon in Phenomenology and in Husserl's philosophy in particular see Kuhn and Geniusas (Geniusas, 2012; Kuhn, 1940).

paint a picture of the empathic relationship that is closer to what would happen in an experimental setting than to what happens in our intersubjective experiences.

The importance of context becomes clear when ambiguity needs to be resolved in our empathic understanding of others' expressions: "Expressions occur in a given context, and our understanding of the context, of what comes before and after, helps us to understand whether a blush means shame or anger, or is the result of physical exertion" (Zahavi, 2014b, p. 163). Thus, in order to discern the meaning of a particular expression, such as blushing, the empathizer must also grasp some aspects of the specific situation in which the expression occurs, such as what the blushing person is looking at and what she was doing just before the expression. Aron Gurwitsch famously and effectively articulated this point in his 1931 *Human Encounters in the Social World* by claiming that "expressive phenomena smoothly arises from knowledge about the situation in which I am with others, and fits into this knowledge as one of its moments" (Gurwitsch, 1931, p. 162). Depending on the complexity of the expression and the context, this situational grasp can occur both in the first degree and/or in the second degree by following the intentionality of the other.

As Zahavi forcefully points out, the grasp of these kinds of contextual aspects of the other's expression (e.g., the gaze following or the assessment of the immediate situation) can still be characterized as direct (Zahavi, 2014b, pp. 163–165). In particular, the empathic grasp of the situational context is carried out both quasi-perceptually (first degree) and/or quasi-imaginatively (second degree). This is not to say that the same context and expression cannot be understood using different tools, such as inference, simulation, or perspective-taking, or that these tools cannot be used in combination with empathy. The point is that phenomenological empathy has the resources to directly grasp, however imperfectly, some elements of the particular context in which the empathized foreign expression or internal state is taking place.

Besides the strictly immediate context in which the particular expression of the other person takes place (e.g., the treadmill next to the blushing person), phenomenological empathy seems to be able to provide a grasp of another kind of context, that is, the character of the other person, of which the particular expression we are trying to empathically grasp is an instance. More specifically, an empathic grasp of the other's character is achieved only through multiple and repeated acts of empathy.

On this point, as said, Stein explicitly argued that it is through repeated acts of empathy that I can begin to grasp the other's inner states as located within the specific context of his or her individual character. Having repeatedly empathized with a person, I have gained an understanding of some of his or her character traits and habits, which should serve as a kind of standard of correctness or disambiguation reference for future acts of empathy. For example, since I have empathically grasped the other as a temperate person, I will be justified, only *prima facie*, in grasping the other's silence as an expression of temperance rather than indifference.[6]

Moreover, in the empathic act, the influence of the shared horizon also comes into play: just as the particular inner state is located within the subject's character, this character is also the result of and in active relation to the broader historical, social, and cultural context in which the subject lives. As said (see Chapter 7), according to Stein, the development of our character is strongly influenced by the specific characteristics of our living bodies and by the external circumstances in which the individual was born, raised, and embedded that allow or limit the development of our personality.

While these influences are undeniable, there is one element of our personality, our "personal structure," which does not change and therefore constitutes our identity: "I can think of Caesar in a village instead of Rome and can think of him transferred into the twentieth century. Certainly, his historically settled individuality would then go through some changes, but just as surely he would remain Caesar" (Stein, PE, p. 100). Note that Stein is not suggesting that the Caesar of ancient Rome would be the same Caesar if he lived in Italy today. Instead, Stein suggests that Caesar, despite the different context and because of his personal structure, would still be characterized as a person, i.e., a living body and a bearer of motives and values. In this sense, the personal structure reveals the dynamic and dialogical relationship between the individual and the common horizon in which he develops: "The personal structure marks off a range of possibilities of variation within which the person's real distinctiveness can be developed 'ever according to circumstances'" (Stein, PE, p. 100).

Because of this interplay between the other's expression or inner state, her character, and her broader context, "empathizing with others implies the ability to be directed to another horizon," where the empathically grasped internal states reveal aspects of both the individual and the shared context and, at the same time, require the empathizer to refer to that context in order to fully understand it (Magrì, 2019, p. 336).

Another way to frame the interaction between the specific empathized state, the personal individuality of the subject, and the historical and sociocul-

6 In Stein's words: "But having thus gotten a picture of the foreign 'character' as a unity of these attributes, this itself serves me as a point of departure for the verification of further empathic acts" (Stein, *PE*, p. 80).

tural context is to refer to the idea of typification. As Joona Taipale defines it, typification consists of "the process whereby features that are not experientially present are smuggled into the anticipatory horizon of our present experience" (Taipale, 2015). When we encounter others, we understand them primarily as individuals who belong to a certain type (e.g., people of this gender, race, age, and way of dressing) and thus have some underlying characteristics that we associate with that type but that are not afforded in experience (e.g., being weak or strong and arrogant or humble).

According to Taipale, this very basic way of understanding others is the most common because of the double constraint of prior knowledge and interest. Since I have neither a particular interest nor the prior knowledge necessary to understand the broader personal and cultural context in which the smile of the person on the bus is situated, I will empathically understand that the other person is grinning because she is probably looking at a meme on her phone since I believe her to be a millennial. This would be an instance of second-degree experiential empathy. In contrast, in cases where I have both the interest and the epistemic resources necessary to go one step further in my empathic act, I can try to grasp the specificity of that individual, i.e., I can empathically grasp the motivational and axiological context of the person smiling on the bus and locate her experience within our shared horizon, as happens in instances of personal empathy, especially when repeated over time.

Most importantly, even when we engage in more complex acts of empathy, namely personal empathy, and are interested in understanding the other's individuality by revealing the deeper level of his or her personality and character, we do not achieve this by abandoning the typification process. Instead, in order to understand the other's inner states more deeply, we try to uncover how these typicalities are realized in that particular person.[7] This is because

7 For a preliminary definition of "type" in Husserl's philosophy see the one provided by Moran and Cohen: "Perceptual experience is primarily directed at individuals but it also identifies groups of individuals according to certain loose generalizations or 'types' constituted on the basis of similarity. In a 1925 letter to Landgrebe, Husserl says he is interested in the idea of 'type' as found in Dilthey and that of ideal type in Weber (*Briefwechsel* IV 247) In *Ideas II* § 60, Husserl claims personal life manifests a typicality. There is what is typical for human beings as such, but also what is typical for this individual. (…) Types do not emerge through active conceptual consideration, but rather through the meaningful connection of experiences. Unlike the Kantian schematism (which seeks to apply the pure concepts to the raw material of sensibility), types are not images, either in the form of mere examples or as simpler figures. There can be types of individual, e.g. my 'type' (stereotype) of how I think about John, or types of humanness or humanity (e.g. Indian, Chinese, and so on)" (Moran & Cohen, 2012, pp. 336–337).

"as univocally emphasized by classical phenomenologists, personal uniqueness is not gained by way of stripping off the supraindividual (cultural, historical, biological, etc.) typicalities, but by way of appropriating and thus *clothing oneself* with these typicalities in a unique and hence personal manner" (Taipale, 2015). Our unique personality, and the unique meaning that our inner states have within it, is in part the result of how we thematize and realize the influences that the broader context has on us: "Initially others are present to us as fellow citizens, as children or adults, as men or women, as clerks or police officers, as Europeans or Asians, as patients, as ice-hockey players, as rock stars, as 'just that kind of persons', and so on, and their singularity is discovered and recognized – more or less extensively, *if at all* – underneath, yet in the light of, such typifications" (Taipale, 2015).[8]

As both Taipale and Summa point out, Stein considered the process of typification to be part of the empathic act, especially in the second degree: "[Stein] defends the claim that typological recognition (primarily concerning the body, but, more specifically also concerning cultural or social background, etc.) enable us to take over, via presentification, the other's person point of view without ever giving up ours" (Summa, 2017, p. 102). Thus, because we have this typological way of framing others (and ourselves), especially when it comes to our roles in social and cultural contexts, we are able to follow and be guided by the other's intentionality without having to simulate or infer the other's expressions or internal states. Ultimately, it is because of our typological recognition of others that we are able to empathize with them.

Two clarifications are in order. First, is not the involvement of typification in our empathic understanding of others just a glorified and more sophisticated way of saying that empathy is modulated by prejudice and bias, which, if true, would expose phenomenological empathy to the same objections raised against cognitive and affective empathy (see Part II)? Second, if we accept the influences of the broader context on our empathic understanding, are we bound to claim that phenomenology is *de facto* able to capture the complexity of that context in its entirety?

I am rather skeptical about a possible equivalence between the biased nature of affective empathy and cognitive empathy and the presence of typification in phenomenological empathy. In the SD, cognitive and affective biases modulate not only the accuracy of the empathic process, but also the presence or absence of what the SD identifies as empathy since the activation of mirroring or affective sharing are directly dependent on our biased categorization

8 Taipale's claim directly echoes Schütz's position that in every encounter we have with others, we have already a typification involved (Schutz, 1972).

of others (e.g., as in-group members or out-group members). Conversely, in phenomenological empathy, the most basic form of recognition of the other as an embodied mind – that is, the first-degree of experiential empathy – is not immediately modulated by typification as second-degree instances of empathy seem to be. It is not modulated by anything at all; it is the default way we exist and directly experience the world we share with others.

This fundamental difference also explains why phenomenological empathy is better equipped to deal with its potential inaccuracies and resulting morally problematic consequences than the SD of empathy. While the inclusion of typification in empathy can clearly lead to epistemic inaccuracies and morally questionable attitudes, such as when "my social typifications are derogatory – e.g., if I were a white settler in colonial Williamsburg in whom are sedimented negative typifications of the indigenous people" (Burns, 2016, p. 275), I would also argue that it is possible, and indeed easier, to overcome this problem within the framework of phenomenological empathy because it does not depend entirely on or consist of our typification. Specifically, second-degree empathy, especially in the case of personal empathy and in cases of repeated empathy, aims precisely at gasping the personal motivational and axiological context of the specific other, which should allow for a correction, however partial, of inaccurate typifications.

Nevertheless, negative typifications that are so deeply ingrained and sedimented may prevent the empathizer from going beyond a basic recognition of the objective correlate of the other's expression filtered through the lens of her negative typifications. The advantage, however, is that basic recognition is always granted, which in turn should pose fewer problems from both an epistemic and a moral perspective, especially since phenomenological empathy is not expected to play a foundational role in morality, nor is it considered the only or most trustworthy source of information about others (see Chapter 9).

Everything that has been said so far should explain why phenomenological empathy seems less prone to promoting instances of epistemic injustice, especially in asymmetrical relationships. Not only a phenomenological account of empathy is inherently aware of the context of the empathic relationship and thus of possible power imbalances between the subjects, but it is also less prone to inaccuracy, mischaracterization, and usurpation of the other's perspective because in it empathy does not consist of simulation, projection, or perspective-taking. Specifically, the compatibility of phenomenological empathy with the practice of what Nancy Tuana has called "loving ignorance" seems to make the former particularly capable of both preventing and mitigating epistemically unjust practices (Tuana 2006, p. 15).

Because phenomenological empathy allows the empathizer to understand whether an accurate and respectful empathic understanding is possible, while always recognizing the other person as a bearer of motives and values regardless of the possibility of that understanding, it is also capable of signaling to the subject when it is appropriate to cultivate loving ignorance. Being lovingly ignorant means "recogni[zing] that there are modalities that exceed our own and cannot be fully comprehended" (Tuana 2006, p. 16). Phenomenological empathy and loving ignorance can thus be fruitfully intertwined, as the former seems capable of grasping which perspectives and conditions, given the situatedness of the particular empathizer, require an approach based on the latter. This is justified, once again, by the fact that a phenomenological understanding of empathy, particularly a critical one, inherently acknowledges that "the social background [unequal distribution of power included] is connected to how we thematize the *visibility* of the subjects we encounter" (Magrì & McQueen, 2023, p. 96).

The cooperation between phenomenological empathy and loving ignorance seems to have both an epistemic and a moral advantage. First, it seems to return some epistemic power to marginalized people. Understanding that a privileged empathizer cannot understand some aspects of a marginalized person's lived experience means that epistemic space is freed up to allow that person to be the person most entitled to speak about that experience. Incidentally, this does not mean that the empathizer has no active responsibility, both moral and epistemic, toward the other marginalized person. Rather, this understanding of a lack of understanding enhances the epistemic credibility and trustworthiness of their testimony, which promotes the acquisition and sharing of knowledge within the broader epistemic community.

At the same time, prioritizing the testimony of the marginalized person mitigates some of the potential immoral consequences of inaccurate empathic understanding, such as the projection of the empathizer's perspective with the consequent obscuring of the lived experience of the marginalized person, the risk of usurping ownership of that experience, or the misuse of that empathic understanding for immoral purposes, that have always been evident to the phenomenological tradition since it first addressed the empathic phenomenon.

This brings me to my final point. A phenomenological account of empathy is fully aware of the need for more tools to understand others in general and the socio-cultural context in which they are embedded. Consequently, phenomenological empathy does not claim exclusivity when it comes to social cognition. On the contrary, as Zahavi effectively emphasizes, "there is a limit to how far empathy (plus sensitivity to the context) can get us. Our everyday understanding of others draws on other resources as well. If we wish to unearth *why* somebody is feeling the way he does or *why* he is acting the way he does, we might have to consider the larger social, cultural, and historical context and thereby go beyond the offerings of empathy" (Zahavi, 2014b, p. 168).

Thus, empathy is not sufficient to explore and understand the broader context in all its complexity and its interactions with the specific inner states of others. According to a phenomenological approach, while we are undoubtedly always influenced by this context and are able to partially grasp and bring to light this influence through mechanisms such as typification, we will never be able to fully understand it through empathy alone.

More precisely, phenomenological empathy seems to be able to partially grasp what we can call the "subjective individual why" of the other's expressions and inner states through the second degree of empathy (i.e., by grasping the intentional object and motivational context of the other).[9] However, it will never be the right tool to fully understand what we call the "shared why," that is, all the complex and interrelated social, historical, cultural, and economic reasons behind the other's interiority and resulting behavior.

Note that phenomenological empathy will still never be able to *fully* understand the "subjective individual why" or the depth of the other's inner world, especially in asymmetrical relationships. The epistemic and ontological asymmetry between how we access ourselves and how we access others makes it impossible to achieve a truly complete understanding of the other. In the next and final chapter, I will explore this crucial asymmetry, which underlies the entire phenomenological account of empathy and is one of the reasons why I believe phenomenological empathy to be such an attractive account of the phenomenon.

---

9 On this point, I am in partial disagreement with Zahavi (see Chapter 9).

CHAPTER 9

Phenomenological Empathy and Its Role in Deliberation

It is now time to see phenomenological empathy in action. In this final chapter, I will redefine the role that phenomenological empathy plays in the deliberative process. In particular, I will argue that phenomenological empathy has an eminently epistemic role, but one that is greatly diminished from the role ascribed to empathy as defined in the SD. Phenomenological empathy allows the empathizer to grasp the other's inner states and motivational context, but without claiming to understand it in its entirety and complexity. While phenomenological empathy can sometimes be the source of our reasons for holding believes about others, acting toward them, and judging their actions, these reasons can only provide a *prima facie* justification for the outcomes of our deliberations and thus seem incapable of carrying normative weight or guaranteeing their morality.

Moreover, a specific epistemic achievement of phenomenological empathy is its ability to grasp the values of the other person as revealed in their emotions. As a result, by empathizing with the other's emotions, the empathizer recognizes the other as a person, that is, as a bearer of motives and values. However, the epistemic-evaluative function of emotions, and the consequent ability of empathy to grasp the other's values through emotions, does not seem capable of grounding normative judgments about the appropriateness of the other's emotions. Similarly, recognizing the other as a person has no moral value in itself and thus cannot normatively ground our actions toward or judgments about others. But even if this epistemic achievement is not moral in itself, it seems hard to deny that it has something to do with morality, namely that it seems capable of providing the space for it.

1 The Revised Epistemic Role

Phenomenological empathy and cognitive (and affective) empathy have one thing in common, that is, both are said to play an epistemic role in our lives and deliberative processes. However, because of its essential difference from the SD of empathy, phenomenological empathy seems to raise fewer issues than the competing account. More precisely, although both phenomenologi-

 | HTTPS://DOI.ORG/10.1163/9789004745360-011

cal empathy and cognitive (and affective) empathy can be considered as knowledge providers, they differ greatly in the *kind* of knowledge they provide. This difference is closely related to and depends on the different ways in which the two phenomena achieve this knowledge. As noted above (see Chapter 8), phenomenological empathy does not consist of imaginative perspective-taking or a simulation-plus-projection process, and does not require affective matching or sharing. Despite this apparent limitation in its toolkit, it can still provide the empathizer with some valuable information about what is going on with the other person.

From the beginning, the phenomenological approach to empathy has developed the key insight that empathy is a limited but crucial tool for understanding others. The idea that empathy is the way we encounter other people and recognize them as living bodies experiencing mental and emotional states is constitutively accompanied by the awareness that our empathic grasp of others will necessarily never be as deep as the understanding we have of our own minds and, consequently, that the grasp of others will always be limited.

It is because we access other people's minds in a different way that we recognize their minds as different from our own, for if we could have exactly the same access to other people's minds that we have to our own, their otherness would disappear, which – and this is the point – never actually happens, even with people we consider closest and think we know better (Husserl, 1931). Moreover, it is the existence of this asymmetry that makes objective knowledge of the world we all share possible. By empathically grasping others as others and not as exactly like me, we lay the foundation for an intersubjective, i.e., objective, understanding of the world. Note that it is this Husserlian idea that motivates Stein's interest in further exploring the topic of empathy, which, incidentally, seems to support the core claim that its role is specifically epistemic (see Chapter 7).

In this regard, Zahavi, following Husserl (Husserl, 1928), points out that empathy can only take us so far in our understanding of others: "Experiential directness doesn't entail infallibility or exhaustiveness. Another person's mind is never exposed in such a way that we immediately, effortlessly, and infallibly have complete access to its innermost thoughts and feelings" (Zahavi, 2014b, p. 167). Some aspects of the other's inner world are constitutively inaccessible to us, to our empathic grasp, and ultimately to any other tools at our disposal, but again, it is precisely the impossibility of complete epistemic permeability of the other's mind that makes us identify the other as other than ourselves. At the same time, however, the phenomenological approach is able to strike the right balance between this awareness and the recognition that we are still capable of empathically understanding some of the inner states of the other.

Every act of empathy is an act of grasping something that is there and something that is not there: the other is experiencing something, but that something will never be fully accessible through my act of empathy. As Zahavi puts it, in empathy "we experience bodily and behavioral expressions as expressive of an experiential life that transcends the expressions" (Zahavi, 2014b, p. 166).[1] Thus, the kind of epistemic access that phenomenological empathy provides is always limited and can also vary in its outcomes. Andrews emphasizes this tension even more forcefully: "The Other remains wholly other, even as it is given through language, embodied encounter, and memory. Such encounter with transcendence points to a particular kind of un-knowing, to an experience of a non-experience, to a non-cognitive experience of alterity given beyond reason, beyond thought, beyond metaphysical propositions, even beyond Being" (Andrews, 2022, p. 237).

This is also clear in Stein's account since empathy comes in different levels of depth, depending on the object toward which it is directed and the interest of the empathizer. At its most basic level, phenomenological empathy allows us to recognize others as embodied minds. We can also grasp, always partially, that is, not primordially, in the first degrees of both experiential and personal empathy, that the other person is experiencing a certain inner state, such as pain or pleasure, is in a certain mood, has a certain emotion, is thinking about or desiring something, or feels some way, such as love or hate, toward others. Finally, if we so choose, we can also partially grasp some aspects of the motivational and/or axiological context in which these states are situated by following the intentionality of the other.

It follows that the epistemic contribution that phenomenological empathy can make is markedly different from that of cognitive empathy, understood as imaginative perspective-taking. While the kind of epistemic achievement that cognitive empathy is supposed to provide is extremely complex and rich, phenomenological empathy is not expected to do the same. Cognitive empathy is supposed to be able to understand what the other is thinking and feeling in her particular situation, to understand and reproduce, even from the other's first-person point of view, as in other-oriented perspective-taking, her particular situation in both its internal and external components or characteristics, and even to understand the reasons behind her decisions and reactions, which can also be judged in terms of their appropriateness to the situation. In this

1 I have previously examined Zahavi's phenomenological account of empathy and demonstrated its advantages over cognitive and affective empathy in the context of narrative medicine. Specifically, I argued that phenomenological empathy better aligns with the practices, values, and theoretical framework of narrative medicine while resolving the conceptual ambiguities that arise from alternative definitions of empathy in clinical practice (Stefanello, 2024b).

sense, the kind of understanding provided by cognitive empathy is of a "thick" kind since the inner world and situation of the other are considered to be knowable in detail.

In contrast, phenomenological empathy aims to achieve a "thinner" kind of understanding. Through phenomenological empathy, the empathizer can grasp the other's expressions as expressions of her internal states, and she can sometimes also grasp the intentional, motivational, and axiological context of the internal states. This difference in the nature of the epistemic result provided by cognitive empathy and phenomenological empathy is emphasized by the choice of verb used to denote their respective activities: cognitive empathy allows one to *understand* the other's internal states, whereas phenomenological empathy *grasps* them. The specificity of the epistemic product provided by phenomenological empathy is once again made clear by Zahavi: "When saying that empathy can provide a special kind of experiential understanding, this is not meant to suggest that empathy provides an especially profound or deep kind of understanding. (…). No, the specificity of the access is due to the fact that it is basic and intuitive, i.e., the empathized experience is given directly as existing here and now" (Zahavi, 2017, p. 39).

In partial disagreement with Zahavi, however, I believe that phenomenological empathy, especially personal empathy in its most complete form, is capable of providing some insight into what I have called the "subjective individual why" of the other's internal states, which is just another way of saying that phenomenological (personal) empathy in its second degree is capable of grasping that the other's internal states are always the result of a larger motivational and axiological context (see Chapter 8). In this sense, I agree with Zahavi that phenomenological empathy need not and cannot provide a deep and complete understanding of "the why" behind other people's expressions, especially what I have called the "shared why." At the same time, I think that phenomenological empathy, precisely because of its nature as a specific form of other-directed intentionality, can help us to partially experience the other's interiority as part of that person's broader personality.

Note that the incompleteness and limitations of our empathic grasp are built-in features of phenomenological empathy, not some sort of corollary added to solve some of the problems discussed above. Precisely because of its nature as a direct quasi-perceptual and quasi-imaginative experience of another's consciousness, phenomenological empathy is already limited in what it can accomplish.[2] It seems to me that it is this awareness that our empathic

2 Zahavi on this point: "The fact that my experiential access to and acquaintance with the minds of others differs from my first-person acquaintance with my own mind is precisely

grasp of the other is not only multifaceted and more basic but that it will always be limited, combined with a rejection of any perspective-taking or simulationist mechanism, that gives phenomenological empathy a leg up for its epistemic role in other-oriented deliberation since it seems able to guarantee greater accuracy and respect for the other's agency.

Thus, far from being a weakness, this limitation is one of, if not the most important strength of a phenomenological account of empathy, since it not only mitigates the pitfalls we have discussed, but also prevents the risk of mislabeling other phenomena as empathy, ultimately allowing for a more precise and faithful definition of what we experience when we empathize.

Recall for the last time our "white lie" case. Pam has decided not to tell Jim about his partner's affair, and Michael is deliberating about what Pam is thinking and feeling in making this decision, and ultimately about whether or not Pam is a good friend to Jim. What epistemic role, if any, does phenomenological empathy play in this kind of deliberative process, that is, in other-directed theoretical deliberation? First, phenomenological empathy allows Michael to grasp that Pam is an embodied and minded living body who shares the same world. Second, Michael can grasp Pam's facial expressions, bodily movements, and tone of voice as she briefly recounts her decision to withhold this information from Jim. When she says, "I'm not going to tell Jim about the cheating, it will only make him suffer more," Michael empathetically grasps that her tone is slightly anxious, her face is tense, her arms are crossed, and overall, Pam is distraught but determined. This is the kind of direct and fundamental epistemic grasp that phenomenological empathy provides. Michael can also repeat the empathic act if Pam's expressions or words signal to him that his initial grasp was inaccurate.

Michael is also able to empathically grasp something else about Pam, namely, that Pam's decision is situated within a complex and interrelated motivational context that was partially revealed in her reference to her concern for Jim's suffering. Michael, through an act of personal empathy directed at Pam's love for Jim and by following Pam's intentionality, is able to grasp that Pam's decision is the result of a specific set of motivations and also reflects her hierarchy of values; the content of both motivations and values are only *partially* graspable because full access is not possible through empathy alone.

This empathic act is not aimed at understanding the specific reasons for Pam's choice and/or its appropriateness. In fact, phenomenological empathy

not an imperfection or shortcoming. On the contrary, it is a difference that is constitutional. It is precisely because of this difference, precisely because of this asymmetry, that we can claim that the minds we experience are other minds" (Zahavi, 2014b, p. 166).

does not require any of Michael's inferential or simulative skills, nor does it involve Pam's unconscious background, all of which should reduce the risk of projection and of limiting Pam's agency. Nevertheless, phenomenological empathy, however basic it may be, directly and inherently allows the empathizer to recognize that the other person's internal states are always expressions of a broader motivational and axiological context that makes her not only a living body that expresses feelings and has thoughts but also a person with motives and values.

To reiterate, the point is not to deny that Michael could have used perspective-taking in this case, but rather to argue that, on the one hand, if Michael were to use perspective-taking, he would not be empathizing, at least not on the phenomenological account I am defending here, and, on the other hand, that phenomenological empathy seems to be a more accurate source for Michael's deliberation than perspective-taking. When the result of an act of phenomenological empathy is the epistemic source for our other-directed deliberative processes, we seem less likely to adopt an inaccurate belief about the other person, if only because the actual information gained through phenomenological empathy is necessarily incomplete, which consequently motivates the subject to use other means to ensure that his or her understanding of the other is epistemically accurate and to assign less weight to the reasons provided by the act of empathy.

More importantly, phenomenological empathy can only provide *prima facie* reasons for our other-directed theoretical deliberative processes. Thus, if Michael empathically understands that Pam is distressed about her lie, and that this decision is situated in her motivational and axiological context, and therefore deliberates that Pam is a good friend, his deliberation is only *prima facie* justified (see Chapter 8). The fact that phenomenological empathy can only provide a *prima facie* justification for our deliberations explains why, on a phenomenological account, empathy can never be the normative source of our motivating reasons in other-directed practical deliberations, especially when moral principles are involved.

It is one thing to say that because Michael empathically grasped Pam's distress, he decided to spend the night keeping her company rather than going to the movies. Another thing is to say that because of what Michael empathically perceived when he talked to Pam, he *should* keep her company instead of going to the movies. The result of Michael's other-directed practical deliberative process is only *prima facie* justified, so the reasons provided by the empathic act do not seem sufficient to ground a normative claim.

This is even more true in cases of moral other-directed practical deliberation. The empathically grasped information about the other's inner states may constitute part of the motivating reasons for the subject's decision, but it cannot normatively justify it or guarantee its morality. It follows that, for example, the fact that Michael decided not to show up for his shift at the soup kitchen in order to keep Pam company does not seem to be normatively justified by the fact that he empathically grasped her distress. On an empathy-based account of morality, the mere fact that empathy is involved in the deliberative process should ensure the morality of the resulting action. However, the moral status of Michael's decision does not seem to depend solely on his empathic act. For it to be moral, we need something more than what empathy has accomplished since it can be argued that Michael's decision not to honor his previous commitment to help people in need because of his friend's distress over something quite manageable seems morally dubious, if not outright immoral.

The same can be said about the role of phenomenological empathy in formulating moral judgments about the actions of others. Phenomenological empathy can, under certain circumstances, provide information about the others' actions, but if our moral judgments about their actions are based solely or primarily on empathy, they do not seem sufficiently justified.[3] If Michael's judgment of Pam's action as moral is based on his empathic grasp of Pam's inner states at the moment of their encounter, it seems incapable of making any normative claims about its justification and validity. Similarly, in some cases the mere grasping of the other's sensations or emotional state does not guarantee that the empathizer will be able to formulate a judgment about its intelligibility. Thus, especially in complex situations, both moral judgments and intelligibility judgments about the other's inner states need to be justified – both epistemically and normatively – by something more than the act of empathizing.

As noted earlier (see Chapter 8), in a phenomenological account of empathy, none of the information grasped by the empathic act is the result of, and therefore does not require, any kind of affective sharing. Michael does not consider keeping Pam company instead of serving dinner to people in need

3 Jesse Prinz forcefully denies any normative role of empathy: "Even in cases where it is descriptively true that people appeal to empathy, the crucial question is whether such appeals do any important normative work. I think they do not. What makes an action wrong in cases where empathy is invoked is the harm it causes, not our vicarious experience of that harm. What makes an action good is the pleasure it brings to beneficiaries of that action, not the shared feelings in those who assess it. Thus, the emotions we feel during assessment cannot be advanced as reasons for a moral verdict. They are, at best, ways of drawing attention to our reasons – that is, to actual harms and benefits. Thus, empathy is playing only an epistemic role in justification" (Prinz, 2011, p. 225). While I do not necessarily subscribe to the consequentialist approach, I think Prinz is right to argue that empathy is at best an epistemic spotlight for our reasons, which must come from some other source.

because he has shared Pam's distress, nor does he judge Pam's action to be moral because he has shared her empathic concern for Jim or because he has approved of Pam's emotional response to Jim's situation, i.e., judged it to be appropriate from the perspective of an ideal spectator. Again, I am not suggesting that Michael cannot share and be moved by Pam's distress. My point is that, on the one hand, sharing the other's emotion would be a different process from phenomenological empathy and thus not empathic by my definition, and, on the other hand, it would still not guarantee the morality of the action it motivates (or the judgments it grounds).

Moreover, from a phenomenological perspective, Michael's deliberative process – theoretical, practical, and moral – regarding Pam's decision will necessarily require him to explore the broader context in which his and Pam's decisions are situated. For this reason, empathy alone is not enough. The sociocultural context in which their decisions are made, as well as Pam's and Michael's overall character, has an enormous impact on their deliberative processes: does Pam have a habit of lying? How is cheating perceived and judged in her culture? Is divorce socially acceptable? How problematic is lying and lying for the sake of a friend? Are Michael's and Pam's social, cultural, and economic backgrounds the same? And, most importantly, how do these play into and influence Pam and Michael's inner states and decisions? These questions cannot be answered by empathy. Other tools must be used by the deliberating subject to grasp not only what the broader context is but also how it may affect the inner state of the other.

Thus, the contribution that empathy seems to make to our other-directed deliberative processes is eminently epistemic. More specifically, empathy can sometimes be the source of our reasons for holding believes about others, acting toward them, and judging their actions. But these empathy-based reasons can only – and not even always – provide a *prima facie* justification for the outcomes of our deliberations. For this reason, empathy-based reasons seem incapable of carrying normative weight or guaranteeing their morality.

The phenomenological perspective seems to have understood that the centrality of empathy is not that it can sometimes constitute some of the reasons for our decisions, actions, and judgments involving others, but, more fundamentally, that empathy is the basic and direct way in which we experience others as we encounter them in our shared world. In other words, phenomenology recognizes that empathy is a pervasive and crucial aspect of human nature, but it also does not overstate its contribution to our lives. While empathy plays a central role in our interpersonal lives, it is not understood as an epistemic *passe-partout* of other people's minds. Empathy is only one, albeit fundamental, of the many tools we have at our disposal to understand the other's condition and situation, always aware that a complete understanding of the other will never be achieved and thus that the weight of the reasons it can offer the deliberating subject must always be critically evaluated and, if necessary, revised.

2 The Axiological Role

According to Stein's account, in instances of mental empathy (what I have called personal empathy), that is, when we empathize with the feelings and sentiments of others, it is possible to grasp the other's hierarchically organized values (see Chapter 7). In order to properly understand and ultimately justify this claim, we need to better understand how, according to Stein, affective states, especially feelings and sentiments, relate to values.[4] The theoretical starting point of Stein's account of affectivity and its relation to values is the idea, inspired by one of Brentano's seminal intuitions (Brentano, 1874), that emotional states are intentionally directed toward the world, which means that they can provide information about that world.

However, intentionality does not operate in the same way in all affective states. Sensual feelings are not really intentional since they are only causally directed to the objects or states that cause them. Similarly, although general feelings are intentionally directed to the world and specifically to "vital values" such as tiredness, vitality, and irritability, they can only indicate these values, not grasp them (Vendrell Ferran, 2018, p. 72).

With regard to moods, Stein argued that they are intentionally directed toward the world in a particular way, since "for him who is cheerful, the world is bathed in a rosy glow; for him who is depressed, bathed in black" (Stein, PE, p. 92). It follows that since "moods constitute the background structure of our experience and are enduring affective states that influence and 'color' the way in which we are directed toward the world," their intentionality is "a 'background' intentionality that does not have values as its objects" (Vendrell Ferran, 2018, p. 72).

In contrast, feelings – what we would also call emotions – are intentionally directed toward two specific aspects of the world. First, feelings are directed toward their object (e.g., the poisonous snake that scares me), and second, they are directed toward the value associated with that object (e.g., the scariness of the poisonous snake). Claiming, as Stein and other phenomenologists such as

4 I follow Vendrell Ferran's interpretation of Stein's account of the relationship between emotions, empathy, and values (Vendrell Ferran, 2015a, 2015a).

Brentano and Husserl do, that feelings are directed toward an object of the world, namely humans, nonhuman animals, material objects, states of affairs, and abstract entities, constitutes a particular theoretical stance that we can define in contemporary terms as "emotional cognitivism" (Vendrell Ferran, 2015). According to this view, "the material objects of the emotions are given to us thanks to cognitions, [which means that], emotions have a founded nature" (Vendrell Ferran, 2018, p. 74). Importantly, the cognitive basis on which feelings are founded is not only made up of judgments but also "perceptions, imagining, and deductive thoughts count chiefly as theoretical acts" such as when we react emotionally to something we have only imagined or assumed (Vendrell Ferran, 2018, p. 74).

In addition, although the material objects of emotions may vary, there is a specific correlation between the emotion and the evaluative category to which it is related. This means, as Vendrell Ferran points out, that "in relation to these restricted objects, emotions may thus be appropriate or inappropriate. To feel joy with regard to something dangerous is inappropriate in the same sense that it is inappropriate to feel fear with regard to something joyful" (Vendrell Ferran, 2018, p. 75). The appropriateness or inappropriateness of feelings is judged by their relationship to the values to which they are intentionally directed (e.g., fear must always be directed toward something frightening).

Finally, sentiments are intentionally directed toward other people's personal inherent value (e.g., loving someone for who she is). The kind of intentionality involved in sentiments differs from that of feelings because sentiments do not maintain the distinction between subject and object as feelings do. Rather, sentiments "'stream' from the subject to the object, bridging the gap between both poles" (Vendrell Ferran, 2018, p. 75). Furthermore, sentiments do not have to be felt in the same way by all people, as the hedonic experience of love and hate can vary drastically depending on the situation and the subjects involved (e.g., hate can bring pleasure and love can bring pain) (Vendrell Ferran, 2018, p. 75).

In short, affective states are characterized by different kinds of intentionality and, most importantly, they relate to values in different ways: "General feelings indicate values without apprehending them, emotions grasp values, moods show a background intentionality and sentiments aim for bridging the gap between subject and object" (Vendrell Ferran, 2018, p. 76). Here, I am particularly interested in the ability of emotions to grasp and disclose value, and how this function operates within the empathic act. I will begin by trying to better define what it means for emotions to be able to capture values.

Although with relevant theoretical differences, the idea that feelings are responsible for revealing values is one of the common features of the early phenomenological tradition of which Stein is a prominent example (Husserl, 1900–1; Scheler, 1916).[5] To explain this specific function of emotions, she argued for the well-known analogy between how emotions grasp values and how perception grasps the external world. Just as we can directly perceive some characteristics of a physical object, we can also directly feel, and thus grasp, that something has a certain value (Stein, 1922, p. 158).[6] Importantly, while Stein shares the idea that values are revealed in feelings, she rejects Scheler's distinction between "feeling" and "the feeling," that is, between the act of feeling (i.e., grasping the value) and the emotional reaction to this grasping, since she does not believe that "these two designations indicate different kinds of experiences, but only different 'directions' of the same experience' (Stein, PE, p. 89–90).[7]

As Vendrell Ferran argues, Stein's position achieves two results. On the one hand, it paints a more coherent picture of how we grasp values since we often experience the grasping of values and the emotion that accompanies it as two sides of the same coin, and on the other hand, it does not collapse these two moments, making it possible to "explain those cases in which it is possible to grasp a value without having the corresponding emotion" or, conversely, it is possible to experience something without grasping its value (Vendrell Ferran, 2018, p. 77–78).[8]

---

5 For a discussion of values in early phenomenology see Reicher (Reicher, 2009).

6 In Stein's words: "(...) Just as with perception, a mental apprehension springs up on account of the egoic contents, turning them into bearers of a gift of sense, and that those egoic contents in their 'function of manifestation' reveal to the subject the view into a new object world. This new object world which unfolds before us as we feel, is the world of value" (Stein, 1922, p. 158).

7 Although Stein did not explicitly mention Scheler, the reference to, and consequent, rejection of his conceptualization of the two concepts and their relationship is clear. See Stein's complete passage: "People want to distinguish between 'feeling' [*Fühlen*] and 'the feeling' [*Gefühl*]. I do not believe that these two designations indicate different kinds of experiences, but only different 'directions' of the same experience. Feeling is an experience when it gives us an object or else something about an object. The feeling is the same act when it appears to be originating out of the 'I' or unveiling a level of the 'I'" (Stein, PE, pp. 89–90). On this point see also Vendrell Ferran (Vendrell Ferran, 2018, p. 76).

8 In Stein's words: "Thus, the completely fulfilled value-perception is always a feel in which the value-intention and the response-reaction are united. And where live egoic participation is lacking, an unfulfilled intention still substitutes for it" (Stein, 1922, p. 159). She also described cases in which there is a mismatch between the two moments of value perception: "1. You can confront a bodily present thing without having any hunch that it's the bearer of a value. 2. You can have a thing in front of you and know, on the basis of a message,

Admittedly, much more could be said about Stein's theory of values and about the early phenomenologists' understanding of values in general. For the purposes of my work, however, the most relevant aspect is the claim that feelings and emotions are responsible for grasping values. It follows that empathy seems to be able to do something similar when it comes to the values of others since when we empathize with the feelings and emotions of another person, we should be able to grasp not only those feelings and emotions but also the values to which they are related (see Section 7.3).

As Lebech points out, feelings "cause something in me (the blood to rush, the hands to sweat, the knees to weaken) and they are motivated by something that comes to me as a massage sounding something like 'this is valuable', 'dangerous', 'horrid', 'beautiful'" (Lebech, 2015, p. 33). Thus, feelings and emotions display both the causality that governs the psycho-physical individual and the motivation that governs the person. Thus, when I empathize with other people's feelings, I can grasp not only that they are the causes of the physical modifications in the other's body via experiential empathy but also the evaluative category that "motivates" that emotional response (e.g., the other person's fear of something or someone is motivated by the fact that the thing or person is dangerous to them) via personal empathy.

It is precisely in this sense that personal empathy is able to recognize the other as a person and to grasp their motivational and axiological context. Specifically, personal empathy "involves understanding the other's motivations (why he thinks he does what he does, as distinct from why he does what he does – I can also know the latter of animals and plants [thanks to experiential empathy]), and these motivations can be followed in so far as what it felt gets expressed in a glance, an attitude, in language or in art" (Lebech, 2015, p. 25). Consequently, according to Stein, values have two functions: "As values are what allows us to conceptualize what type of motivatedness we have in front of us, they also explain why something is done. When this is their function, we call them motives" (Lebech, 2015, p. 28).

For example, I empathize with my friend's joy and, guided by his intentionality, I can grasp not only the material object of his emotion, namely the birth of his first child, but also the evaluative category related to that material object, namely joyousness, and revealed by that emotion, namely joy. In this sense, I understand that his joy at the birth of his first child is related to the fact

that it possesses a value, without catching sight of this value yourself. (…) 3. You can have an object in front of you and catch a glimpse of its value without being inwardly filled up with it" (Stein, 1922, p. 162).

that he values this state of affairs as joyous, and that his response is therefore motivated by this value stance, which in turn signals to me that his response is located within his broader motivational and axiological context.

Grasping our own motives or those of others through personal empathy provides a crucial window into our own and others' personalities. First and foremost, by grasping that others' feelings and general behavior are motivated by their evaluative stances, I not only recognize, as already mentioned, that these values may be different from my own, but I also understand that my own emotional reactions and decisions are the result of my personal values. This bi-directional act of empathy (from me to others and from others to me) is what Stein calls "reiterated empathy" (PE, p. 58–59), which can show both me and others that the world "can be explained by (my) motivation" (Lebech, 2015, p. 31). More generally, the empathic act inherently involves reciprocity, which explains how and why self-understanding and one's own constitution as unity of body, spirit, and soul are possible only through others and, thus, through empathy. Jolly summarizes this tenet of a phenomenological understanding of empathy (see Chapter 7): "Not only do I empathize with others and constitute their I's, but, at the same time, through reiterated empathy, I empathically understand my individual acts through the others' constitution of me" (Jolly, p. 35). As said, Husserl also argued for the inherently intersubjective nature of the constitution of the person in his work (see Chapter 7). For example, in *Ideas II*, he claims that "when we inquired into the essence of the person, then nature presented itself as something constituted in an intersubjective association of persons, hence presupposing it" (Husserl, *Ideas II*, p. 220).

Second, because the motives can be endorsed or not by each of us, that is, we can allow them to motivate our actions or not, they are capable of explaining our personality. In other words, when I choose to be motivated by a particular value, I am *de facto* accepting that value not only as my motivation, but also as part of who I am as a person, as part of my character. This means that we can choose not to follow all the values that emerge in our emotional responses and instead be motivated by another value that we find more appropriate to the context, more powerful in its motivational power, or more representative of our personality. Because of this possibility, each of us forms and maintains a hierarchy of values. I can glimpse the hierarchy of others by focusing on the intensity of the other person's emotion through the act of empathy. By empathically experiencing my friend's joy over his first child, I can also get an idea, albeit a very loose one, of how the value revealed by that joy ranks in his axiological hierarchy, since, simply put, the more intense the reaction, the higher that value ranks.

At this point, one might wonder whether this way of understanding phenomenological empathy's ability to grasp the values of others is different from cognitive empathy. The fact that phenomenological empathy can grasp the motivational and axiological context of others could be interpreted as essentially compatible with Stueber's position that empathy can grasp the reasons for others' thoughts, feelings, actions, and decisions, or with Bailey's concept of humane understanding, in which empathy is responsible for grasping the intelligibility of others' emotional reactions.

I do not think this interpretation is justified for two main reasons. First, the ways in which phenomenological empathy and cognitive empathy in Stueber's and Bailey's accounts achieve their results are extremely different. As said, phenomenological empathy does not gain epistemic access to another's interiority by reenacting or imaginatively taking up the other's perspective, but rather through a combination of a quasi-perceptual and a quasi-imaginative act of directly grasping the other's behavior and intentionality (see Chapter 8).

Second, the substantial difference in the nature of these accesses leads to a difference in the quality of their epistemic results. Because of this, I resist the idea that the grasp of the motivational and axiological context provided by phenomenological empathy is *qualitatively* similar to the understanding of the other's internal states provided by cognitive empathy. Whereas in cognitive empathy the desired epistemic outcome is either an understanding of the other's deliberative process and its reasons, or an appreciation of the intelligibility of the other's emotions, in a phenomenological account of empathy the outcome seems less epistemically ambitious, though still crucial to our interpersonal understanding. The empathic grasp of the motivational and axiological context of the other person does not imply a complete understanding of all or even most of the reasons for a particular thought, emotion, or action, and does not determine its intelligibility.

For example, by empathically grasping my friend's joy, I have access to a range of information. First, I recognize him as a living body; second, I grasp directly in his bodily gestures and facial expressions that he is experiencing joy; third, by being guided by the intentionality of his emotion, I grasp that his joy is directed toward the birth of his first child; fourth, I can also grasp the evaluative category associated with this event, i.e., that he values it positively, and the intensity of his emotion can also reveal to me that he highly values this event. Finally, I can place his joy in his motivational and axiological context and thus recognize him as a person who has motives and values.

Although the empathic act just described provides relevant information about the other's condition, it still does not seem to achieve the same (supposed) epistemic result as cognitive empathy, since it does not allow me to reproduce and thus understand my friend's joy at the birth of his child from his perspective, nor the complex reasons for this particular emotional response. Moreover, the fact that not every empathic act is intended or required to go through all three levels of empathy, and that not every act of empathy is an act of personal empathy further proves that phenomenological empathy does not aim to achieve the same epistemic result as cognitive empathy, nor does it claim to be the most epistemically effective tool for understanding the reasons behind the other's inner states.

In my phenomenological account, the depth of understanding of the other's motivational and axiological context is determined by what can be directly quasi-perceived and quasi-imagined in the empathic act. By rejecting the imaginative processes of perspective-taking and simulation, a phenomenological account of empathy severely limits the *quantity* and *quality* of information available to the empathizer, since both the empathizer's experience, which is the epistemic source for self-oriented perspective-taking, and the other person's imaginatively simulated background, which is the epistemic source for other-oriented perspective-taking, are not available.

Thus, while it is true that phenomenological empathy, in grasping the motivational and axiological context of the other, is able to glimpse the "subjective individual why," it is also true that it is always able to do so only in a limited way. It will never be able to fully grasp this context, given its immediate quasi-perceptual and quasi-imaginative nature on the one hand, and its inability to grasp the "shared why" on the other. To understand that my friend feels joy because he highly values the birth of his first child is to have only a minimal, though valuable, insight into his motivational and axiological context of what he is experiencing as a first-time parent. However, far from being a flaw, the inherent limitations of the phenomenological empathic act seem to protect the empathic act from the pitfalls of the SD of empathy when involved in deliberation.

So far, it has become clear that phenomenological empathy has an eminently epistemic role, in that it allows us to access, in a very specific way, a certain kind of information about the other person. Even what I have defined as the "axiological role" is in fact a specific aspect of the more general epistemic role of empathy. The prerogative of emotions to reveal values, and the ability of empathy to grasp the feelings or sentiments of others, and consequently their values, is entirely epistemic in nature, scope, and aim. In this sense, as noted above, the empathic grasp that, on the one hand, the other person's feelings reveal what he or she values, and, on the other hand, that his or her world of values is hierarchically organized, can also provide *prima facie* motivating reasons for our moral other-oriented theoretical and practical deliberations.

For example, in deliberating about Pam's decision not to tell Jim about his partner's cheating, by empathically grasping that she is concerned about Jim's welfare, Michael can also grasp that she values, i.e., is motivated by, the other person's welfare more than truthfulness. As a result, Michael can decide what to think of her decision and how to act toward her, but there is no guarantee of the morality of his beliefs, actions, and judgments.

It follows that the ability of emotions to grasp values in general, and the ability of empathy to grasp the values of others in particular, seem unable to carry normative weight when involved in other-directed deliberation. While it is true that empathically grasped emotions can sometimes provide some motivating reasons for moral actions toward others and moral judgments about their behavior, it does not follow that empathically grasped emotions, or emotions in general, are always capable of guaranteeing moral actions or judgments, or that they should be the sole source of either moral motivation or judgment. This is consistent with the phenomenological approach to the role of emotions in our moral deliberations, according to which "an ethics grounded only in emotion would be mistaken, and the emotions always need the corrective of reason" or "the mediation of evaluative thinking" (Vendrell Ferran, 2015b, p. 350).

Stein herself believed that reasoning is responsible for "estimating motivating power," meaning that reason is the one faculty responsible for determining whether the state of affairs actually calls for the motivation that emerges from my initial emotional response (Lebech, 2015, p. 37). If the answer is negative, then the subject can choose not to actualize that particular motivational force or, in her words, she "can make it inoperative" (Stein, 1922, p. 49). Calcagno also points out that this cooperation between emotions and reason is a crucial feature of Stein's account of motivation and, ultimately, human action: "In motivation, often psychic affects will accompany a motivation, and though there is a psychic affect, motivation will often draw upon judgment and reason (all acts that lie within the domain of spirit) in order that the will may freely respond to what motivation brings forward" (Calcagno, 2020, p. 631).[9] This is further evidence that the values and motives captured through personal empathy are never guaranteed to be the definitive and all-encompassing motivating reasons for the other's behavior since they can always be critically

9 Calcagno provides an insightful example of this dynamic: "For example, I learn that someone I know requires books to carry on further study. The person has no money, but I have the funds to help. A situation arises, and I may feel sympathy for the person and I may even empathize with the other's desire for further study. I feel sad that the other person cannot study. Reason tells or motivates me that I can afford to pay and I freely decide or will to help the person" (Calcagno, 2020, p. 631).

revised and thus modified, making them a potentially unreliable source for our other-directed deliberations, both epistemically and normatively.

There still seems to be one particularly controversial aspect of the phenomenological account of empathy that requires further discussion. The fact that others' emotions reveal their world of values, and that I can grasp this fact through empathy, leads to a recognition of them as persons, indicating precisely that they are bearers of motives and values. Does this recognition have any moral value or relevance in our other-directed deliberations? Now, the controversy arises not only because the concept of personhood and its definition is an incredibly complex and open question (Shoemaker, 2021) but also because to argue that the recognition of others as persons depends entirely on the empathic act, and that the moral status of others depends on this recognition, can potentially lead to the exclusion from the moral community of those with whom we do not empathize.

First of all, it is important to distinguish between two different claims. One thing is to say that empathy is responsible for recognizing others as value bearers and the other is to say that this recognition grounds how we treat them. To me, the first claim seems more plausible and less problematic than the second. If we look at our everyday experience, we always consider those around us as embodied and minded beings who are also bearers of motives and values, without having to reflect on or explicitly attribute this qualification to them. Since empathy is the mode of experiencing and encountering other people, and since it is always active, it seems theoretically plausible to ascribe to it the specific epistemic ability to recognize others as persons.

One might wonder whether the distinction between experiential and personal empathy might be problematic, and whether it is only in instances of personal empathy, that is, when we empathize with the emotions of others, that we recognize them as persons rather than mere psycho-physical individuals. This is not my position, and I suspect it is not Stein's either. Even in an act of experiential empathy, we are already grasping something beyond the fact that the other is a psychophysical individual experiencing a particular state such as pain or pleasure. This "something more" is precisely the fact that the other is also part of the realm of values, that is, that she is value-oriented. This does not mean that every time we experience an act of experiential empathy we can grasp the motivational context of the other. It simply means that any act of empathy is capable of immediately and directly signaling to the empathizer the presence of another person as an embodied, minded individual with motives and values, without identifying what those specifically are.

Nevertheless, I would resist the temptation to ascribe an inherent moral value to this recognition. Recognizing others as persons alone does not guarantee that we will act morally toward them, or that we will grant them the moral status they deserve, since it does not prevent the empathizer from using the empathically gathered information about the other to abuse him or her. Rather, it is sometimes the very fact that we recognize the other as a person that makes immoral actions possible. Some of the harm we inflict on others seems to be motivated precisely by the fact that we recognize them as persons; otherwise we would not bother to engage in immoral actions such as psychological abuse, gaslighting, or public shaming, where our specific goal is not to physically harm the other but to threaten the other's values (e.g., privacy, autonomy, self-worth, and their role as a member of a community). Once again, recognizing others as persons seems to be primarily an epistemic achievement, not something that can provide normative weight to empathy-based deliberative processes.

At the same time, however, even on an intuitive level, the act of recognizing the other as a person seems to have something to do with morality. Several moral norms and behaviors seem to implicitly or explicitly refer to recognizing that the other is a person rather than an inanimate object. While there is much more to be said about the relationship between recognizing personhood and morality than I can do here, let me sketch a preliminary way of framing the issue.

Recognizing the other as a person through empathy means experiencing and grasping, albeit very fleetingly, a part of her personality as especially revealed in her affective acts, which at the same time allows us to recognize her (and ourselves) as "subjects that experience themselves as value-related, as motivated," that is, as persons (Lebech, 2015, p. 39).[10] This empathic recognition has an ambivalent relationship to morality because, as Drummond convincingly argues, recognizing the other (and myself because of the other's empathy toward me) as a person is an epistemic act "that has no moral content" since "by itself, it is insufficient to account either for our evaluations of things and situations in our emotional life or for our choices regarding moral action" (Drummond, 2023, p. 14). This is because the ultimate and only goal of empathic recognition is to reveal "the fundamental structure present in concrete experiences of other persons," that is, "similarity-in-irreducible-difference" (Drummond, 2023, p. 14). Recognizing this basic feature of all our encounters, and ultimately of ourselves as persons, is a fundamental *epistemic*, not moral, achievement that does not automatically translate into an attitude of respect or care for the other.

---

10 In Stein's words: "every time we advance in the value realm, we also make acquisitions in the realm of our own personality" (Stein, PE, p. 92).

However, and this is the point, this recognition is also crucial in opening up "the logical space in which we can situate our discussions of ethics and morality" (Drummond, 2023, p. 14). Thus, the empathy-based recognition of others as persons is adjacent to morality in the sense that it allows – from a logical standpoint – for the cultivation of our moral discourse and related practices. In other words, without it we would not be able to consider how to treat those around us because we would not be able to make sense of who they are and why – only part of the "subjective why" – they behave as they do.

However, unlike our choice to behave morally or not, this recognition is never optional. As I said, in a phenomenological account, empathy is always ongoing, and so is the recognition of others as persons that depends on it. For this reason, I would still avoid framing the issue in terms of empathy being a necessary condition for morality. I find this phrasing potentially misleading since it seems to imply inappropriately that there is a possibility that this empathic recognition might not be present in our encounters with others, regardless of its relation to morality.

One last aspect of the axiological role of phenomenological empathy needs to be discussed, and it concerns its supposed objectivity. Precisely because of the correlation between personality and values, Stein argued that the empathizer can judge them to be right or wrong (Stein, PE, p. 92):

> This correlation makes feelings and their firm establishment in the "I" rationally lawful as well as making possible decisions about "right" and "wrong" in this domain. If someone is "overcome" by the loss of his wealth (i.e., if it gets him at the kernel point of his "I"), he feels "irrational." He inverts the value hierarchy or loses sensitive insight into higher values altogether, causing him to lack the correlative personal levels.

Thus, from this passage, it seems that I can judge that the other's emotional reaction is appropriate because it is directed toward the right value or, conversely, that it is inappropriate because it is directed toward the wrong value (recall the example of grief over the loss of a loved one versus the loss of a piece of jewelry). Moreover, as already discussed, since our value hierarchies are the result of the broader sociocultural, historical, economic, and political context in which we are embedded, (reiterated) empathy is also the tool that can help us recognize the differences between our own values and those of others, and, if necessary, revise our initial understanding of the other's values or even our own personal hierarchy (Vendrell Ferran, 2015, p. 497).

The problem with this position is that for empathy to function effectively as a normative ground for our judgments about the rightness and wrongness of others' emotional reactions and value hierarchies, we must accept two highly controversial ontological claims about values, namely value realism and the objectivity of values and their hierarchy. First, according to value realism, an ontological claim shared by early phenomenologists, including Stein, "values exist independently of the subjects who grasp them and of the material objects in which they are given" (Vendrell Ferran, 2015a, p. 496). Following Husserl, Stein argued that values are constituted in the subject who grasps them, which means that the subject does not create these values; instead, the subject is "the space in which the values become possible" (Vendrell Ferran, 2015a, p. 496).[11]

Second, because values exist independently of subjects and objects, and can be grasped in feelings in much the same way that we grasp the physical properties of material objects in the external world, Stein argued that they are objective. Most importantly, their objectivity should explain why we can have an appropriate or inappropriate response to them, and we can judge others' emotional responses to these values in the same way. Although the objective character of values is somewhat counterbalanced by the awareness that we may see them differently because of individual and contextual variations, and that empathy is supposed to signal these differences, values are still characterized by Stein as capable of "the constitution of super-individual objects," i.e., as objective (Stein, 1922, p. 164).

The ontological and phenomenological status of values that value realism and the objectivity of the values implies is not only controversial but also not explicitly discussed by Stein, further complicating the matter (Mulligan, 2009; Szanto & Moran, 2024). For these reasons, I suggest that by adopting a more moderate version of Stein's claim about empathy and values, we might be able to avoid having to engage directly with her ontological positions on values. It seems possible to accept Stein's epistemological claim about the capacity of emotions, and consequently of empathy, to grasp values, without either rejecting or accepting value realism and the objectivity of values.

At the same time, it is also possible to interpret Stein's claim about the appropriateness of emotions (both of the subject herself and of others) in terms of "fittingness," i.e., "an emotion is fitting, if it picks out *those* evaluative features of the target that really matters *to the emoter herself*," rather than "moral, practical, and prudential appropriateness" (Szanto & Moran, 2024). In this particular interpretation, "fittingness is an essentially subject-relative

11 Again in Vendrell Ferran's words: "The idea of constitution implies that the valuing subject and the values themselves are related to one another, that there is a direction from the subject toward the object, and that in being directed the subject plays an active role: values are dependent on valuing persons and the emotional experiences they are able to arouse" (Vendrell Ferran, 2018, p. 82).

notion. It doesn't concern any objective (axiological or moral) proprieties" (Szanto & Moran, 2024). Thus, our emotions can be appropriate or inappropriate depending on whether or not they actually correspond to the values that are important to the subject (for a similar claim see De Monticelli, 2020).

The same is true of other people's emotions, the fittingness of which, understood in this way, can be grasped through empathy. If someone reacts with relief to the loss of her wedding ring because of her abusive husband, we, empathizing with her, grasp this reaction as fitting, given the value it reveals. In contrast, if this person had reacted to this loss with sadness, we would have grasped this emotional response as unfitting with the evaluative category she ascribed to her marriage. Crucially, the empathic grasp of the appropriateness of the other's emotion is not a normative judgment about the rightness or wrongness of that particular response.[12]

Accordingly, in my phenomenological account, empathy is capable of recognizing the other as a person, directly grasping the other's internal states, and, in the second degree, also grasping that they are part of the other's motivational context. In particular, in empathizing with the other's emotions and feelings, the empathizer can partially grasp their hierarchically organized values and the fittingness between that emotion, its intentional object, and what the other person values, but this cannot provide the normative basis for judging the other's emotional responses as right or wrong. Note that this grasp of the other's values and this specific kind of fittingness does not occur every time we empathize with someone and is not equivalent to a reproduction of the other's reasons for their deliberative process or emotional responses to their situation.

In conclusion, while I share Stein's claim about the "epistemic-evaluative function" of emotion, i.e., the capacity of empathy to partially grasp the values that the other's emotions reveal, which is also what makes the empathic rec-

12 Incidentally, and very broadly, this reading of Stein's account seems consistent with a "minimal" version of value realism (Da Re, 2013). In this approach to value realism, following, among others, McDowell, the content of values is undoubtedly socially, culturally, and subjectively determined, rather than objective in the strong sense of the word, i.e., in the sense of the objectivity that belongs to primary qualities investigated by the scientific method (McDowell, 1985). However, it is still possible to assign a kind of objective weight to values, especially those related to the so-called secondary qualities, i.e. those qualities that refer to the subject. Thus, within this minimal framework, values (and our judgments about them) are not some bizarre entities or mere expressions of emotions, while at the same time one adopts minimal versions of the claims about the ontological, epistemic, and normative nature of these values. This is, however, only a preliminary and tentative remark on the subject and by no means exhaustive. For a discussion of these problems see von Kutschera (Kutschera, 1999).

ognition of the other as a person morally colored, I suspend judgments about the ontological status of values. At the same time, while recognizing that there is a connection between emotions, values, and personality, I am inclined to reject a "normative" reading of Stein's claim about the appropriateness of emotions. Instead, following the above interpretation that does not rely on value realism, I understand appropriateness in terms of fittingness, whose criterion is not normative but subject-based.

Finally, even if one were to reject Stein's and my epistemological claim *tout court*, and deny that values are perceivable in emotions, and thus argue against the fact that other people's values are empathically graspable, my phenomenological account of empathy would not lose its strength relative to the SD. I would argue that it might even benefit from it. By claiming that the epistemic role of empathy does not include the specific ability to grasp the other's values, but only the other's internal states and their intentional objects, the chance for the empathizer to inaccurately understand or misinterpret the other's interiority would be further reduced. This would, of course, imply a narrowing of the epistemic scope of empathy, which I do not see as a negative outcome per se. On the contrary, it would still be compatible with what I have argued, namely that empathy plays a crucial, albeit limited, epistemic role in our other-directed deliberations, and precisely because of its nature and limitations, it seems to be a better ally for our other-directed deliberative processes than how the SD (inaccurately) defines empathy.

Conclusion

I began work on this topic, moved by a desire to better understand the peculiar yet so common experience we usually call empathy and its less-discussed interaction with our deliberative processes. One of the most common ways to frame the issue is to suggest that empathy, defined as a combination of perspective-taking, affective sharing, and concern for the welfare of others, can motivate, ground, or justify our deliberations and judgments about the thoughts, emotional reactions, actions, and decisions of others. However, as the potential negative consequences of including empathy in our other-directed deliberations and, more generally, of this way of understanding empathy – which I have called the SD of empathy – became apparent, I grew increasingly dissatisfied with this framing.

As a result, I began to explore possible alternatives for better explaining what happens when we empathize with others, and how to avoid or mitigate some of the problems that arise when empathy, as understood in the SD, is involved in our deliberations about them. I was initially tempted to simply point out how flawed and problematic, both epistemically and morally, the SD of empathy and its involvement in the deliberative process seem to be, by offering a systematic critique of those accounts that ascribe to it a foundational or essential role in morality. I even considered arguing, *a la* Paul Bloom or Jesse Prinz – whose works were my entry point into the debate on the dark sides of empathy – for the need to replace empathy altogether with another concept.

However, once I discovered how Phenomenology has dealt with the empathic phenomenon – especially in the prolific work of Dan Zahavi, which introduced me to the relevance of Classical Phenomenology for empathy – I realized that replacing empathy with something else was not necessary. Instead, what was (and still is) needed is a more precise definition of what empathy is, so as to avoid mislabeling other phenomena as empathy. The ultimate goal of this book was precisely to show that the phenomenological approach succeeds in doing just that.

In particular, I find Stein's account compelling because it manages to provide a very complex yet clear picture of how we empathize with each other and what this experience means for us as human beings. After reading her work on empathy, I realized that most of the problems I had with the relationship between empathy and deliberation could be reduced, if not resolved, by adopting a different definition of the empathic phenomenon and shifting the overall theoretical framework to describe what happens when we encounter others in our shared world.

 | HTTPS://DOI.ORG/10.1163/9789004745360-012

Inspired by her theoretical proposal and other early phenomenologists such as Husserl and Scheler, as well as contemporary authors and commentators, I have offered an alternative definition of empathy, that is, phenomenological empathy understood as the direct quasi-perceptual and quasi-imaginative experience of the inner states of others and their recognition as persons. At the same time, I have outlined a specific kind of deliberative process, namely other-directed theoretical and practical deliberation, as the mental activity in which we decide, by weighing different kinds of reasons, what to think about or do to others.

On the one hand, the account of empathy I have defended seems better able to capture what happens when we empathize with others by distinguishing empathy from other phenomena involved in interpersonal understanding. On the other hand, it seems to be a more effective ally for our other-directed deliberative processes because, by limiting the role of phenomenological empathy, it is better equipped to avoid or deal with the potentially problematic implications that the SD of empathy seems to have when involved in these processes.

As I have argued in the last two chapters, a phenomenological account of empathy – both its experiential and personal aspects – seems, because of its multifaceted, direct, and always ongoing nature, to allow the empathizer to grasp the other's inner states and motivational and evaluative contexts without claiming to understand them in their entirety and complexity. When this happens, the empathizer recognizes the other as a person, that is, as someone with motives and hierarchically organized values.

This reconceptualization of what the empathic phenomenon amounts to has also allowed me to redefine its role in deliberation. In my account, empathy has an exclusively epistemic role in other-directed deliberative processes, but it can only provide *prima facie* and always incomplete – rather than normative – reasons for our deliberations. Moreover, while the recognition that others (including myself) are persons is not itself moral, it is responsible for making space for morality.

Thus, while it is true that we cannot and should not abandon the influence of the empathic phenomenon on our interactions and decisions, we should not settle for an unsatisfactory, fuzzy, or overly broad definition of it. For this reason, as I have argued, we should consider a phenomenologically informed account of empathy as the best conceptual candidate both for defining the empathic phenomenon and for playing a role in our other-directed deliberative processes.

Bibliography

Ales Bello, A. (with Calcagno, A.). (2025). *Edith Stein and Edmund Husserl: Philosophical Exchanges* (1st ed). Lexington Books/Fortress Academic.

Ames, D. R. (2004). Inside the Mind Reader's Tool Kit: Projection and Stereotyping in Mental State Inference. *Journal of Personality and Social Psychology, 87*, 340–353. https://doi.org/10.1037/0022-3514.87.3.340.

Ames, D. R., Weber, E. U., & Zou, X. (2012). Mind-Reading in Strategic Interaction: The Impact of Perceived Similarity on Projection and Stereotyping. *Organizational Behavior and Human Decision Processes, 117*(1), 96–110. https://doi.org/10.1016/j.obhdp.2011.07.007.

Andrade, E. B., & Ariely, D. (2009). The Enduring Impact of Transient Emotions on Decision Making. *Organizational Behavior and Human Decision Processes, 109*(1), 1–8. https://doi.org/10.1016/j.obhdp.2009.02.003.

Andrews, M. F. (2022). Edith Stein's Understanding of the Personal Attitude: Applications and Implications for a New Ethics. In M. F. Andrews & A. Calcagno (Eds.), *Ethics and Metaphysics in the Philosophy of Edith Stein: Applications and Implications* (pp. 225–239). Springer International Publishing.

Anscombe, G. E. M. (2000). *Intention*. Harvard University Press.

Arpaly, N., & Schroeder, T. (2014). *In Praise of Desire*. Oxford University Press.

Avenanti, A., Sirigu, A., & Aglioti, S. M. (2010). Racial Bias Reduces Empathic Sensorimotor Resonance with Other-Race Pain. *Current Biology: CB, 20*(11), 1018–1022. https://doi.org/10.1016/j.cub.2010.03.071.

Bailey, O. (2018). Empathy and Testimonial Trust. *Royal Institute of Philosophy Supplement, 84*, 139–160. https://doi.org/10.1017/S1358246118000589.

Bailey, O. (2020). Empathy and the Value of Humane Understanding. *Philosophy and Phenomenological Research*, phpr.12744. https://doi.org/10.1111/phpr.12744.

Baron, J. (2008). *Thinking and Deciding* (4th ed). Cambridge University Press.

Baron-Cohen, S. (2011). *The Science of Evil: On Empathy and the Origins of Cruelty*. Basic Books.

Bartels, D. M., Bauman, C. W., Cushman, F. A., Pizarro, D. A., & McGraw, A. P. (2015). Moral Judgment and Decision Making. In G. Keren & G. Wu (Eds.), *The Wiley Blackwell Handbook of Judgment and Decision Making* (pp. 478–515). John Wiley & Sons, Ltd. https://doi.org/10.1002/9781118468333.ch17.

Batson, C. D. (2009). These Things Called Empathy: Eight Related but Distinct Phenomena. In J. Decety & W. Ickes (Eds.), *Social Neuroscience. The Social Neuroscience of Empathy* (pp. 3–15). MIT Press.

Batson, C. D. (2011). *Altruism in Humans*. Oxford University Press.

Batson, C. D. (2014). Empathy-Induced Altruism and Morality: No Necessary Connection. In H. L. Maibom (Ed.), *Empathy and Morality* (pp. 42–58). Oxford University

Press. https://doi.org/10.1093/acprof:oso/9780199969470.003.0002.

Batson, C. D., Klein, T. R., Highberger, L., & Shaw, L. L. (1995). Immorality from Empathy-Induced Altruism: When Compassion and Justice Conflict. *Journal of Personality and Social Psychology, 68*(6), 1042–1054. https://doi.org/10.1037/0022-3514.68.6.1042.

Batson, C. D., Lishner, D. A., Carpenter, A., Dulin, L., Harjusola-Webb, S., Stocks, E. L., Gale, S., Hassan, O., & Sampat, B. (2003). "... As you Would have Them Do Unto You": Does Imagining Yourself in the Other's Place Stimulate Moral Action? *Personality and Social Psychology Bulletin, 29*(9), 1190–1201. https://doi.org/10.1177/0146167203254600.

Battaly, H. D. (2011). Is Empathy a Virtue? In A. Coplan & P. Goldie (Eds.), *Empathy: Philosophical and Psychological Perspectives* (pp. 277–301). Oxford University Press. https://doi.org/10.1093/acprof:oso/9780199539956.003.0017.

Bechara, A. (2004). The Role of Emotion in Decision-making: Evidence from Neurological Patients with Orbitofrontal Damage. *Brain and Cognition, 55*(1), 30–40. https://doi.org/10.1016/j.bandc.2003.04.001.

Ben-Moshe, N. (2020). Making Sense of Smith on Sympathy and Approbation: Other-Oriented Sympathy as a Psychological and Normative Achievement. *British Journal for the History of Philosophy, 28*(4), 735–755. https://doi.org/10.1080/09608788.2019.1667292.

Betzler, M. (2019). The Relational Value of Empathy. *International Journal of Philosophical Studies, 27*(2), 136–161. https://doi.org/10.1080/09672559.2019.1598081.

Beyer, C. (2022). Edmund Husserl. In E. N. Zalta & U. Nodelman (Eds.), *The Stanford Encyclopedia of Philosophy* (Winter 2022). Metaphysics Research Lab, Stanford University. https://plato.stanford.edu/archives/win2022/entries/husserl/.

Bloom, P. (2016). *Against Empathy: The Case for Rational Compassion*. Ecco.

Boella, L. (2018). *Empatie: L'esperienza empatica nella società del conflitto* (1st ed). Raffaello Cortina editore.

Bohman, J., & Rehg, W. (1997). *Deliberative Democracy: Essays on Reason and Politics*. MIT Press.

Borg, E. (2007). If Mirror Neurons Are the Answer, What Was the Question? *Journal of Consciousness Studies, 14*(8), 5–19.

Brentano, F. (1874). *Psychology from an Empirical Standpoint*. Routledge.

Bubandt, N., & Willerslev, R. (2015). The Dark Side of Empathy: Mimesis, Deception, and the Magic of Alterity. *Comparative Studies in Society and History, 57*(1), 5–34. https://doi.org/10.1017/S0010417514000589.

Burns, T. (2022). Theodor Lipps on the Concept of Einfühlung (Empathy). In D. Romand & S. Tchougounnikov, *Theodor Lipps, (1851–1914): Psychologie, Philosophie, Esthétique, Langage/Psychology, Philosophy, Aesthetics, Language* (1st ed). sdvig press. https://doi.org/10.19079/138650.5.

Burns, T. A. (2016). Review: Phenomenology of Sociality. *Husserl Studies*, *32*(3), 271–278. https://doi.org/10.1007/s10743-016-9197-5.

Calcagno, A. (2007). *The Philosophy of Edith Stein*. Duquesne University Press. https://muse.jhu.edu/pub/149/monograph/book/5384.

Calcagno, A. (2014). *Lived Experience from the Inside Out: Social and Political Philosophy in Edith Stein*. Duquesne University Press.

Calcagno, A. (2017). The Role of Identification in Experiencing Community: Edith Stein, Empathy, and Max Scheler. In E. Magrì & D. Moran (Eds.), *Empathy, Sociality, and Personhood: Essays on Edith Stein's Phenomenological Investigations* (pp. 143–159). Springer International Publishing. https://doi.org/10.1007/978-3-319-71096-9_8.

Calcagno, A. (2020). Edith Stein. In *The Routledge Handbook of Phenomenology and Phenomenological Philosophy*. Routledge.

Cameron, C. D., & Payne, B. K. (2011). Escaping Affect: How Motivated Emotion Regulation Creates Insensitivity to Mass Suffering. *Journal of Personality and Social Psychology*, *100*(1), 1–15. https://doi.org/10.1037/a0021643.

Carel, H., & Kidd, I. J. (2014). Epistemic Injustice in Healthcare: A Philosophical Analysis. *Medicine, Health Care, and Philosophy*, *17*(4), 529–540. https://doi.org/10.1007/s11019-014-9560-2.

Carr, L., Iacoboni, M., Dubeau, M.-C., Mazziotta, J. C., & Lenzi, G. L. (2003). Neural Mechanisms of Empathy in Humans: A Relay from Neural Systems for Imitation to Limbic Areas. *Proceedings of the National Academy of Sciences of the United States of America*, *100*(9), 5497–5502. https://doi.org/10.1073/pnas.0935845100.

Cassels, T. G., Chan, S., & Chung, W. (2010). The Role of Culture in Affective Empathy: Cultural and Bicultural Differences. *Journal of Cognition and Culture*, *10*(3–4), 309–326. https://doi.org/10.1163/156853710X531203.

Cheng, Y., Chen, C., Lin, C.-P., Chou, K.-H., & Decety, J. (2010). Love Hurts: An fMRI Study. *NeuroImage*, *51*(2), 923–929. https://doi.org/10.1016/j.neuroimage.2010.02.047.

Chiao, J. Y., Iidaka, T., Gordon, H. L., Nogawa, J., Bar, M., Aminoff, E., Sadato, N., & Ambady, N. (2008). Cultural Specificity in Amygdala Response to Fear Faces. *Journal of Cognitive Neuroscience*, *20*(12), 2167–2174. https://doi.org/10.1162/jocn.2008.20151.

Chopik, W. J., O'Brien, E., & Konrath, S. H. (2017). Differences in Empathic Concern and Perspective Taking Across 63 Countries. *Journal of Cross-Cultural Psychology*, *48*(1), 23–38. https://doi.org/10.1177/0022022116673910.

Cognition. (2023). In *Lexico*. Oxford University Press. https://web.archive.org/web/20200715113427/https://www.lexico.com/definition/cognition

Cohen, J. (1989). Deliberation and Democratic Legitimacy. *The Good Polity*.

Cohen, J. (2007). Deliberative Democracy. In S. W. Rosenberg (Ed.), *Deliberation, Participation and Democracy: Can the People Govern?* (pp. 219–236). Palgrave Macmillan UK. https://doi.org/10.1057/9780230591080_10.

Coplan, A. (2011a). Understanding Empathy: Its Features and Effects. In A. Coplan & P. Goldie (Eds.), *Empathy: Philosophical and Psychological Perspectives* (pp. 3–18). Oxford University Press.

Coplan, A. (2011b). Will the Real Empathy Please Stand Up? A Case for a Narrow Conceptualization. *The Southern Journal of Philosophy, 49*, 40–65. https://doi.org/10.1111/j.2041-6962.2011.00056.x.

Cordaro, D. T., Sun, R., Keltner, D., Kamble, S., Huddar, N., & McNeil, G. (2018). Universals and Cultural Variations in 22 Emotional Expressions Across Five Cultures. *Emotion, 18*, 75–93. https://doi.org/10.1037/emo0000302.

Corrigan, P. W., & Watson, A. C. (2002). Understanding the Impact of Stigma on People with Mental Illness. *World Psychiatry, 1*(1), 16.

Costa, V. (2010). *Fenomenologia dell'Intersoggettività: Empatia, Socialità, Cultura*. Carocci.

Cuddy, A. J. C., Rock, M. S., & Norton, M. I. (2007). Aid in the Aftermath of Hurricane Katrina: Inferences of Secondary Emotions and Intergroup Helping. *Group Processes & Intergroup Relations, 10*(1), 107–118. https://doi.org/10.1177/1368430207071344.

Cuff, B. M. P., Brown, S. J., Taylor, L., & Howat, D. J. (2016). Empathy: A Review of the Concept. *Emotion Review, 8*(2), 144–153. https://doi.org/10.1177/1754073914558466.

Da Re, A. (2013). Realismo Morale Minimo e Massimo. *Perché Essere Realisti: una Sfida Filosofica.*, 179–194.

Dahlstrom, D. (2021). Experiencing Others: Stein's Critique of Scheler. *American Catholic Philosophical Quarterly, 95*(3), 433–453. https://doi.org/10.5840/acpq2021526224.

Damasio, A. R. (1994). *Descartes Error: Emotion, Reason and the Human Brain*. Vintage books.

Darley, J. M., & Latane, B. (1968). Bystander Intervention in Emergencies: Diffusion of Responsibility. *Journal of Personality and Social Psychology, 8*, 377–383. https://doi.org/10.1037/h0025589.

D'Arms, J. (2011). Empathy, Approval, and Disapproval in Moral Sentimentalism. *The Southern Journal of Philosophy, 49*, 134–141. https://doi.org/10.1111/j.2041-6962.2011.00062.x.

Darwall, S. (1998). Empathy, Sympathy, Care. *Philosophical Studies: An International Journal for Philosophy in the Analytic Tradition, 89*(2/3), 261–282.

Darwall, S. (2009). *The Second-Person Standpoint: Morality, Respect, and Accountability*. Harvard University Press.

Darwall, S. (2010). Sentiment, Care, and Respect. *Theory and Research in Education, 8*(2), 153–162. https://doi.org/10.1177/1477878510368618.

Darwall, S. L. (1977). Two Kinds of Respect. *Ethics, 88*(1), 36–49.

Davidson, D. (2001). Actions, Reasons, and Causes. In D. Davidson (Ed.), *Essays on Actions and Events* (pp. 3–20). Oxford University Press. https://doi.org/10.1093/0199246270.003.0001.

Davis, Z., & Steinbock, A. (2024). Max Scheler. In E. N. Zalta & U. Nodelman (Eds.), *The Stanford Encyclopedia of Philosophy* (Spring 2024). Metaphysics Research Lab, Stanford University. https://plato.stanford.edu/archives/spr2024/entries/scheler/.

De Monticelli, R. (2020). Values, Norms, Justification and the Appropriateness of Emotions. In T. Szanto & H. Landweer (Eds.), *The Routledge Handbook of Phenomenology of Emotion* (1st ed., pp. 275–287). Routledge. https://doi.org/10.4324/9781315180786-27.

de Vignemont, F., & Jacob, P. (2012). What Is It like to Feel Another's Pain? *Philosophy of Science*, *79*(2), 295–316. https://doi.org/10.1086/664742.

de Vignemont, F., & Singer, T. (2006). The Empathic Brain: How, When and Why? *Trends in Cognitive Sciences*, *10*(10), 435–441. https://doi.org/10.1016/j.tics.2006.08.008.

Debes, R. (2016). Adam Smith and the Sympathetic Imagination. In R. Hanley (Ed.), *Adam Smith* (pp. 192–207). Princeton University Press. https://doi.org/10.1515/9781400873487-015.

Decety, J., & Cowell, J. M. (2014). Friends or Foes: Is Empathy Necessary for Moral Behavior? *Perspectives on Psychological Science*, *9*(5), 525–537. https://doi.org/10.1177/1745691614545130.

Decety, J., Echols, S., & Correll, J. (2010). The Blame Game: The Effect of Responsibility and Social Stigma on Empathy for Pain. *Journal of Cognitive Neuroscience*, *22*(5), 985–997. https://doi.org/10.1162/jocn.2009.21266.

Decety, J., & Jackson, P. L. (2004). The Functional Architecture of Human Empathy. *Behavioral and Cognitive Neuroscience Reviews*, *3*(2), 71–100. https://doi.org/10.1177/1534582304267187.

Decety, J., & Yoder, K. J. (2016). Empathy and Motivation for Justice: Cognitive Empathy and Concern, but Not Emotional Empathy, Predict Sensitivity to Injustice for Others. *Social Neuroscience*, *11*(1), 1–14. https://doi.org/10.1080/17470919.2015.1029593.

Denham, A. E. (2017). Empathy and Moral Motivation. In H. L. Maibom (Ed.), *The Routledge Handbook of Philosophy of Empathy* (pp. 227–241). Routledge.

DeSteno, D. (2015). Compassion and Altruism: How Our Minds Determine Who Is Worthy of Help. *Current Opinion in Behavioral Sciences*, *3*. https://doi.org/10.1016/j.cobeha.2015.02.002.

di Pellegrino, G., Fadiga, L., Fogassi, L., Gallese, V., & Rizzolatti, G. (1992). Understanding Motor Events: A Neurophysiological Study. *Experimental Brain Research*, *91*(1), 176–180. https://doi.org/10.1007/BF00230027.

Donise, A. (2019). *Critica della Ragione Empatica: Fenomenologia dell'Altruismo e della Crudeltà*. Il mulino.

Donise, A. (2024). Understanding Others: Theodor Lipps as Philosopher of Gestures. In G. Maddalena, F. Ferrucci, M. Bella, & M. Santarelli (Eds.), *Gestures: Approaches,*

Uses, and Developments (pp. 81–94). De Gruyter. https://doi.org/10.1515/9783110785845-006.

Döring, S. A. (2007). Seeing What to Do: Affective Perception and Rational Motivation. *Dialectica, 61*(3), 363–394. https://doi.org/10.1111/j.1746-8361.2007.01105.x.

Drummond, J. J. (2022). Empathy, Sympathetic Respect, and the Foundations of Morality. In *Empathy, Sympathetic Respect, and the Foundations of Morality* (pp. 345–362). De Gruyter. https://doi.org/10.1515/9783110698787-018.

Drummond, J. J. (2023). Why Empathy Means Nothing – and Everything – for Ethics. In M. Englander & S. Ferrarello (Eds.), *Empathy and Ethics* (pp. 9–28). Rowman & Littlefield.

Dryzek, J. S., & Braithwaite, V. (2000). On the Prospects for Democratic Deliberation: Values Analysis Applied to Australian Politics. *Political Psychology, 21*(2), 241–266. https://doi.org/10.1111/0162-895X.00186.

Dullstein, M. (2013). Direct Perception and Simulation: Stein's Account of Empathy. *Review of Philosophy and Psychology, 4*(2), 333–350. https://doi.org/10.1007/s13164-013-0139-2.

Echols, S., & Correll, J. (2011). It's More than Skin Deep: Empathy and Helping Behavior across Social Groups. In J. Decety (Ed.), *Empathy: From Bench to Bedside* (pp. 55–72). MIT Press. https://doi.org/10.7551/mitpress/9780262016612.003.0004.

Ehrlinger, J., Readinger, W. O., & Kim, B. (2016). Decision-Making and Cognitive Biases. In *Encyclopedia of Mental Health* (pp. 5–12). Elsevier. https://doi.org/10.1016/B978-0-12-397045-9.00206-8.

Eisenberg, N. (1992). *The Caring Child.* Harvard University Press.

Elfenbein, H. A. (2013). Nonverbal Dialects and Accents in Facial Expressions of Emotion. *Emotion Review, 5*(1), 90–96. https://doi.org/10.1177/1754073912451332.

Elfenbein, H. A., Beaupré, M., Lévesque, M., & Hess, U. (2007). Toward a Dialect Theory: Cultural Differences in the Expression and Recognition of Posed Facial Expressions. *Emotion, 7*, 131–146. https://doi.org/10.1037/1528-3542.7.1.131.

Elster, J. (Ed.). (1998a). *Deliberative Democracy.* Cambridge University Press. https://doi.org/10.1017/CBO9781139175005.

Elster, J. (1998b). Introduction. In J. Elster (Ed.), *Deliberative Democracy* (pp. 1–18). Cambridge University Press. https://doi.org/10.1017/CBO9781139175005.002.

Eyal, T., Steffel, M., & Epley, N. (2018). Perspective Mistaking: Accurately Understanding the Mind of Another Requires Getting Perspective, Not Taking Perspective. *Journal of Personality and Social Psychology, 114*(4), 547–571. https://doi.org/10.1037/pspa0000115.

Ferencz-Flatz, C. (2015). The Element of Intersubjectivity. Heidegger's Early Conception of Empathy. *Continental Philosophy Review, 48*(4), 479–496. https://doi.org/10.1007/s11007-015-9350-4

Ferrari, P. F., & Coudé, G. (2018). Mirror Neurons, Embodied Emotions, and Empathy. In K. Z. Meyza & E. Knapska (Eds.), *Neuronal Correlates of Empathy* (pp. 67–77).

Academic Press. https://doi.org/10.1016/B978-0-12-805397-3.00006-1.

Finlay, S., & Schroeder, M. (2017). Reasons for Action: Internal Vs. External. In E. N. Zalta (Ed.), *The Stanford Encyclopedia of Philosophy* (Fall 2017). Metaphysics Research Lab, Stanford University. https://plato.stanford.edu/archives/fall2017/entries/reasons-internal-external/.

Firman, T., Surbakti, I. M., Idroes, I. C., & Simarmata, H. A. (2011). Potential Climate-Change Related Vulnerabilities in Jakarta: Challenges and Current Status. *Habitat International, 35*(2), 372–378. https://doi.org/10.1016/j.habitatint.2010.11.011.

Fischer, P., Krueger, J. I., Greitemeyer, T., Vogrincic, C., Kastenmüller, A., Frey, D., Heene, M., Wicher, M., & Kainbacher, M. (2011). The Bystander-Effect: A Meta-analytic Review on Bystander Intervention in Dangerous and Non-dangerous Emergencies. *Psychological Bulletin, 137*, 517–537. https://doi.org/10.1037/a0023304.

Fishkin, J. S. (2021). Deliberative Public Consultation via Deliberative Polling: Criteria and Methods. *Hastings Center Report, 51*(S2). https://doi.org/10.1002/hast.1316.

Fleischacker, S. (2012). Sympathy in Hume and Smith: A Contrast, Critique, and Reconstruction. In C. Fricke & D. Føllesdal (Eds.), *Intersubjectivity and Objectivity in Adam Smith and Edmund Husserl* (pp. 273–311). Ontos.

Fricker, M. (2007). *EpistemicIinjustice: Power and the Ethics of Knowing*. Oxford University Press.

Fudenberg, D., & Tirole, J. (1991). *Game Theory*. MIT Press.

Gallagher, S. (2007). Simulation Trouble. *Social Neuroscience, 2*(3–4), 353–365. https://doi.org/10.1080/17470910601183549.

Gallagher, S. (2012). Empathy, Simulation, and Narrative. *Science in Context, 25*(3), 355–381. https://doi.org/10.1017/S0269889712000117.

Gallese, V. (2001). The Shared Manifold Hypothesis. From Mirror Neurons to Empathy. *Journal of Consciousness Studies*.

Ganczarek, J., Hünefeldt, T., & Olivetti Belardinelli, M. (2018). From "Einfühlung" to Empathy: Exploring the Relationship between Aesthetic and Interpersonal Experience. *Cognitive Processing, 19*(2), 141–145. https://doi.org/10.1007/s10339-018-0861-x.

Garden, R. E. (2007). The Problem of Empathy: Medicine and the Humanities. *New Literary History, 38*(3), 551–567. https://doi.org/10.1353/nlh.2007.0037.

Gardner, C. (2015). Medicine's Uncanny Valley: The Problem of Standardising Empathy. *The Lancet (British Edition), 386*(9998), 1032–1033. https://doi.org/10.1016/S0140-6736(15)00161-0.

Gaut, B. (1993). Moral Pluralism. *Philosophical Papers, 22*(1), 17–40. https://doi.org/10.1080/05568649309506391.

Gazzola, V., Rizzolatti, G., Wicker, B., & Keysers, C. (2007). The Anthropomorphic Brain: The Mirror Neuron System Responds to Human and Robotic Actions. *NeuroImage, 35*(4), 1674–1684. https://doi.org/10.1016/j.neuroimage.2007.02.003.

Gehlbach, H., & Mu, N. (2023). How We Understand Others: A Theory of How Social Perspective Taking Unfolds. *Review of General Psychology*, 282–302. https://doi org/10.1177/10892680231152595.

Geniusas, S. (2012). *The Origins of the Horizon in Husserl's Phenomenology*. Springer.

Gleichgerrcht, E., & Decety, J. (2013). Empathy in Clinical Practice: How Individual Dispositions, Gender, and Experience Moderate Empathic Concern, Burnout, and Emotional Distress in Physicians. *PloS One*, *8*(4), e61526–e61526. https://doi.org/10.1371/journal.pone.0061526.

Goldie, P. (2011). Anti-empathy. In A. Coplan & P. Goldie (Eds.), *Empathy Philosophical and Psychological Perspectives* (pp. 302–317). Oxford University Press.

Goldman, A. I. (2002). Simulation Theory and Mental Concepts. In *Simulation and Knowledge of Action* (pp. 1–19). John Benjamins Publishing Company. https://doi.org/10.1075/aicr.45.02gol.

Goldman, A. I. (2005). Imitation, Mind Reading, and Simulation. In *Perspectives on Imitation: From Neuroscience to Social Science: Vol. 2: Imitation, Human Development, and Culture* (pp. 79–93). MIT Press.

Goldman, A. I. (2006). *Simulating Minds: The Philosophy, Psychology, and Neuroscience of Mindreading*. Oxford University Press.

Goldman, A. I. (2011). Two Routes to Empathy: Insights from Cognitive Neuroscience. In *Empathy*. Oxford University Press. https://doi.org/10.1093/acprof:oso/9780199539956.003.0004.

Goodin, R. E. (2003). *Reflective Democracy*. Oxford University Press.

Gordon, R. M. (1986). Folk Psychology as Simulation. *Mind & Language*, *1*(2), 158–171. https://doi.org/10.1111/j.1468-0017.1986.tb00324.x.

Greenspan, P. (2019). The Evaluative Content of Emotion. *Royal Institute of Philosophy Supplements*, *85*, 75–86. https://doi.org/10.1017/S1358246118000693.

Greenspan, P. (2020). Emotions in Practical Reasoning. In R. Chang & K. Sylvan (Eds.), *The Routledge Handbook of Practical Reason*. Routledge.

Griffin, A. S., Callen, A., Klop-Toker, K., Scanlon, R. J., & Hayward, M. W. (2020). Compassionate Conservation Clashes with Conservation Biology: Should Empathy, Compassion, and Deontological Moral Principles Drive Conservation Practice? *Frontiers in Psychology*, *11*, 1139. https://doi.org/10.3389/fpsyg.2020.01139.

Grigoletto, S. (2019). *Only through Complexity. Morality and the Case of Supererogation*. Padova University Press.

Guo, C. C. (2017). The Neuroscience of Empathy. In H. L. Maibom (Ed.), *The Routledge Handbook of Philosophy of Empathy*. Routledge.

Gupta, R., Koscik, T. R., Bechara, A., & Tranel, D. (2011). The Amygdala and Decision-Making. *Neuropsychologia*, *49*(4), 760–766. https://doi.org/10.1016/j.neuropsychologia.2010.09.029

Gurwitsch, A. (1931). *Human Encounters in the Social World*. Duquesne University Press.

Gutmann, A., & Thompson, D. (1997). Deliberating about Bioethics. *The Hastings Center Report*, *27*(3), 38–41. https://doi.org/10.2307/3528667.

Gutsell, J. N., & Inzlicht, M. (2010). Empathy Constrained: Prejudice Predicts Reduced Mental Simulation of Actions during Observation of Outgroups. *Journal of Experimental Social Psychology*, *46*(5), 841–845. https://doi.org/10.1016/j.jesp.2010.03.011.

Habermas, J. (1998). *Between Facts and Norms* (W. Rehg, Trans.; 2nd printing). MIT Press.

Hagiwara, N., Kron, F. W., Scerbo, M. W., & Watson, G. S. (2020). A Call for Grounding Implicit Bias Training in Clinical and Translational Frameworks. *The Lancet*, *395*(10234), 1457–1460. https://doi.org/10.1016/S0140-6736(20)30846-1.

Haidt, J. (2001). The Emotional Dog and Its Rational Tail: A Social Intuitionist Approach to Moral Judgment. *Psychological Review*, *108*, 814–834. https://doi.org/10.1037/0033-295X.108.4.814.

Harman, G. (2011). Moral Reasoning. In M. Timmons (Ed.), *Oxford Studies in Normative Ethics* (Vol. 6, pp. 263–276). Oxford University Press.

Harsanyi, J. C. (1977). Morality and the Theory of Rational Behavior. *Social Research*, *44*(4), 623–656.

Haryanto, B. (2018). Climate Change and Urban Air Pollution Health Impacts in Indonesia. In R. Akhtar & C. Palagiano (Eds.), *Climate Change and Air Pollution: The Impact on Human Health in Developed and Developing Countries* (pp. 215–239). Springer. https://doi.org/10.1007/978-3-319-61346-8_14.

Hayward, M. W., Callen, A., Allen, B. L., Ballard, G., Broekhuis, F., Bugir, C., Clarke, R. H., Clulow, J., Clulow, S., Daltry, J. C., Davies-Mostert, H. T., Fleming, P. J. S., Griffin, A. S., Howell, L. G., Kerley, G. I. H., Klop-Toker, K., Legge, S., Major, T., Meyer, N., … Wüster, W. (2019). Deconstructing Compassionate Conservation. *Conservation Biology*, *33*(4), 760–768. https://doi.org/10.1111/cobi.13366.

Heal, J. (Ed.). (1986). Replication and Functionalism. In *Mind, Reason and Imagination: Selected Essays in Philosophy of Mind and Language* (pp. 11–27). Cambridge University Press. https://doi.org/10.1017/CBO9780511615894.004.

Heal, J. (1996). Simulation, Theory, and Content. In P. Carruthers & P. K. Smith (Eds.), *Theories of Theories of Mind* (pp. 75–89). Cambridge University Press.

Hein, G., Silani, G., Preuschoff, K., Batson, C. D., & Singer, T. (2010). Neural Responses to Ingroup and Outgroup Members' Suffering Predict Individual Differences in Costly Helping. *Neuron*, *68*(1), 149–160. https://doi.org/10.1016/j.neuron.2010.09.003.

Hein, G., & Singer, T. (2008). I Feel How You Feel but Not Always: The Empathic Brain and Its Modulation. *Current Opinion in Neurobiology*, *18*(2), 153–158. https://doi.org/10.1016/j.conb.2008.07.012.

Herder, J. G. von. (1778). *Plastik: Einige Wahrnehmungen über Form und Gestalt aus Pygmalions bildendem Traume*. https://doi.org/10.11588/diglit.1222.

Heyd, D. (2019). Supererogation. In E. N. Zalta (Ed.), *The Stanford Encyclopedia of Philosophy* (Winter 2019). Metaphysics Research Lab, Stanford University. https://plato.stanford.edu/archives/win2019/entries/supererogation/.

Hieronymi, P. (2011). Reasons for Action. *Proceedings of the Aristotelian Society, 111* (3pt3), 407–427. https://doi.org/10.1111/j.1467-9264.2011.00316.x.

Hilbert, M. (2012). Toward a Synthesis of Cognitive Biases: How Noisy Information Processing Can Bias Human Decision Making. *Psychological Bulletin, 138*(2), 211–237. https://doi.org/10.1037/a0025940.

Hippel, W. von, & Trivers, R. (2011). The Evolution and Psychology of Self-Deception. *Behavioral and Brain Sciences, 34*(1), 1–16. https://doi.org/10.1017/S0140525X10001354.

Hodges, S. D. (2005). Is How Much You Understand Me in Your Head or Mine? In B. F. Malle & S. D. Hodges (Eds.), *Other Minds: How Humans Bridge the Divide between Self and Others* (pp. 298–309). Guilford Publications.

Hodges, S. D., Kiel, K. J., Kramer, A. D. I., Veach, D., & Villanueva, B. R. (2010). Giving Birth to Empathy: The Effects of Similar Experience on Empathic Accuracy, Empathic Concern, and Perceived Empathy. *Personality and Social Psychology Bulletin, 36*(3), 398–409. https://doi.org/10.1177/0146167209350326.

Hodges, S. D., Lewis, K. L., & Ickes, W. (2015). The Matter of Other Minds: Empathic Accuracy and the Factors that Influence It. In M. Mikulincer, P. R. Shaver, J. A. Simpson, & J. F. Dovidio (Eds.), *APA Handbook of Personality and Social Psychology, Volume 3: Interpersonal Relations* (pp. 319–348). American Psychological Association. https://doi.org/10.1037/14344-012.

Hodges, S. D., & Wegner, D. M. (1997). Automatic and Controlled Empathy. In *Empathic Accuracy* (pp. 311–339). The Guilford Press.

Hoffman, M. L. (2000). *Empathy and Moral Development: Implications for Caring and Justice*. Cambridge University Press. https://doi.org/10.1017/CBO9780511805851.

Hoffman, M. L. (2011). Empathy, Justice, and the Law. In A. Coplan & P. Goldie (Eds.), *Empathy: Philosophical and Psychological Perspectives* (pp. 230–254). Oxford University Press.

Hollan, D. (2008). Being There: On the Imaginative Aspects of Understanding Others and Being Understood. *Ethos, 36*(4), 475–489.

Hollan, D. (2012). Emerging Issues in the Cross-Cultural Study of Empathy. *Emotion Review, 4*(1), 70–78. https://doi.org/10.1177/1754073911421376.

Hollan, D. (2017). Empathy across Cultures. In H. L. Maibom (Ed.), *The Routledge Handbook of Philosophy of Empathy* (pp. 341–352). Routledge.

Horgan, T., & Timmons, M. (2022). Expressing Gratitude as What's Morally Expected: A Phenomenological Approach. *Ethical Theory and Moral Practice, 25*(1), 139–155. https://doi.org/10.1007/s10677-021-10261-w.

Hume, D. (with Beauchamp, T. L.). (1748). *An Enquiry Concerning the Principles of Morals*. Oxford University Press.

Hume, D. (with Mossner, E. C.). (1739). *A Treatise of Human Nature.* Penguin Books.

Husserl, Edmund. (1952). Ideas Pertaining to a Pure Phenomenology and to a Phenomenological Philosophy – Second Book: Studies in the Phenomenology of Constitution. Kluwer Academic Publishers.

Husserl, Edmund. (1913). *Ideas: General Introduction to Pure Phenomenology.* (Dermot Moran, Ed; W. R. Boyce Gibson, Trans). Routledge.

Husserl, E. (1928). *Zur Phänomenologie des inneren Zeitbewusstseins: Mit den Texten aus der Erstausgabe und dem Nachlass.* Felix Meiner Verlag.

Husserl, E. (1931). *Cartesian meditations: An introduction to phenomenology.* Kluwer Academic Publishers.

Husserl, E. (2000). *Logical investigations.* Humanity Books.

Husserl, E. (2006). *The basic problems of phenomenology: From the lectures, winter semester, 1910–1911 from the German "Aus den Vorlesungen, Grundprobleme der Phänomenologie, Wintersemester 1910/1911" in "Zur Phänomenologie der Intersubjektivität, Husserliana XIII" edited by Iso Kern* (I. Farin & J. G. Hart, Trans.). Springer.

Hutchison, K. (2020). Four Types of Gender Bias Affecting Women Surgeons and Their Cumulative Impact. *Journal of Medical Ethics, 46*(4), 236–241. https://doi.org/10.1136/medethics-2019-105552.

Iacoboni, M. (2009). Imitation, Empathy, and Mirror Neurons. *Annual Review of Psychology, 60*(1), 653–670. https://doi.org/10.1146/annurev.psych.60.110707.163604.

Ickes, W. (1993). Empathic Accuracy. *Journal of Personality, 61*(4), 587–610. https://doi.org/10.1111/j.1467-6494.1993.tb00783.x.

Ickes, W., Stinson, L., Bissonnette, V., & Garcia, S. (1990). Naturalistic Social Cognition: Empathic Accuracy in Mixed-sex Dyads. *Journal of Personality and Social Psychology, 59*(4), 730–742. https://doi.org/10.1037/0022-3514.59.4.730.

Ilyes, I. (2017). Empathy in Hume and Smith. In H. L. Maibom (Ed.), *The Routledge Handbook of Philosophy of Empathy* (pp. 98–109). Routledge.

Jahoda, G. (2005). Theodor Lipps and the Shift from "Sympathy" to "Empathy." *Journal of the History of the Behavioral Sciences, 41*(2), 151–163. https://doi.org/10.1002/jhbs.20080.

Jami, P. Y., Walker, D. I., & Mansouri, B. (2023). Interaction of Empathy and Culture: A Review. *Current Psychology.* https://doi.org/10.1007/s12144-023-04422-6.

Jardine, J. (2015). Stein and Honneth on Empathy and Emotional Recognition. *Human Studies, 38*(4), 567–589. https://doi.org/10.1007/s10746-015-9361-5.

Jardine, J. (2017). Elementary Recognition and Empathy. *Metodo. International Studies in Phenomenology and Philosophy, 5.* https://metodo-rivista.eu/pub-138301.

Jardine, J., & Szanto, T. (2017). Empathy in the Phenomenological Tradition. In H. L. Maibom (Ed.), *The Routledge Handbook of Philosophy of Empathy* (pp. 86–97). Routledge.

Jenni, K., & Loewenstein, G. (1997). Explaining the Identifiable Victim Effect. *Journal of Risk and Uncertainty, 14*(3), 235–257. https://doi.org/10.1023/A:1007740225484.

Jolly, M. (2022). Putting the Emotion Back into Empathy: Edith Stein's Understanding of Empathy Applied to Contemporary Issues. In M. F. Andrews & A. Calcagno (Eds.), *Ethics and Metaphysics in the Philosophy of Edith Stein: Applications and Implications* (pp. 29–42). Springer. https://doi.org/10.1007/978-3-030-91198-0_3.

Jones, J. (2022). Disappearing Black People through Failures of White Empathy. In K. Maitra & J. McWeeny (Eds.), *Feminist Philosophy of Mind* (pp. 86–102). Oxford University Press. https://doi.org/10.1093/oso/9780190867614.003.0005.

Kant, I. (1784). *An Answer to the Question: What Is Enlightenment?* (T. Humphrey, Trans.). Hackett Publishing.

Kant, I. (2011). *Groundwork of the Metaphysics of Morals* (M. Gregor & J. Timmermann, Eds.; 1st ed.). Cambridge University Press. https://doi.org/10.1017/CBO9780511973741.

Kaplan, E. A. (2011). Empathy and Trauma Culture: Imaging Catastrophe. In A. Coplan & P. Goldie (Eds.), *Empathy: Philosophical and Psychological Perspectives* (pp. 255–276). Oxford University Press. https://doi.org/10.1093/acprof:oso/9780199539956.003.0016.

Kaplan, J. T., & Iacoboni, M. (2006). Getting a Grip on Other Minds: Mirror Neurons, Intention Understanding, and Cognitive Empathy. *Social Neuroscience*, *1*(3–4), 175–183. https://doi.org/10.1080/17470910600985605.

Kauppinen, A. (2014). Empathy, Emotion Regulation, and Moral Judgment. In H. L. Maibom (Ed.), *Empathy and Morality*. Oxford University Press. https://doi.org/10.1093/acprof:oso/9780199969470.003.0005.

Kekes, J. (1996). The Morality of Pluralism. In *The Morality of Pluralism*. Princeton University Press. https://doi.org/10.1515/9781400821105.

Keltner, D., Sauter, D., Tracy, J., & Cowen, A. (2019). Emotional Expression: Advances in Basic Emotion Theory. *Journal of Nonverbal Behavior*, *43*(2), 133–160. https://doi.org/10.1007/s10919-019-00293-3.

Kennett, J. (2002). Autism, Empathy and Moral Agency. *The Philosophical Quarterly*, *52*(208), 340–357. https://doi.org/10.1111/1467-9213.00272.

Kennett, J., & Maibom, H. L. (2017). Empathy and Psychopathology. In *The Routledge Handbook of Philosophy of Empathy* (pp. 364–376). Routledge.

Kern, I. (2018). Husserl's Phenomenology of Intersubjectivity. In *Husserl's Phenomenology of Intersubjectivity*. Routledge.

Kidd, I. J., & Carel, H. (2017). Epistemic Injustice and Illness. *Journal of Applied Philosophy*, *34*(2), 172–190. https://doi.org/10.1111/japp.12172.

Korsgaard, C. M. (1986). Skepticism about Practical Reason. *Journal of Philosophy*, *83*(1), 5–25. https://doi.org/10.2307/2026464.

Korsgaard, C. M. (1996). *The Sources of Normativity*. Cambridge University Press. https://doi.org/10.1017/CBO9780511554476.

Krause, S. R. (2008). *Civil Passions: Moral Sentiment and Democratic Deliberation*. Princeton University Press. https://press.princeton.edu/books/hardcover/9780691137254/civil-passions.

Kuhn, H. (1940). The Phenomenological Concept of "Horizon" (pp. 106–123). Harvard University Press. https://doi.org/10.4159/harvard.9780674333512.c6.

Kutschera, F. V. (1999). *Grundlagen der Ethik*. De Gruyter. https://doi.org/10.1515/9783110813869.

La fallacia naturalistica e la neuroetica. Un ponte indiretto tra descrittivo e prescrittivo?. In C. Chiurco, M. Deodati (Ed.), Etica e Natura (pp. 383–395). Orthotes Edizioni.

Lamothe, M., Boujut, E., Zenasni, F., & Sultan, S. (2014). To Be or Not to Be Empathic: The Combined Role of Empathic Concern and Perspective Taking in Understanding Burnout in General Practice. *BMC Family Practice*, *15*(1), 15–15. https://doi.org/10.1186/1471-2296-15-15.

Lebech, M. (2015). *The Ohilosophy of Edith Stein: From Phenomenology to Metaphysics*. Peter Lang.

Lerner, J. S., Li, Y., Valdesolo, P., & Kassam, K. S. (2015). Emotion and Decision Making. *Annual Review of Psychology*, *66*(1), 799–823. https://doi.org/10.1146/annurev-psych-010213-115043.

Levy, S. R., & Macdonald, J. L. (2016). Progress on Understanding Ageism. *Journal of Social Issues*, *72*(1), 5–25. https://doi.org/10.1111/josi.12153.

Lewis, K. L., Hodges, S. D., Laurent, S. M., Srivastava, S., & Biancarosa, G. (2012). Reading between the Minds: The Use of Stereotypes in Empathic Accuracy. *Psychological Science*, *23*(9), 1040–1046. https://doi.org/10.1177/0956797612439719.

Leyens, J.-P., Cortes, B., Demoulin, S., Dovidio, J. F., Fiske, S. T., Gaunt, R., Paladino, M.-P., Rodriguez-Perez, A., Rodriguez-Torres, R., & Vaes, J. (2003). Emotional Prejudice, Essentialism, and Nationalism The 2002 Tajfel lecture. *European Journal of Social Psychology*, *33*(6), 703–717. https://doi.org/10.1002/ejsp.170.

Leyens, J.-P., Paladino, P. M., Rodriguez-Torres, R., Vaes, J., Demoulin, S., Rodriguez-Perez, A., & Gaunt, R. (2000). The Emotional Side of Prejudice: The Attribution of Secondary Emotions to Ingroups and Outgroups. *Personality and Social Psychology Review*, *4*(2), 186–197. https://doi.org/10.1207/S15327957PSPR0402_06.

Liebow, N., & Ades, R. L. (2022). "I Know What It's Like": Epistemic Arrogance, Disability, and Race. *Journal of the American Philosophical Association*, *8*(3), 531–551. https://doi.org/10.1017/apa.2021.27.

Likowski, K. U., Mühlberger, A., Seibt, B., Pauli, P., & Weyers, P. (2008). Modulation of Facial Mimicry by Attitudes. *Journal of Experimental Social Psychology*, *44*, 1065–1072. https://doi.org/10.1016/j.jesp.2007.10.007.

Lipps, T. (1907). The Knowledge of Other Egos (T. Burns & M. Cavallaro, Trans.). In *The New Yearbook for Phenomenology and Phenomenological Philosophy* (pp. 261–282). Routledge.

Lipps, T. (1909). *Leitfaden der Psychologie* (3. teilweise umgearb. Aufl). W. Engelmann.

Lipps, T. (1903). *Ästhetik: Psychologie des Schönen und der Kunst*. Voss Publisher. http://archive.org/details/sthetikpsycholoo2lippgoog

Loewenstein, G., & Lerner, J. S. (2003). The Eole of Affect in Decision Making. In *Handbook of Affective Sciences* (pp. 619–642). Oxford University Press.

Magrì, E. (2015). Subjectivity and Empathy: A Steinian Approach. *Discipline Filosofiche*, *25*(2), 129–147. https://doi.org/10.1400/239315.

Magrì, E. (2018). An Inquiry on Radical Empathy and the Phenomenological Reduction in Sartre and Merleau-Ponty. *Continental Philosophy Review*, *51*(3), 323–341. https://doi.org/10.1007/s11007-018-9445-9.

Magrì, E. (2019). Empathy, Respect, and Vulnerability. *International Journal of Philosophical Studies: IJPS*, *27*(2), 327–346. https://doi.org/10.1080/09672559.2019.1587260.

Magrì, E., & McQueen, P. (2023). *Critical Phenomenology: An Introduction*. Polity Press.

Maibom, H. (2009). In Defence of (Model) Theory Theory. *Journal of Consciousness Studies*, *16*. https://www.academia.edu/1230850/In_Defence_of_Model_Theory_Theory.

Maibom, H. (2014). Introduction: (Almost) Everything You Ever Wanted to Know about Empathy. In H. L. Maibom (Ed.), *Empathy and Morality* (pp. 1–40). Oxford University Press. https://doi.org/10.1093/acprof:oso/9780199969470.003.0001.

Maibom, H. L. (2010). Imagining Others. *Les Ateliers de l'éthique/The Ethics Forum*, *5*(1), 34–49.

Maibom, H. L. (2012). The Many Faces of Empathy and Their Relation to Prosocial Action and Aggression Inhibition. *WIREs Cognitive Science*, *3*(2), 253–263. https://doi.org/10.1002/wcs.1165.

Maibom, H. L. (2016). Knowing Me, Knowing You. In A. Kind & P. Kung (Eds.), *Knowledge Through Imagination* (pp. 185–206). Oxford University Press. https://doi.org/10.1093/acprof:oso/9780198716808.003.0009.

Maibom, H. L. (2017). Affective Empathy. In H. L. Maibom (Ed.), *The Routledge Handbook of Philosophy of Empathy* (pp. 22–32). Routledge.

Marsh, A. A. (2014). Empathy and Moral Deficits in Psychopathy. In H. L. Maibom (Ed.), *Empathy and Morality* (pp. 139–154). Oxford University Press. https://doi.org/10.1093/acprof:oso/9780199969470.003.0007.

Masto, M. (2015). Empathy and Its Role in Morality. *The Southern Journal of Philosophy*, *53*(1), 74–96. https://doi.org/10.1111/sjp.12097.

Matravers, D. (2017). Empathy in the Aesthetic Tradition. In H. L. Maibom (Ed.), *The Routledge Handbook of Philosophy of Empathy* (pp. 77–85). Routledge.

Matthiesen, N., & Klitmøller, J. (2019). Encountering the Stranger: Hannah Arendt and the Shortcomings of Empathy as a Moral Compass. *Theory & Psychology*, 29(2), 182–199. https://doi.org/10.1177/0959354319828174.

McDowell, J. (1985). Values and Secondary Qualities. In T. Honderich (Ed.), *Morality and Objectivity* (pp. 110–129). Routledge.

McMullin, I. (2019). *Existential Flourishing: A Phenomenology of the Virtue*. Cambridge University Press.

Medina, J. (2012). *The Epistemology of Resistance: Gender and Racial Oppression, Epistemic Injustice, and Resistant Imaginations*. Oxford University Press.

Meltzoff, A. N., & Brooks, R. (2001). "Like Me" as a Building Block for Understanding Other Minds: Bodily Acts, Attention, and Intention. In *Intentions and Intentionality: Foundations of Social Cognition* (pp. 171–191). MIT Press.

Michel, C., Rossion, B., Han, J., Chung, C.-S., & Caldara, R. (2006). Holistic Processing Is Finely Tuned for Faces of One's Own Race. *Psychological Science*, *17*(7), 608–615. https://doi.org/10.1111/j.1467-9280.2006.01752.x.

Mill, J. S. (1861). *Utilitarianism* (3rd ed). Longmans, Green, Reader, and Dyer Publisher.

Mill, J. S. (1865). *An Examination of Sir William Hamilton's Philosophy, and of the Principal Philosophical Questions Discussed in His Writings*. Longman, Green, Longman, Roberts. http://archive.org/details/examinationofsiroomill.

Moran, D. (2004). The Problem of Empathy: Lipps, Scheler, Husserl and Stein. In T. Kelly & P. Rosemann (Eds.), *Amor Amicitiae: On the Love that Is Friendship. Essays in Medieval Thought and Beyond in Honor of the Rev. Professor James McEvoy*. Peteers Publishers.

Moran, D., & Cohen, J. D. (2012). *The Husserl Dictionary*. Continuum.

Morrell, M. E. (2015). Empathy and Democracy: Feeling, Thinking, and Deliberation. In *Empathy and Democracy*. Penn State University Press. https://doi.org/10.1515/9780271051222.

Morton, A. (2017). Empathy and Imagination. In H. L. Maibom (Ed.), *The Routledge Handbook of Philosophy of Empathy* (pp. 180–189). Routledge, Taylor & Francis Group.

Mulligan, K. (2009). Emotions and Values. In P. Goldie (Ed.), *The Oxford Handbook of Philosophy of Emotion* (pp. 475–500). Oxford University Press.

Nagel, T. (1978). *The Possibility of Altruism*. Princeton University Press.

Nichols, S. (2001). Mindreading and the Cognitive Architecture Underlying Altruistic Motivation. *Mind & Language*, *16*(4), 425–455. https://doi.org/10.1111/1468-0017.00178.

Nichols, S., & Stich, S. P. (2003). *Mindreading: An Integrated Account of Pretence, Self-Awareness, and Understanding Other Minds*. Oxford University Press. https://doi.org/10.1093/0198236107.001.0001.

Nisbett, R. E., & Wilson, T. D. (1977). Telling More than We Can Know: Verbal Reports on Mental Processes. *Psychological Review, 84*, 231–259. https://doi.org/10.1037/0033-295X.84.3.231.

Nowak, M. (2011). The Complicated History of Einfühlung. *Argument: Biannual Philosophical Journal, 1*(2), 301–326.

Nussbaum, M. C. (2001a). *The Fragility of Goodness: Luck and Ethics in Greek Tragedy and Philosophy* (2nd ed.). Cambridge University Press. https://doi.org/10.1017/CBO9780511817915.

Nussbaum, M. C. (2001b). *Upheavals of Thought: The Intelligence of Emotions*. Cambridge University Press.

Oxlely, J. C. (2011). *The Moral Dimensions of Empathy: Limits and Applications in Ethical Theory and Practice*. Palgrave Macmillan.

Pedersen, R. (2008). Empathy: A Wolf in Sheep's Clothing? *Medicine, Health Care and Philosophy, 11*(3), 325–335. https://doi.org/10.1007/s11019-007-9104-0.

Persson, I., & Savulescu, J. (2018). The Moral Importance of Reflective Empathy. *Neuroethics, 11*(2), 183–193. https://doi.org/10.1007/s12152-017-9350-7.

Price, D. D. (2000). Psychological and Neural Mechanisms of the Affective Dimension of Pain. *Science, 288*(5472), 1769–1772. https://doi.org/10.1126/science.288.5472.1769.

Prinz, J. (2009). Emotions: Motivating Feelings. In A. Beckermann, B. P. McLaughlin, & S. Walter (Eds.), *The Oxford Handbook of Philosophy of Mind* (pp. 678–690). Oxford University Press. https://doi.org/10.1093/oxfordhb/9780199262618.003.0040.

Prinz, J. (2011a). Against Empathy. *The Southern Journal of Philosophy, 49*, 214–233. https://doi.org/10.1111/j.2041-6962.2011.00069.x.

Prinz, J. (2011b). Is Empathy Necessary for Morality? In A. Coplan & P. Goldie (Eds.), *Empathy Philosophical and Psychological Perspectives* (pp. 211–229). Oxford University Press.

Ravenscroft, I. (1998). What Is It Like to Be Someone Else? Simulation and Empathy. *Ratio, 11*(2), 170–185. https://doi.org/10.1111/1467-9329.00062.

Raz, J. (2010). *Engaging Reason: On the Theory of Value and Action*. Oxford University Press.

Reicher, M. E. (2009). Value Facts and Value Experiences in Early Phenomenology. In W. Huemer & B. Centi (Eds.), *Value and Ontology* (pp. 105–135). Ontos-Verlag. https://doi.org/10.1515/9783110325522.105.

Rick, J. (2007). Hume's and Smith's Partial Sympathies and Impartial Stances. *Journal of Scottish Philosophy, 5*(2), 135–158. https://doi.org/10.3366/jsp.2007.5.2.135.

Rifkin, J. (2009). *The Empathic Civilization: The Race to Global Consciousness in a World in Crisis*. Penguin Publishing Group.

Rizzolatti, G., Fogassi, L., & Gallese, V. (2006). Mirrors of the Mind. *Scientific American, 295*(5), 54–61. https://doi.org/10.1038/scientificamerican1106-54.

Rosaldo, R. (1984). Grief and a Headhunter's Rage: On the Cultural Force of Emotions. *Text, Play and Story: The Construction and Reconstruction of Self and Society*, 178–195.

Ross, D. (1930). *The Right and the Good*. Oxford University Press.

Salice, A. (2025). The Phenomenology of the Munich and Göttingen Circles. In E. N. Zalta & U. Nodelman (Eds.), *The Stanford Encyclopedia of Philosophy* (Fall 2025). Metaphysics Research Lab, Stanford University. https://plato.stanford.edu/archives/fall2025/entries/phenomenology-mg/.

Sayre-McCord, G. (2013). Hume and Smith on Sympathy, Approbation, and Moral Judgment. *Social Philosophy and Policy*, *30*(1–2), 208–236. https://doi.org/10.1017/s0265052513000101

Scheler, M. (1913). *The Nature of Sympathy* (W. Stark, Trans.). Routledge and KPaul.

Scheler, M. (1916). *Formalism in Ethics and Non-formal Ethics of Values: A New Attempt toward the Foundation of an Ethical Personalism*. Northwestern University Press.

Schramme, T. (2017). Empathy and Altruism. In H. Maibom (Ed.), *The Routledge Handbook of Philosophy of Empathy* (pp. 203–214). Routledge. https://livrepository.liverpool.ac.uk/3013058.

Schroeder, M. A. (2007). *Slaves of the Passions*. Oxford University Press.

Schutz, A. (1972). *The Phenomenology of the Social World*. Northwestern University Press.

Sen, A. (1980). Plural Utility. *Proceedings of the Aristotelian Society*, *81*, 193–215.

Sherman, G. D., Haidt, J., Iyer, R., & Coan, J. A. (2013). Individual Differences in the Physical Embodiment of Care: Prosocially Oriented Women Respond to Cuteness by Becoming More Physically Careful. *Emotion*, *13*, 151–158. https://doi.org/10.1037/a0029259.

Shoemaker, D. (2021). Personal Identity and Ethics. In K. Witt, A. Dufner, & E. N. Zalta (Eds.), *The Stanford Encyclopedia of Philosophy* (Fall 2021). https://plato.stanford.edu/archives/fall2021/entries/identity-ethics/.

Sidgwick, H. (1962). *The Methods of Ethics* (7. ed). MacMillan and Co LTD.

Simmons, A. (2013). In Defense of the Moral Significance of Empathy. *Ethical Theory and Moral Practice*, *17*(1), 97–111. https://doi.org/10.1007/s10677-013-9417-4.

Singer, T., Seymour, B., O'Doherty, J. P., Stephan, K. E., Dolan, R. J., & Frith, C. D. (2006). Empathic Neural Responses Are Modulated by the Perceived Fairness of Others. *Nature*, *439*(7075), 466–469. https://doi.org/10.1038/nature04271.

Slote, M. (2004). Moral Sentimentalism. *Ethical Theory and Moral Practice*, *7*(1), 3–14.

Slote, M. (2005). Moral Sentimentalism and Moral Psychology. In D. Copp (Ed.), *The Oxford Handbook of Ethical Theory* (pp. 219–239). Oxford University Press. https://doi.org/10.1093/0195147790.003.0009.

Slote, M. (2007). *The Ethics of Care and Empathy*. Routledge.

Slote, M. (2009). *Moral Sentimentalism*. Oxford University Press. https://doi.org/10.1093/acprof:oso/9780195391442.001.0001.

Slote, M. (2015). The Roots of Empathy. In N. Snow (Ed.), *Cultivating Virtue: Perspectives from Philosophy, Theology, and Psychology* (pp. 65–86). Oxford University Press.

Slote, M. (2016). Saucers of Mud: Why Sympathy and Altruism Require Empathy. *Etica & Politica /Ethics & Politics, 17*(2), 12–26.

Smith, A. (1759). *The Theory of Moral Sentiments* (D. D. Raphael & A. L. Macfie, Eds.). Clarendon Press.

Smith, A. (2006). Cognitive Empathy and Emotional Empathy in Human Behavior and Evolution. *The Psychological Record, 56*(1), 3–21. https://doi.org/10.1007/BF03395534.

Solomon, R. C. (1993). *The Passions: Emotions and the Meaning of Life*. Hackett.

Song, Y. (2015). How to Be a Proponent of Empathy. *Ethical Theory and Moral Practice, 18*(3), 437–451. https://doi.org/10.1007/s10677-014-9525-9.

Songhorian, S. (2015). Against a Broad Definition of "Empathy." *Rivista Internazionale di Filosofia e Psicologia, 6*(1), 56–69. https://doi.org/10.4453/rifp.2015.0005.

Songhorian, S. (2019). The Contribution of Empathy to Ethics. *International Journal of Philosophical Studies, 27*(2), 244–264. https://doi.org/10.1080/09672559.2019.1619266.

Spaulding, S. (2016). Mind Misreading. *Philosophical Issues, 26*(1), 422–440. https://doi.org/10.1111/phis.12070.

Spaulding, S. (2017). Cognitive Empathy. In H. L. Maibom (Ed.), *The Routledge Handbook of Philosophy of Empathy* (pp. 13–21). Routledge.

Stanley, D. A., Sokol-Hessner, P., Banaji, M. R., & Phelps, E. A. (2011). Implicit Race Attitudes Predict Trustworthiness Judgments and Economic Trust Decisions. *Proceedings of the National Academy of Sciences, 108*(19), 7710–7715. https://doi.org/10.1073/pnas.1014345108.

Stefanello, E. (2021a). Empatia: Un Possibile Ponte Tra Autonomia E Vulnerabilità. In F. Marin & B. Giacomini (Eds.), *Paradosso: Autonomia e Vulnerabilità* (pp. 121–140). Il poligrafo.

Stefanello, E. (2021b). Your Pain Is Not Mine: A Critique of Clinical Empathy. *Bioethics*, bioe.12980. https://doi.org/10.1111/bioe.12980.

Stefanello, E. (2024a). Empathy, Environmental Motivation, and Phenomenology. *Metodo, 12*. https://metodo-rivista.eu/pub-267695.

Stefanello, E. (2024b). Narrative Medicine and Empathy: A Phenomenological Perspective. *Journal of the British Society for Phenomenology, 55*(2), 167–183. https://doi.org/10.1080/00071773.2024.2314119.

Stein, E. (1917). *On the Problem of Empathy* (W. Stein, Trans.). Springer Netherlands. https://doi.org/10.1007/978-94-017-5546-7.

Stein, E. (1922). *Philosophy of Psychology and the Humanities: The Collected Works of Edith Stein, vol. 7*. ICS Publications.

Stein, E. (1986). *Life in a Jewish Family*. ICS Publications.

Stein, E. (2002). *Finite and Eternal Being: An Attempt at an Ascent to the Meaning of Being*. ICS Publications, Institute of Carmelite Studies.

Stein, E. (2009). *Potency and Act: Studies Toward a Philosophy of Being: The Collected Works of Edith Stein, vol. 11*. ICS Publications.

Stueber, K. (2019). Empathy. In E. N. Zalta (Ed.), *The Stanford Encyclopedia of Philosophy* (Fall 2019). Metaphysics Research Lab, Stanford University. https://plato.stanford.edu/archives/fall2019/entries/empathy/.

Stueber, K. R. (2006). *Rediscovering Empathy: Agency, Folk Psychology, and the Human Sciences*. MIT Press.

Stueber, K. R. (2009). The Ethical Dimension of Folk Psychology? *Inquiry*, *52*(5), 532–547. https://doi.org/10.1080/00201740903302717.

Stueber, K. R. (2011). Moral Approval and the Dimensions of Empathy: Comments on Micheal Slote's Moral Sentimentalism. *Analytic Philosophy*, *52*(4), 328–336. https://doi.org/10.1111/j.2153-960X.2011.00540.x.

Summa, M. (2017). Empathy and Anti-empathy: Which Are the Problems? In E. Magrì & D. Moran (Eds.), *Empathy, Sociality, and Personhood* (pp. 87–105). Springer.

Svenaeus, F. (2016). The Phenomenology of Empathy: A Steinian Emotional Account. *Phenomenology and the Cognitive Sciences*, *15*(2), 227–245. https://doi.org/10.1007/s11097-014-9411-x.

Svenaeus, F. (2018). Edith Stein's Phenomenology of Sensual and Emotional Empathy. *Phenomenology and the Cognitive Sciences*, *17*(4), 741–760. https://doi.org/10.1007/s11097-017-9544-9.

Szanto, T., & Moran, D. (2024). Edith Stein. In E. N. Zalta & U. Nodelman (Eds.), *The Stanford Encyclopedia of Philosophy* (Fall 2024). Metaphysics Research Lab, Stanford University. https://plato.stanford.edu/archives/fall2024/entries/stein/.

Ta, V. P., & Ickes, W. (2017). Empathic Accuracy. In H. L. Maibom (Ed.), *The Routledge Handbook of Philosophy of Empathy* (pp. 353–363). Routledge.

Taipale, J. (2015). From Types to Tokens: Empathy and Typification. In T. Szanto & D. Moran (Eds.), *Phenomenology of Sociality* (pp. 143–158). Routledge.

Tappolet, C. (2009). *Emotion, Motivation, and Action: The Case of Fear*. Oxford University Press. https://doi.org/10.1093/oxfordhb/9780199235018.003.0015.

Thornton, S. (2024). Levinas on Empathy, Desire, and the Caress. *Human Studies*, *47*(3), 553–572. https://doi.org/10.1007/s10746-024-09714-9.

Throop, C. J., & Zahavi, D. (2020). Dark and Bright Empathy: Phenomenological and Anthropological Reflections. *Current Anthropology*, *61*(3), 283–303. https://doi.org/10.1086/708844.

Titchener, E. B. (1909). *Lectures on the Experimental Psychology of the Thought-Processes* (pp. x, 318). MacMillan Co. https://doi.org/10.1037/10877-000.

Tuana, N. (2006). The Speculum of Ignorance: The Women's Health Movement and Epistemologies of Ignorance. *Hypatia*, *21*(3), 1–19.

Ugazio, G., Majdandžić, J., & Lamm, C. (2014). Are Empathy and Morality Linked? Insights from Moral Psychology, Social and Decision Neuroscience, and Philosophy. In H. L. Maibom (Ed.), *Empathy and Morality* (pp. 155–172). Oxford University Press. https://doi.org/10.1093/acprof:oso/9780199969470.003.0008.

Van Bavel, J. J., Packer, D. J., & Cunningham, W. A. (2008). The Neural Substrates of In-Group Bias: A Functional Magnetic Resonance Imaging Investigation. *Psychological Science*, *19*(11), 1131–1139. https://doi.org/10.1111/j.1467-9280.2008.02214.x.

Vendrell Ferran, Í. (2015a). Empathy, Emotional Sharing and Feelings in Stein's Early Work. *Human Studies*, *38*(4), 481–502. https://doi.org/10.1007/s10746-015-9346-4.

Vendrell Ferran, Í. (2015b). The Emotions in Early Phenomenology. *Studia Phaenomenologica*, *15*, 349–374. https://doi.org/10.5840/studphaen20151518.

Vendrell Ferran, I. (2018). Intentionality, Value Disclosure and Constitution: Stein's Model. In E. Magrì & D. Moran (Eds.), *Empathy, Sociality and Personhood. Essays on Edith Stein's Phenomenological Investigations.* (pp. 65–85). https://philarchive org/rec/FERIVD-2.

Vischer, R. (1873). *Über das optische Formgefühl: E. Beitrag zur Aesthetik.* Credner.

Vischer, F. T. von. (1846). *Ästhetik oder Wissenschaft des Schönen.* Mäcken.

Waal, F. B. M. de. (2009). *The Age of Empathy: Nature's Lessons for a Kinder Society.* Three Rivers Press.

Wallace, R. J. (1999). Three Conceptions of Rational Agency. *Ethical Theory and Moral Practice*, *2*(3), 217–242.

Wallace, R. J. (2020). Practical Reason. In E. N. Zalta (Ed.), *The Stanford Encyclopedia of Philosophy* (Spring 2020). Metaphysics Research Lab, Stanford University. https://plato.stanford.edu/archives/spr2020/entries/practical-reason/.

Wedgwood, R. (2009). Intrinsic Values and Reasons for Action. In E. Sosa & E. Villanueva (Eds.), *Metaethics* (pp. 342–363). Wiley Periodicals.

Wedgwood, R. (2013). The Weight of Moral Reasons. In M. Timmons (Ed.), *Oxford Studies in Normative Ethics: Volume 3* (pp. 35–58). Oxford University Press. https://doi.org/10.1093/acprof:oso/9780199685905.003.0003.

Wellman, H. M., Harris, P. L., Banerjee, M., & Sinclair, A. (1995). Early Understanding of Emotion: Evidence from Natural Language. *Cognition and Emotion*, *9*(2–3), 117–149. https://doi.org/10.1080/02699939508409005.

Westra, E. (2019). Stereotypes, Theory of Mind, and the Action–Prediction Hierarchy. *Synthese*, *196*(7), 2821–2846. https://doi.org/10.1007/s11229-017-1575-9.

Westra, E. (2020). When Is Mindreading Accurate? A Commentary on Shannon Spaulding's How We Understand Others: Philosophy and Social Cognition. *Philosophical Psychology*, *33*(6), 868–882. https://doi.org/10.1080/09515089.2020.1765326.

Williams, B. (Ed.). (1973). Ethical Consistency. In *Problems of the Self: Philosophical Papers 1956–1972* (pp. 166–186). Cambridge University Press. https://doi.org/10.1017/CBO9780511621253.013.

Williams, B. (Ed.). (1981). Internal and External Reasons. In *Moral Luck: Philosophical Papers 1973–1980* (pp. 101–113). Cambridge University Press. https://doi.org/10.1017/CBO9781139165860.009.

Wispé, L. (1986). The Distinction between Sympathy and Empathy: To Call Forth a Concept, a Word Is Needed. *Journal of Personality and Social Psychology*, *50*(2), 314–321. https://doi.org/10.1037/0022-3514.50.2.314.

Wispé, L. (1987). History of the Concept of Empathy. In N. Eisenberg & J. Strayer (Eds.), *Empathy and Its Development* (pp. 17–37). Cambridge University Press.

Wu, S., & Keysar, B. (2007). The Effect of Culture on Perspective Taking. *Psychological Science*, *18*(7), 600–606. https://doi.org/10.1111/j.1467-9280.2007.01946.x.

Xu, X., Zuo, X., Wang, X., & Han, S. (2009). Do You Feel My Pain? Racial Group Membership Modulates Empathic Neural Responses. *The Journal of Neuroscience*, *29*(26), 8525–8529. https://doi.org/10.1523/jneurosci.2418-09.2009.

Yang, Q., Zhou, S., Gu, R., & Wu, Y. (2020). How Do Different Kinds of Incidental Emotions Influence Risk Decision Making? *Biological Psychology*, *154*, 107920. https://doi.org/10.1016/j.biopsycho.2020.107920.

Zagzebski, L. (2015). Admiration and the Admirable. *Proceedings of the Aristotelian Society, Supplementary Volumes*, *89*, 205–221.

Zagzebski, L. (2017). *Exemplarist Moral Theory*. Oxford University Press.

Zahavi, D. (2008). Simulation, Projection and Empathy. *Consciousness and Cognition*, *17*(2), 514–522. https://doi.org/10.1016/j.concog.2008.03.010.

Zahavi, D. (2011). Empathy and Direct Social Perception: A Phenomenological Proposal. *Review of Philosophy and Psychology*, *2*(3), 541–558. https://doi.org/10.1007/s13164-011-0070-3.

Zahavi, D. (2014a). Empathy and Other-Directed Intentionality. *Topoi*, *33*(1), 129–142. https://doi.org/10.1007/s11245-013-9197-4.

Zahavi, D. (2014b). *Self and Other: Exploring Subjectivity, Empathy, and Shame*. Oxford University Press.

Zahavi, D. (2017). Phenomenology, Empathy, and Mindreading. In H. L. Maibom (Ed.), *The Routledge Handbook of Philosophy of Empathy* (pp. 33–43). Routledge.

Zahavi, D., & Overgaard, S. (2011). Empathy without Isomorphism: A Phenomenological Account. In J. Decety (Ed.), *Empathy: From Bench to Bedside* (pp. 2–20). The MIT Press. https://doi.org/10.7551/mitpress/9780262016612.003.0001.

Zahavi, D., & Rochat, P. (2015). Empathy≠sharing: Perspectives from Phenomenology and Developmental Psychology. *Consciousness and Cognition*, *36*, 543–553. https://doi.org/10.1016/j.concog.2015.05.008.

Zahn-Waxler, C., Radke-Yarrow, M., Wagner, E., & Chapman, M. (1992). Development of Concern for Others. *Developmental Psychology*, *28*, 126–136. https://doi.org/10.1037/0012-1649.28.1.126.

Zaki, J., & Cikara, M. (2015). Addressing Empathic Failures. *Current Directions in Psychological Science: A Journal of the American Psychological Society*, *24*(6), 471–476. https://doi.org/10.1177/0963721415599978.

Zaki, J., & Ochsner, K. (2011). The Cognitive Neuroscience of Sharing and Understanding Others' Emotions. In J. Decety (Ed.), *Empathy: From Bench to Bedside* (pp. 207–226). MIT Press. https://doi.org/10.7551/mitpress/9780262016612.003.0012.

Zilio, F. (2021). La fallacia naturalistica e la neuroetica. Un ponte indiretto tra descrittivo e prescrittivo?. In C. Chiurco, M. Deodati (Ed.), Etica e Natura (pp. 383–395). Orthotes Edizioni.

Index

www.ingramcontent.com/pod-product-compliance
Lightning Source LLC
Chambersburg PA
CBHW051401240926
51852CB00002B/82
9789004745353